Lecture Notes in Computer Science 1997

Edited by G. Goos, J. Hartmanis and J. van Leeuwen

T0232334

Springer

Berlin
Heidelberg
New York
Barcelona
Hong Kong
London
Milan
Paris
Singapore
Tokyo

Dan Suciu   Gottfried Vossen (Eds.)

The
World Wide Web
and Databases

Third International Workshop WebDB 2000
Dallas, TX, USA, May 18-19, 2000
Selected Papers

 Springer

Series Editors

Gerhard Goos, Karlsruhe University, Germany
Juris Hartmanis, Cornell University, NY, USA
Jan van Leeuwen, Utrecht University, The Netherlands

Volume Editors

Dan Suciu
University of Washington, Computer Science and Engineering
Seattle, WA 98195-2350, USA
E-mail: suciu@cs.washington.edu

Gottfried Vossen
Universität Münster, Wirtschaftsinformatik
Steinfurter Str. 109, 48149 Münster, Germany
E-mail: vossen@helios.uni-muenster.de

Cataloging-in-Publication Data applied for

Die Deutsche Bibliothek - CIP-Einheitsaufnahme

The World Wide Web and databases : selected papers / Third
International Workshop WebDB 2000, Dallas, TX, May 18 - 19, 2000. Dan
Suciu ; Gottfried Vossen (ed.). - Berlin ; Heidelberg ; New York ;
Barcelona ; Hong Kong ; London ; Milan ; Paris ; Singapore ; Tokyo :
Springer, 2001
    (Lecture notes in computer science ; Vol. 1997)
    ISBN 3-540-41826-1

CR Subject Classification (1998): H.5, C.2.4, H.4.3, H.2, H.3

ISSN 0302-9743
ISBN 3-540-41826-1 Springer-Verlag Berlin Heidelberg New York

Springer-Verlag Berlin Heidelberg New York
a member of BertelsmannSpringer Science+Business Media GmbH

http://www.springer.de

© Springer-Verlag Berlin Heidelberg 2001
Printed in Germany

Typesetting: Camera-ready by author, data conversion by PTP Berlin, Stefan Sossna
Printed on acid-free paper   SPIN 10782175   06/3142   5 4 3 2 1 0

Preface

With the development of the World-Wide Web, data management problems have branched out from the traditional framework in which tabular data is processed under the strict control of an application, and address today the rich variety of information that is found on the Web, considering a variety of flexible environments under which such data can be searched, classified, and processed. Database systems are coming forward today in a new role as the primary backend for the information provided on the Web. Most of today's Web accesses trigger some form of content generation from a database, while electronic commerce often triggers intensive DBMS-based applications. The research community has begun to revise data models, query languages, data integration techniques, indexes, query processing algorithms, and transaction concepts in order to cope with the characteristics and scale of the data on the Web. New problems have been identified, among them goal-oriented information gathering, management of semi-structured data, or database-style query languages for Web data, to name just a few. The *International Workshop on the Web and Databases* (WebDB) is a series of workshops intended to bring together researchers interested in the interaction between databases and the Web. This year's WebDB 2000 was the third in the series, and was held in Dallas, Texas, in conjunction with the ACM SIGMOD International Conference on Management of Data. After receiving a record number of paper submissions (69) the program committee accepted twenty papers to be presented during the workshop, in addition to an invited paper. The workshop attracted over 160 participants.

This volume contains a selection of the papers presented during the workshop, including the invited contribution. All papers contained herein have been further expanded by their authors and have undergone a final round of reviewing.

As could be seen from the workshop's papers, as well as from the selection of papers included in this volume, many researchers today relate their work to XML. Indeed, XML, an industry standard, offers a unifying format for the rich variety of data being shared today on the Web. There is tremendous potential here for the data management community. For the past years, research in avant-guard fields like semi-structured data, data integration, text databases, and combining database with relevance searches, applied only to very narrow settings, often hampering researchers' efforts to branch out of the traditional tabular-data processing framework. Today, XML makes these research areas not only relevant, but even imperative, opening the door for a dramatic impact. For researchers in data management, XML is seen as a linguistic framework which can express both data and meta data, and that can be stored as well as queried in a way that is familiar to a DBMS. This current interest was manifested in the workshop program through sessions on caching, querying, structuring and versioning, schema issues, and query processing, all centering around XML in one way or another.

The invited contribution is by Don Chamberlin (IBM ARC), one of the "fathers" of SQL, Jonathan Robie (Software AG USA), and Daniela Florescu (INRIA) on *Quilt: An XML Query Language for Heterogeneous Data Sources*. Quilt is a recent proposal for a query language that operates on collections of XML documents, and that searches them in a style that is familiar to the database user. It grew out of earlier proposals such XML-QL, XPath, and XQL, and combines features found there with properties of languages such as SQL and OQL. In particular, Quilt is a *functional* language whose main syntactical construct is the FLWR ("flower") expression which can bind variables in a *For* as well as a *Let* clause, then apply a predicate in a *Where* clause, and finally construct a result in a *Return* clause.

The section on *Information Gathering* has three contributions: In *Theme-Based Retrieval of Web News*, Nuno Maria and Mario J. Silva (Univ. Lisboa, Portugal) study the problem of populating a complex database of Web news with articles retrieved from heterogeneous Web sources. In *Using Metadata to Enhance a Web Information Gathering System*, Neel Sundaresan (IBM ARC), Jeonghee Yi (UCLA), and Anita Huang (IBM ARC) present the Grand Central Station (GCS) Web gathering system that enables users to find information regardless of location and format. GCS is composed of crawlers and summarizers, the former of which collect data, while the latter do content summarization in RDF, XML, or some custom format. In *Architecting a Network Query Engine for Producing Partial Results*, Jayavel Shanmugasundaram (Univ. Wisconsin and IBM ARC), Kristin Tufte (OGI), David DeWitt (Univ. Wisconsin), Jeffrey Naughton (Univ. Wisconsin), and Dave Maier (OGI) look at a new way of computing query results, namely by basing the processing on an initial part of the input instead of a complete input, which may be expensive to wait for on the Web.

The next section concentrates on techniques for *Caching* Web pages or views to speed up the handling of future requests. Luping Quan, Li Chen, and Elke A. Rundensteiner (Worcester Polytech) present *Argos: Efficient Refresh in an XQL-Based Web Caching System*. Qiong Luo, Jeffrey Naughton, Rajesekar Krishnamurthy, Pei Cao, and Yunrui Li (Univ. Wisconsin) study *Active Query Caching for Database Web Servers* as well as techniques for answering at a proxy server.

The first section devoted to XML is on *Querying XML*. Anja Theobald and Gerhard Weikum (Univ. Saarland, Germany) argue that XML query languages proposed so far are inadequate for Web searching since they do *Boolean* retrieval only and vastly ignore semantic relationships of data. They suggest *Adding Relevance to XML* by combining XML querying with an information retrieval search engine that has ontological knowledge. In *Evaluating Queries on Structure with eXtended Access Support Relations*, Thorsten Fiebig and Guido Moerkotte (Univ. Mannheim, Germany) present a scalable index structure that supports queries over the structure of XML documents. Next, Albrecht Schmidt, Martin Kersten, Menzo Windhouwer, and Florian Waas (CWI) present a data and an execution model for *Efficient Relational Storage and Retrieval of XML Documents*.

The second XML section is on *XML Structuring and Versioning*. It is started by Meike Klettke and Holger Meyer (Univ. Rostock, Germany) with *XML and Object-Relational Database Systems — Enhancing Structural Mappings Based on Statistics*. Arnaud Sahuguet (Univ. Pennsylvania), following a well-known movie title, discusses *Everything You Ever Wanted to Know About DTDs, but Were Afraid to Ask*. He explores how XML DTDs are being used today for specifying document structure and how and why they are abused. One of his findings is that most DTDs are incorrect, as they seem to be used more for documentation than for validation; moreover, many of the syntactic features of XML are not used in current DTDs. Finally several replacement candidates are discussed, such as XML Schemas, Schematron, and XDuce. The section concludes with *Version Management of XML Documents* by Shu-Yao Chien (UCLA), Vassilis Tsotras (UC Riverside), and Carlo Zaniolo (UCLA).

In the section entitled *Web Modeling*, Aldo Bongio, Stefano Ceri, Piero Fraternali, and Andrea Maurino (Politecnico di Milano, Italy) report on *Modeling Data Entry and Operations in WebML*. WebML, the Web Modeling Language, is an XML-based language for the conceptual and visual specification of Web sites that comes with a variety of design tools.

The next topic area to be studied is *Query Processing*. Gösta Grahne and Alex Thomo (Concordia University) present *An Optimization Technique for Answering Regular Path Queries* that does query rewriting in the context of semistructured data. Haruo Hosoya and Benjamin C. Pierce (University of Pennsylvania) present a preliminary report on *XDuce: A Typed XML Processing Language*. XDuce is a statically typed functional programming language for tree transformations and hence XML processing, which guarantees that programs never crash at run-time, and that resulting values always conform to specified types.

The final area is *Classification and Retrieval*. Panagiotis G. Ipeirotis, Luis Gravano (Columbia University), and Mehran Sahami (E.piphany, Inc.) discuss *Automatic Classification of Text Databases Through Query Probing*. David W. Embley and L. Xu (Brigham Young University) present *Record Location and Reconfiguration in Unstructured Multiple-Record Web Documents*, where the objective is to convert unstructured Web documents into structured database tables. The major technique employed for record location is a record recognition measure that is based on vector space modeling.

As can be seen from the above, WebDB 2000 covered a variety of topics and gave good insight into current research projects that are carried out at the intersection of databases and the Web. It clearly showed the rapidly increasing interest in issues related to Internet databases, and to applying database techniques to the Web; it also put the current XML hype somewhat into perspective.

We are particularly grateful to the members of our program committee, who had to do a lot of reading within very short time, and to Maggie Dunham,

Leonidas Fegaras, Alex Delis, and the SIGMOD 2000 staff for doing almost all of the financial transactions as well as the local organization for us.

November 2000   Dan Suciu and Gottfried Vossen

Organization

WebDB 2000 took place for the third time, on May 18 and 19, 2000, at the Adam's Mark Hotel in Dallas, Texas, as in the previous year right after the ACM PODS/SIGMOD conferences.

Program Committee

Program Co-chairs:	Dan Suciu (University of Washington, USA)
	Gottfried Vossen (University of Münster, Germany)
Members:	Peter Buneman (University of Pennsylvania, USA)
	Stefano Ceri (Politecnico di Milano, Italy)
	Daniela Florescu (INRIA, France)
	Juliana Freire (Bell Labs, USA)
	Zoe Lacroix (Genelogic, USA)
	Laks Lakshmanan (Concordia University, Canada)
	Alon Levy (University of Washington, USA)
	Bertram Ludäscher
	(San Diego Supercomputer Center, USA)
	Gianni Mecca (Universita di Roma Tre, Italy)
	Renee Miller (University of Toronto, Canada)
	Guido Moerkotte (University of Mannheim, Germany)
	Frank Neven
	(Limburgs Universitaire Centrum, Belgium)
	Werner Nutt (DFKI Germany)
	Yannis Papakonstantionou
	(University of California, San Diego, USA)
	Louiqa Raschid (University of Maryland, USA)
	Shiva Shivakumar (Stanford University, USA)

Sponsoring Institutions

AT&T Labs Research, Florham Park, New Jersey, USA
Westfälische Wilhelms-Universität Münster, Germany

Table of Contents

Quilt: An XML Query Language for Heterogeneous Data Sources

Don Chamberlin[1], Jonathan Robie[2], and Daniela Florescu[3]

[1]IBM Almaden Research Center, San Jose, CA 95120, USA
chamberlin@almaden.ibm.com

[2] Software AG – USA, 3207 Gibson Road, Durham, NC 27703
Jonathan.Robie@SoftwareAG-USA.com

[3] INRIA, 78153 Le Chesnay cedex, France
Daniela.Florescu@inria.fr

Abstract. The World Wide Web promises to transform human society by making virtually all types of information instantly available everywhere. Two prerequisites for this promise to be realized are a universal markup language and a universal query language. The power and flexibility of XML make it the leading candidate for a universal markup language. XML provides a way to label information from diverse data sources including structured and semi-structured documents, relational databases, and object repositories. Several XML-based query languages have been proposed, each oriented toward a specific category of information. Quilt is a new proposal that attempts to unify concepts from several of these query languages, resulting in a new language that exploits the full versatility of XML. The name Quilt suggests both the way in which features from several languages were assembled to make a new query language, and the way in which Quilt queries can combine information from diverse data sources into a query result with a new structure of its own.

1 Introduction

The Extensible Markup Language, XML[1], is having a profoundly unifying effect on diverse forms of information. For the first time, XML provides an information interchange format that is editable, easily parsed, and capable of representing nearly any kind of structured or semi-structured information.

As an example of the unifying influence of XML, consider the once-divergent worlds of documents and databases. Documents have irregular structure, are deeply nested, use relatively simple datatypes, and place great importance on ordering. Relational databases, on the other hand, have a very regular structure, are relatively flat, use complex datatypes, and usually place little importance on ordering. It is a tribute to the flexibility of XML that it is pulling together these diverse forms of information to the extent that the distinction between a document and a database is quickly vanishing.

D. Suciu and G. Vossen (Eds.): WebDB 2000, LNCS 1997, pp. 1–25, 2001.

In order to realize its potential as a universal format for information exchange, XML needs a query language that is as flexible as XML itself. For querying documents, the language needs to be able to preserve order and hierarchy. For querying databases, the language needs to provide traditional database operations such as joins and grouping. The language must be capable of dealing with all the information structures found in the XML Schema specification[2], and must able to transform information from one structure into another.

Our goal is to design a small, implementable language that meets the requirements identified by the W3C XML Query Working Group[3]. We want a language in which queries are concise but readable. We also want a language that is flexible enough to query a broad spectrum of XML information sources, and we have used examples from the database and document communities as representative of these requirements.

Our strategy in designing the language has been to borrow features from several other languages that seem to have strengths in specific areas. From XPath[4] and XQL[5] we take a syntax for navigating in hierarchical documents. From XML-QL[6] we take the notion of binding variables and then using the bound variables to create new structures. From SQL[7] we take the idea of a series of clauses based on keywords that provide a pattern for restructuring data (the SELECT-FROM-WHERE pattern in SQL). From OQL[8] we take the notion of a functional language composed of several different kinds of expressions that can be nested with full generality. We have also been influenced by reading about other XML query languages such as Lorel[9] and YATL[10]. We decided to name our language Quilt because of its heritage as a patchwork of features from other languages, and also because of its goal of assembling information from multiple diverse sources. Quilt has also been described in [11].

The W3C XML Query Working Group has identified a requirement for both a human-readable query syntax and an XML-based query syntax. Quilt is designed to meet the first of these requirements. We recognize that an alternative, XML-based syntax for the Quilt semantics would be useful for some applications.

2 The Quilt Language

Like OQL, Quilt is a functional language in which a query is represented as an expression. Quilt supports several kinds of expression, and therefore a Quilt query may take several different forms. The various forms of Quilt expressions can be nested with full generality, so the notion of a "subquery" is natural to Quilt.

The input and output of a Quilt query are XML documents, fragments of XML documents, or collections of XML documents. We can think of these inputs and outputs as instances of a data model called the XML Query Data Model, which is under development by the W3C XML Query Working Group[12]. This data model is a refinement of the data model described in the XPath specification[4], in which a document is modeled as a tree of nodes. A fragment of a document, or a collection of documents, may lack a common root and may therefore be modeled as an ordered forest of nodes of various types, including element nodes, attribute nodes, and text nodes, as illustrated in Figure 1.

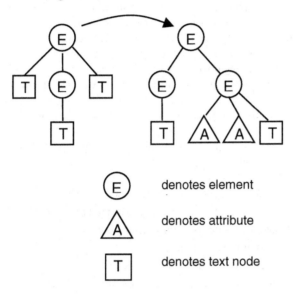

Fig. 1. An instance of the XML Query Data Model: an ordered forest

An informal syntax for Quilt is given in the Appendix of this paper. Formal definition of the syntax and semantics of the language should be considered a work in progress.

The principal forms of Quilt expressions are as follows:
1. Path expressions
2. Element constructors
3. FLWR expressions
4. Expressions involving operators and functions
5. Conditional expressions
6. Quantifiers
7. Variable bindings

Each of these types of expressions is introduced and explained by a series of examples in the following sections. For syntactic details, please refer to the Appendix.

A Quilt query may contain a comment, which is ignored during query processing. As in SQL, the beginning delimiter of a comment is a double hyphen and the ending delimiter is a newline character.

2.1 Path Expressions

Quilt path expressions are based on the abbreviated syntax of XPath, which provides a way to navigate through a hierarchy of nodes. The result of a path expression is an ordered forest consisting of those nodes that satisfy the expression and their descendants. XPath syntax is used in several XML-related applications such as XSLT [13] and XPointer [14].

As in XPath, a Quilt path expression consists of a series of *steps.* Each step represents movement through a document in a particular direction, and each step can apply a predicate to eliminate nodes that fail to satisfy a given condition. The result of each step is a set of nodes that serves as a starting point for the next step.

A path expression can begin with an expression that identifies a specific node, such as the function document(string), which returns the root node of a named document. A Quilt query can also contain a path expression beginning with "/" or "//" which represents an implicit root node, determined by the environment in which the query is executed.

A complete discussion of Xpath abbreviated syntax can be found in [4]. Briefly, the following symbols are used:

.   Denotes the current node.

..   Denotes the parent of the current node.

/   Denotes the root node, or children of the current node

//   Denotes descendants of the current node (closure of /).

@   Denotes attributes of the current node

*   Denotes "any" (node with unrestricted name)

[ ]   Brackets enclose a Boolean expression that serves as a predicate for a given step.

[n]   When a predicate consists of an integer, it serves to select the element with the given ordinal number from a list of elements.

The following example uses a path expression consisting of three steps. The first step locates the root node of a document. The second step locates the second chapter element that is a child of the root element. The third step finds figure elements occurring anywhere within the chapter, but retains only those figure elements that have a caption with the value "Tree Frogs."

(Q1) In the second chapter of the document named "zoo.xml", find the figure(s) with caption "Tree Frogs".

```
document("zoo.xml")/chapter[2]
    //figure[caption = "Tree Frogs"]
```

It is sometimes desirable to return a set of elements whose ordinal numbers span a certain range. For this purpose, Quilt provides a RANGE predicate that is adapted from one of the features of XQL[5], as illustrated in the following example:

(Q2) Find all the figures in chapters 2 through 5 of the document named "zoo.xml."

```
document("zoo.xml")/chapter[RANGE 2 TO 5]//figure
```

In addition to the operators of the XPath abbreviated syntax, Quilt introduces an operator called the dereference operator ("->"). When a dereference operator follows an

IDREF-type attribute or a key, it returns the element(s) that are referenced by the attribute or key. Dereference operators can be used in the steps of a path expression. For example, the following query uses a dereference operator to find the element referenced by the "refid" attribute of a "figref" element.

(Q3) Find captions of figures that are referenced by <figref> elements in the chapter of "zoo.xml" with title "Frogs".

```
document("zoo.xml")/chapter[title = "Frogs"]
    //figref/@refid->/caption
```

The Quilt dereference operator is similar in purpose to the <u>id</u> function of XPath. However, the right-arrow notation is intended to be easier to read, especially in path expressions that involve multiple dereferences. For example, suppose that a given document contains a set of <emp> elements, each of which may contain a "mentor" attribute. The "mentor" attribute is of type IDREF, and it references another <emp> element that represents the mentor of the given employee. The name of each employee is represented by a <name> element nested inside the <emp> element.

(Q4) Find the name of the mentor of the mentor of the employee named "Jack".

```
/emp[name = "Jack"]/@mentor->/@mentor->/name
```

As in XPath, the identifiers used in Quilt expressions can be qualified by namespace prefixes[15]. Quilt provides a syntax for declaring the Universal Resource Identifier (URI) associated with each namespace prefix used in a query, as illustrated in the following example:

(Q5) In the document "zoo.xml", find <tiger> elements in the <u>abc</u> namespace that contain any subelement in the <u>xyz</u> namespace.

```
NAMESPACE abc = "www.abc.com/names"
NAMESPACE xyz = "www.xyz.com/names"
document("zoo.xml")//abc:tiger[xyz:*]
```

2.2 Element Constructors

An element constructor is used to generate an element node. Similar constructors exist for other types of nodes such as comments and processing instructions. An element constructor consists of a start tag and an end tag, enclosing an optional list of expressions that provide the content of the element. The start tag may also specify the values of one or more attributes. The name of the start tag may be specified either by a constant or a variable.

Although an element constructor is an expression in its own right, its typical use is nested inside another expression that binds one or more variables that are used in the element constructor. Both of the following examples are query fragments that refer to variables that are bound in some enclosing expression.

(Q6) Generate an <emp> element containing an "empid" attribute and nested <name> and <job> elements. The values of the attribute and nested elements are specified by variables that are bound in other parts of the query.

```
<emp empid = $id>
    <name> $n </name> ,
    <job> $j </job>
</emp>
```

In the following example, the name of the generated element is specified by a variable named $tagname. Note that, when a start-tag contains a variable name, the matching end-tag must contain the same variable name (see Section 2.8 for a more interesting version of this example.)

(Q7) Generate an element with a computed name, containing nested elements named <description> and <price>.

```
<$tagname>
    <description> $d </description> ,
    <price> $p </price>
</$tagname>
```

2.3   FLWR Expressions

A FLWR (pronounced "flower") expression is constructed from FOR, LET, WHERE, and RETURN clauses. As in an SQL query, these clauses must appear in a specific order. A FLWR expression is used whenever it is necessary to iterate over the elements of a collection.

A FLWR expression begins by binding values to one or more variables, and then uses these variables to construct a result (in general, an ordered forest of nodes). The overall flow of data in a FLWR expression is illustrated in Figure 2.

A FLWR expression begins with a FOR-clause that generates one or more bindings for one or more variables. Each variable introduced in the FOR-clause is associated with an expression (for example, a path expression). In general, each of these expressions returns a list of nodes. The result of the FOR-clause is a list of tuples, each of which contains a binding for each of the variables. The variables are bound to individual nodes returned by their respective expressions, in such a way that the binding-tuples represent the cross-product of the node-lists returned by all the expressions.

The initial FOR-clause in a FLWR expression can be followed by one or more LET-clauses and additional FOR-clauses, which provide bindings for additional variables. A LET-clause simply binds one or more variables to the result of one or more expressions. Unlike a FOR-clause, which iterates over node-lists to generate many bindings for each variable, a LET-clause generates only one binding for each variable. Bindings generated by a FOR-clause bind each variable to a single node (with its descendants), whereas a LET-clause may bind a variable to a forest of nodes.

A FLWR expression may contain several FOR and LET-clauses, and each of these clauses may contain references to variables bound in previous clauses. The result of the sequence of FOR and LET clauses is an ordered list of tuples of bound variables. The number of tuples generated by a FOR/LET sequence is the product of the cardinalities of the node-lists returned by the expressions in the FOR-clauses. The tuples generated by the FOR/LET sequence have an order that is determined by the order of their bound elements in the input document, with the first bound variable taking precedence, followed by the second bound variable, and so on. However, if some expression used in a FOR-clause is unordered (for example, because it contains a distinct function), the tuples generated by the FOR/LET sequence are unordered.

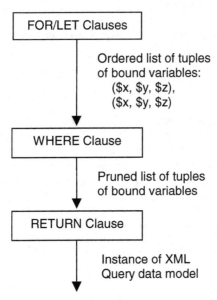

Fig. 2. Flow of data in a FLWR expression

Each of the binding-tuples generated by the FOR and LET clauses is subject to further filtering by an optional WHERE-clause. Only those tuples for which the condition in the WHERE-clause is true are used to invoke the RETURN clause. The WHERE-clause may contain several predicates, connected by AND, OR, and NOT. These predicates usually contain references to the bound variables. Variables bound by a FOR-clause represent a single node (with its descendants) and so they are typically used in scalar predicates such as $p/color = "Red". Variables bound by a LET-clause, on the other hand, may represent collections of nodes, and can be used in collection-oriented predicates such as avg($p/price) > 100. The ordering of the binding-tuples generated by the FOR and LET clauses is preserved by the WHERE-clause.

The RETURN-clause generates the output of the FLWR expression, which may be a node, an ordered forest of nodes, or a primitive value. The RETURN-clause is executed once for each tuple of bindings that is generated by the FOR and LET-clauses and satisfies the condition in the WHERE-clause. If an ordering exists among these tuples, the RETURN-clause is executed on each tuple, in order, and the order of the results is preserved in the output document. The RETURN-clause contains an expression that often contains element constructors, references to bound variables, and nested subexpressions.

We will consider some examples of FLWR expressions based on a document named "bib.xml" that contains a list of <book> elements. Each <book> element, in turn, contains a <title> element, one or more <author> elements, a <publisher> element, a <year> element, and a <price> element. The first example is so simple that it could have been expressed using a path expression, but it is perhaps more readable when expressed as a FLWR expression.

(Q8) List the titles of books published by Morgan Kaufmann in 1998.

```
FOR $b IN document("bib.xml")//book
WHERE $b/publisher = "Morgan Kaufmann"
AND $b/year = "1998"
RETURN $b/title
```

Example Q9 uses a <u>distinct</u> function in the FOR-clause to eliminate duplicates from the list of publishers found in the input document. Two elements are considered to be duplicates if their values (including name, attributes, and normalized content) are equal. The result of the <u>distinct</u> function is an unordered set of elements. Example Q9 then uses a LET-clause to bind a variable to the average price of books published by each of the publishers bound in the FOR-clause.

(Q9) List each publisher and the average price of its books.

```
FOR $p IN distinct(document("bib.xml")//publisher)
LET $a := avg(document("bib.xml")
   /book[publisher = $p]/price)
RETURN
   <publisher>
      <name> $p/text() </name> ,
      <avgprice> $a </avgprice>
   </publisher>
```

The next example uses a LET-clause to bind a variable $b to a set of books, and then uses a WHERE-clause to apply a condition to the set, retaining only bindings in which $b contains more than 100 elements. This query also illustrates the common practice of enclosing a FLWR expression inside an element constructor which provides an enclosing element for the query result.

(Q10) List the publishers who have published more than 100 books.

```
<big_publishers>
   FOR $p IN distinct(document("bib.xml")//publisher)
   LET $b := document("bib.xml")/book[publisher = $p]
   WHERE count($b) > 100
```

```
      RETURN $p
</big_publishers>
```

FLWR expressions are often useful for performing structural transformations on documents, as illustrated by the next query, which inverts a hierarchy. This example also illustrates how one FLWR expression can be nested inside another.

(Q11) Invert the structure of the input document so that, instead of each book element containing a list of authors, each distinct author element contains a list of book-titles.

```
<author_list>
    FOR $a IN distinct(document("bib.xml")//author)
    RETURN
        <author>
            <name> $a/text() </name>,
            FOR $b IN document("bib.xml")//book
            [author = $a]
            RETURN $b/title
        </author>
</author_list>
```

By default, a Quilt query preserves the ordering of elements in the input document(s), as represented by the values of its bound variables. However, it is often important to specify an order for the elements in a query result that supplements or supercedes the order derived from the variable bindings. If a query result contains several levels of nested elements, an ordering may be required among the elements at each level. Quilt provides a SORTBY clause that may be used after an element constructor or path expression to specify an ordering among the resulting elements. The arguments of the SORTBY clause are evaluated within the context of the individual nodes to be sorted, and may be followed by ASCENDING or DESCENDING to specify the direction of the sort (ASCENDING is the default.) The use of SORTBY is illustrated by the following example.

(Q12) Make an alphabetic list of publishers. Within each publisher, make a list of books, each containing a title and a price, in descending order by price.

```
<publisher_list>
    FOR $p IN distinct(document("bib.xml")//publisher)
    RETURN
        <publisher>
            <name> $p/text() </name> ,
            FOR $b IN document("bib.xml")//book
            [publisher = $p]
            RETURN
                <book>
                    $b/title ,
                    $b/price
                </book> SORTBY(price DESCENDING)
        </publisher> SORTBY(name)
</publisher_list>
```

2.4 Operators in Expressions

Like most languages, Quilt allows expressions to be constructed using infix and prefix operators, and allows nested expressions inside parentheses to serve as operands. Quilt supports the usual set of arithmetic and logical operators, and the collection operators UNION, INTERSECT, and EXCEPT. The detailed semantics of these operators, as applied to various kinds of collections including sets, bags, and lists, is left to a more detailed language specification.

From XQL, Quilt inherits the infix operators BEFORE and AFTER, which are useful in searching for information by its ordinal position. Each instance of the XML Query data model (regardless of whether it is a complete document, a fragment of a document, or a list of documents) is a forest that includes a total ordering, called "document order," among all its nodes. BEFORE operates on two collections of elements and returns those elements in the first collection that occur before at least one element of the second collection in document order (of course, this is possible only if the two collections are subsets of the same data model instance.) AFTER is defined in a similar way. Since BEFORE and AFTER are based on global document ordering, they can compare the positions of elements that do not have the same parent. The next two examples illustrate the use of BEFORE and AFTER by retrieving excerpts from a surgical report that includes <procedure>, <incision>, and <anesthesia> elements.

(Q13) Prepare a "critical sequence" report consisting of all elements that occur between the first and second incision in the first procedure.

```
<critical_sequence>
   FOR $p IN //procedure[1],
         $e IN //* AFTER ($p//incision)[1]
             BEFORE ($p//incision)[2]
   RETURN shallow($e)
</critical_sequence>
```

The <u>shallow</u> function strips an element of its subelements.

(Q14) Find procedures in which no anesthesia occurs before the first incision.

```
-- Finds potential lawsuits
FOR $p in //procedure
WHERE empty($p//anesthesia BEFORE ($p//incision)[1])
RETURN $p
```

Another important operator introduced by Quilt is the FILTER operator. FILTER takes two operands, each of which is an expression that, in general, evaluates to an ordered forest of nodes. FILTER returns a subset of the nodes in the forest represented by the first operand, while preserving the hierarchic and sequential relationships among these nodes. The nodes that are returned are those nodes that are present at any level in the first operand and are also top-level nodes in the second operand. Thus the FILTER operator uses the second operand as a "filter" that retains only selected nodes from the forest represented by the first operand. The filtering process is based on node identity—that is, it requires both operands to contain the same node, not just two nodes with the same value. Obviously, if the two operands do not have a common root, the result of the FILTER expression is empty.

The action of a FILTER expression is illustrated by Figures 3a and 3b. Figure 3a shows an ordered forest that might result from evaluating the path expression /C. Each tree is rooted in a node of type C. Figure 3b shows the result when this ordered forest is filtered by the path expression //A | //B. Only nodes of type A and B are retained, but where a hierarchic or sequential relationship exists among these nodes, the relationship is preserved.

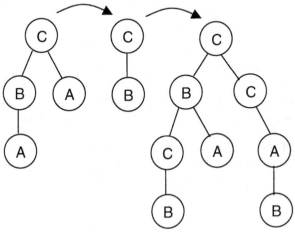

Fig. 3a. Value of /C

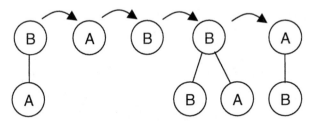

Fig. 3b. Value of /C FILTER //A | //B

FILTER expressions are useful in "projecting" some desired subset of a document, eliminating undesired parts while retaining the document structure. The following example illustrates this process by computing a table of contents for a document that contains many levels of nested sections. The query filters the document, retaining only section elements, title elements nested directly inside section elements, and the text of those title elements. Other elements, such as paragraphs and figure titles, are eliminated, leaving only the "skeleton" of the document.

In this example, the first operand of FILTER is the function call document( ), which returns the root of the implicit document. The second operand is a path expression that identifies the nodes to be preserved from the original document.

(Q15) Prepare a table of contents for an implicit input document, containing nested sections and their titles.

```
<toc>
   document( ) FILTER
   //section | //section/title | //section/title/text()
</toc>
```

2.5 Conditional Expressions

Conditional expressions are useful when the structure of the information to be returned depends on some condition. Of course, like all Quilt expressions, conditional expressions can be nested.

As an example of a conditional expression, consider a library that has many holdings, each described by a <holding> element with a "type" attribute that identifies its type: book, journal, etc. All holdings have a title and other nested elements that depend on the type of holding.

(Q16) Make a list of holdings, ordered by title. For journals, include the editor, and for all other holdings, include the author.

```
FOR $h IN //holding
RETURN
   <holding>
       $h/title,
       IF $h/@type = "Journal"
       THEN $h/editor
       ELSE $h/author
   </holding> SORTBY (title)
```

2.6 Functions

Quilt provides a library of built-in functions for use in queries. We have already used some of the Quilt functions, such as <u>document</u>, which returns the root node of a named document. The Quilt function library contains all the functions of the XPath core function library, all the aggregation functions of SQL (<u>avg</u>, <u>sum</u>, <u>count</u>, <u>max</u>, and <u>min</u>), and a number of other useful functions. For example, the <u>distinct</u> function eliminates duplicates from a collection, and the <u>empty</u> function returns True if and only if its argument is an empty collection.

In addition to the built-in functions, Quilt allows users to define functions of their own. In general, a Quilt query consists of a set of function definitions, followed by an expression that can call the functions that are thus defined. The scope of a function definition is limited to the query in which it is defined. Each function definition must declare the types of its parameters and result.

In another paper, we expect to define an extensibility mechanism whereby function definitions with global scope, written in various programming languages, can be added to the Quilt function library.

Some functions take scalar arguments and some take collections (sets, lists, and bags) as arguments. In general, when a collection is passed to a function that expects a scalar argument, the function returns a collection in which each element is the result of applying the function to one of the elements of the original collection.

A function may be defined recursively—that is, it may be referenced in its own definition. The next query contains an example of a recursive function that computes the depth of a node hierarchy. In its definition, the user-defined function <u>depth</u> calls the built-in functions <u>empty</u> and <u>max</u>.

(Q17) Using a recursive function, compute the maximum depth of the document named "partlist.xml."

```
FUNCTION depth($e ELEMENT) RETURNS integer
    {
    -- An empty element has depth 1
    -- Otherwise, add 1 to max depth of children
    IF empty($e/*) THEN 1
    ELSE max(depth($e/*)) + 1
    }
depth(document("partlist.xml"))
```

To further illustrate the power of functions, we will write a function that returns all the nodes that are "connected" to a given node by child or reference connections, and a recursive function that returns all the nodes that are "reachable" from a given node by child or reference connections. The following example uses these functions to return a connected fragment of the implicit input document.

(Q18) Find all the nodes that are reachable from the employee with serial number 12345 by child or reference connections, preserving the original relationships among the resulting nodes.

```
FUNCTION connected($e ELEMENT) RETURNS SET(ELEMENT)
    { $e/* UNION $e/@*-> }
FUNCTION reachable($e ELEMENT) RETURNS SET(ELEMENT)
    { $e UNION coalesce(reachable(connected($e))) }
document( ) FILTER reachable(//emp[serial="12345"])
```

In the above example, the <u>reachable</u> function invokes itself with a set of elements as argument. Since <u>reachable</u> maps each element to a set of elements, the result of invoking <u>reachable</u> on a set of elements is a set of sets of elements. This intermediate result is passed to the coalesce function, which converts a set of sets to a single set that is the union of its members.

Of course, it is possible to write a recursive function that fails to terminate for some set of arguments. In fact, the reachable function in the previous example will fail to terminate if called on an element that references one of its ancestors. At present, it is the user's responsibility to avoid writing a nonterminating function call. A mechanism to help the user stay out of trouble, such as a fixpoint operator, is a subject for further research.

2.7 Quantifiers

Occasionally it is necessary to test for existence of some element that satisfies a condition, or to determine whether all elements in some category satisfy a condition. For this purpose, Quilt provides existential and universal quantifiers. The existential quantifier is illustrated in Q19, and the universal quantifier is illustrated in Q20.

(Q19) Find titles of books in which both sailing and windsurfing are mentioned in the same paragraph.

```
FOR $b IN //book
WHERE SOME $p IN $b//para SATISFIES
    contains($p, "sailing")
    AND contains($p, "windsurfing")
RETURN $b/title
```

(Q20) Find titles of books in which sailing is mentioned in every paragraph.

```
FOR $b IN //book
WHERE EVERY $p IN $b//para SATISFIES
    contains($p, "sailing")
RETURN $b/title
```

2.8 Variable Bindings

Some queries use the same expression in more than one place. In such a case, it is sometimes helpful to bind the value of the expression to a variable so that the definition of the expression does not need to be repeated. This can be accomplished by a variable binding, which looks like the LET clause of a FLWR expression. A variable binding can be used outside a FLWR expression if it is followed by the word EVAL, which suggests that, after the variable is bound, the expression that follows the binding is evaluated. In the following example, the average price of books is a common subexpression that is bound to variable $a and then used repeatedly in the body of the query.

(Q21) For each book whose price is greater than the average price, return the title of the book and the amount by which the book's price exceeds the average price.

```
LET $a := avg(//book/price)
EVAL
    <result>
       FOR $b IN /book
       WHERE $b/price > $a
       RETURN
           <expensive_book>
              $b/title ,
              <price_difference>
                 $b/price - $a
              </price_difference>
           </expensive_book>
    </result>
```

A variable binding can be used in conjunction with an element constructor to replicate some parts of an existing element, as in the following example. This example uses the XPath functions name(element), which returns the tagname of an element, and number(element), which returns the content of an element expressed as a number. When an expression inside the body of an element constructor evaluates to one or more attributes, those attributes are considered to be attributes of the element that is being constructed.

(Q22) Variable $e is bound to some element with numeric content. Construct a new element having the same name and attributes as $e, and with numeric content equal to twice the content of $e.

```
LET $tagname := name($e)
EVAL
    <$tagname>
       $e/@*,    -- replicates the attributes of $e
       2 * number($e)
    </$tagname>
```

3 Querying Relational Data

Since much of the world's business data is stored in relational databases, access to relational data is a vitally important application for an XML query language. In this section, we will illustrate the use of Quilt to access relational data by a series of examples based on a schema that is often used in relational database tutorials, containing descriptions of suppliers and parts, as shown in Figure 4. In this schema, Table S contains supplier numbers and names; Table P contains part numbers and descriptions, and Table SP contains contains the relationships between suppliers and the parts they supply, including the price of each part from each supplier.

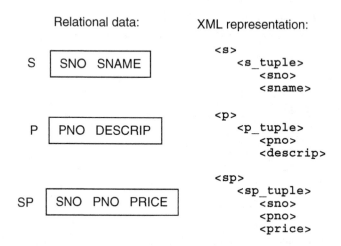

Fig. 4. One possible XML representation of relational data

Figure 4 also shows how the schema of parts and suppliers might be translated into a default XML view in which each table appears as a document, each row of a table appears as an element inside the document, and each value inside a row appears as a nested element. Other, more richly structured views can be defined on top of this default view by means of Quilt queries, as we will illustrate below.

SQL[7] is the standard relational database language. In many cases, SQL queries can be translated into Quilt queries in a straightforward way by mapping SQL query-blocks into FLWR-expressions. We illustrate this mapping by the following query:

(Q23) Find part numbers of gears, in numeric order.

SQL version:

```
SELECT pno
FROM p
WHERE descrip LIKE 'Gear'
ORDER BY pno;
```

Quilt version:

```
FOR $p IN document("p.xml")//p_tuple
WHERE contains($p/descrip, "Gear")
RETURN $p/pno SORTBY(.)
```

In Quilt, the operand of SORTBY is always interpreted within the context of the element to be sorted. Since the <pno> elements generated by Q23 have no internal structure, we use the notation "SORTBY(.)", which causes the <pno> elements to be sorted by their content.

3.1 Grouping

Many relational queries involve forming data into groups and applying some aggregation function such as count or avg to each group. In SQL, these queries are expressed using GROUP BY and HAVING clauses. The following example shows how such a query might be expressed in Quilt:

(Q24) Find the part number and average price for parts that have at least 3 suppliers.

SQL version:

```
SELECT pno, avg(price) AS avgprice
FROM sp
GROUP BY pno
HAVING count(*) >= 3
ORDER BY pno;
```

Quilt version:

```
FOR $pn IN distinct(document("sp.xml")//pno)
LET $sp := document("sp.xml")//sp_tuple[pno = $pn]
WHERE count($sp) >= 3
RETURN
   <well_supplied_item>
       $pn,
       <avgprice> avg($sp/price) </avgprice>
   </well_supplied_item> SORTBY(pno)
```

Note that $pn, bound by a FOR-clause, represents an individual part number, whereas $sp, bound by a LET-clause, represents a set of sp-tuples. The SQL HAVING clause, which applies a predicate to a set, is mapped into a Quilt WHERE-clause that operates on the set-valued variable $sp. The Quilt version of the query also uses an element constructor to enclose each part number and average price in a containing element called <well_supplied_item>.

3.2 Joins

Joins, which combine data from multiple sources into a single query result, are among the most important forms of relational queries. In this section we will illustrate how several types of joins can be expressed in Quilt.

A conventional ("inner") join returns information from two or more related tables, as illustrated by example Q25.

(Q25) Return a "flat" list of supplier names and their part descriptions, in alphabetic order.

```
FOR $sp IN document("sp.xml")//sp_tuple,
    $p IN document("p.xml")//p_tuple[pno = $sp/pno],
    $s IN document("s.xml")//s_tuple[sno = $sp/sno]
RETURN
    <sp_pair>
        $s/sname ,
        $p/descrip
    </sp_pair> SORTBY (sname, descrip)
```

Q25 returns information only about parts that have suppliers and suppliers that have parts. An "outer join" is a join that preserves information from one or more of the participating tables, including those rows that have no matching row in the joined table. For example, a "left outer join" between suppliers and parts might return information about suppliers that have no matching parts. In place of the missing parts data, relational systems usually return null values; but an XML query might represent the missing data by an empty element or the absence of an element. Q26 is an example of a Quilt query that corresponds to a left outer join.

(Q26) Return names of all the suppliers in alphabetic order, including those that supply no parts; inside each supplier element, list the descriptions of all the parts it supplies, in alphabetic order.

```
FOR $s IN document("s.xml")//s_tuple
RETURN
    <supplier>
        $s/sname,
        FOR $sp IN document("sp.xml")//sp_tuple
                [sno = $s/sno],
            $p IN document("p.xml")//p_tuple
                [pno = $sp/pno]
        RETURN $p/descrip SORTBY(.)
    </supplier> SORTBY(sname)
```

Another type of join that is sometimes used in relational systems is a "full outer join," which preserves information from both of the participating tables, including rows of each table that have no matching rows in the other table. In XML, the result of a full outer join can be structured in any of several ways. The example in Q27 uses a format of parts nested inside suppliers, followed by a list of parts that have no supplier. This might be thought of as a "supplier-centered" full outer join. A "part-centered" full outer join, on the other hand, might return a list of suppliers nested inside parts, followed by a list of suppliers that have no parts. Other forms of outer join queries are also possible.

(Q27) Return names of suppliers and descriptions and prices of their parts, including suppliers that supply no parts and parts that have no suppliers.

```
<master_list>
    (FOR $s IN document("s.xml")//s_tuple
    RETURN
        <supplier>
            $s/sname,
            FOR $sp IN document("sp.xml")//sp_tuple
                    [sno = $s/sno],
                $p IN document("p.xml")//p_tuple
                    [pno = $sp/pno]
            RETURN
                <part>
                    $p/descrip,
                    $sp/price
                </part> SORTBY (descrip)
        </supplier> SORTBY(sname)
    )
 UNION
    -- parts that have no supplier
    <orphan_parts>
        FOR $p IN document("p.xml")//p_tuple
        WHERE empty(document("sp.xml")//sp_tuple
            [pno = $p/pno] )
        RETURN $p/descrip SORTBY(.)
    </orphan_parts>
</master_list>
```

Q27 uses an element constructor to enclose its output inside a <master_list> element. The UNION operator, when used as in Q27 to combine two ordered lists, returns the first list with the second list appended at the end. The result is a <master_list> element containing an ordered list of <supplier> elements followed by an <orphan_parts> element that contains descriptions of all the parts that have no supplier.

3.3 Defining Structured Views

An application might prefer a structured XML view of the database of parts and suppliers, such as the "master_list" generated by Q27, rather than a simpler view in which each table appears as a separate document. If a relational database system can present simple default XML views of its tables, the job of constructing more structured views can be left to Quilt. Just as in SQL, a Quilt query can serve as the definition of a persistent view of underlying data. For example, by means of suitable data definition statements, Q27 could be entered into the system catalogs as the definition of a persistent XML view called "master_list". Quilt queries against the master_list could then be automatically merged with the view-definition to form queries against the underlying tables.

4 Conclusion

With the emergence of XML, the distinctions among various forms of information, such as documents and databases, are quickly disappearing. Quilt is designed to support queries against a broad spectrum of information sources by incorporating features from several languages that were originally designed for diverse purposes. This paper has illustrated the versatility of Quilt by using it to express queries against both semi-structured documents and relational databases. We believe that Quilt represents a promising approach to a query language that can help to realize the potential of XML as a universal medium for data interchange.

Acknowledgements. The authors thank Mary Fernandez, Phil Wadler, Jerome Simeon, and Zack Ives for many helpful discussions during the definition of the Quilt language.

Appendix: Quilt Grammar

The following rather permissive grammar will be augmented by a set of typing rules (for example, an expression used in a predicate must return a Boolean value).

```
QuiltQuery ::= NamespaceDeclList? FunctionDefnList? Expr
NamespaceDeclList ::= NamespaceDecl*
NamespaceDecl ::= 'NAMESPACE' Identifier '=' StringLiteral
FunctionDefnList ::= FunctionDefn*
FunctionDefn ::=
      'FUNCTION' FunctionName '(' ParamList? ')' 'RETURNS' Datatype '{' Expr '}'
FunctionName ::= QName
ParamList ::= Parameter ( ',' Parameter )*

/* The name and type of each parameter are declared */
Parameter ::= Variable Datatype
Datatype ::= PrimitiveDatatype
   | Collection '(' Datatype ')'

/* Primitive datatypes will be expanded to all Schema primitive types,
    plus ELEMENT to denote a generic element. We avoid the keyword STRING
    because it would pre-empt the name of a function used in XPath. */
PrimitiveDatatype ::= 'CHARSTRING' | 'INTEGER' | 'ELEMENT'
Collection ::= 'SET' | 'LIST' | 'BAG'
Expr ::= LogicalExpr
   | LogicalExpr 'SORTBY' '(' SortSpecList ')'
```

SortSpecList ::= SortSpec
 | SortSpecList ',' SortSpec
SortSpec ::= Expr
 | Expr 'ASCENDING'
 | Expr 'DESCENDING'
LogicalExpr ::= LogicalTerm
 | LogicalExpr 'OR' LogicalTerm
LogicalTerm ::= LogicalFactor
 | LogicalTerm 'AND' LogicalFactor
LogicalFactor ::= FilteredExpr
 | 'NOT' FilteredExpr
FilteredExpr ::= SetExpr
 | FilteredExpr 'FILTER' SetExpr
SetExpr ::= SetTerm
 | SetExpr 'UNION' SetTerm
SetTerm ::= SequencedValue
 | SetTerm 'INTERSECT' SequencedValue
 | SetTerm 'EXCEPT' SequencedValue
SequencedValue ::= QuiltValue
 | SequencedValue 'BEFORE' QuiltValue
 | SequencedValue 'AFTER' QuiltValue
QuiltValue ::= Comparison
 | SpecialExpr
Comparison ::= ArithExpr
 | Comparison CompareOp ArithExpr
ArithExpr ::= ArithTerm
 | ArithExpr '+' ArithTerm
 | ArithExpr '-' ArithTerm
ArithTerm ::= ArithFactor
 | ArithTerm '*' ArithFactor
 | ArithTerm 'DIV' ArithFactor
 | ArithTerm 'MOD' ArithFactor
ArithFactor ::= ArithPrimitive
 | '+' ArithPrimitive
 | '-' ArithPrimitive
ArithPrimitive ::= BasicExpr Predicate*
 | DisjointPathExpr
DisjointPathExpr ::= PathExpr
 | DisjointPathExpr '|' PathExpr
PathExpr ::= RegularExpr
 | '/' RegularExpr
 | '//' RegularExpr
 | BasicExpr Predicate* '/' RegularExpr
 | BasicExpr Predicate* '//' RegularExpr

/* For now, we support only the '/' and '//' operators of XPath.
    In the future, we may support other forms of regular expressions. */
RegularExpr ::= Step Predicate*
    | RegularExpr '/' Step Predicate*
    | RegularExpr '//' Step Predicate*

/* As in XPath, a step represents movement in an XML document along the
    child, parent, or attribute axis. If followed by '->', the step
    dereferences a key or IDREF attribute and returns the target element
    (this requires information from a schema or Document Type Definition.) */
Step ::= NameTest
    | NodeType '(' ')'
    | '@' NameTest
    | '..'
    | Step '->'

/* An expression in a predicate must evaluate to a Boolean or an ordinal number */
Predicate ::= '[' Expr ']'
    | '[' 'RANGE' Expr 'TO' Expr ']'
BasicExpr ::= Variable
    | Literal
    | FunctionName '(' ExprList? ')'
    | '(' Expr ')'
    | NodeConstructor
    | '.'
Literal ::= StringLiteral
    | IntegerLiteral
    | FloatLiteral
ExprList ::= Expr
    | ExprList ',' Expr
SpecialExpr ::= LetClause 'EVAL' QuiltValue
    | FlwrExpr
    | 'IF' Expr 'THEN' QuiltValue 'ELSE' QuiltValue
    | Quantifier Variable 'IN' Expr 'SATISFIES' QuiltValue
Quantifier ::= 'SOME'
    | 'EVERY'
FlwrExpr ::= ForLetClause WhereReturnClause

/* A ForLetClause has at least one ForClause and any number
    of additional ForClauses and LetClauses */
ForLetClause ::= ForClause
    | ForLetClause ForClause
    | ForLetClause LetClause
ForClause ::= 'FOR' Variable 'IN' Expr
    | ForClause ',' Variable 'IN' Expr

LetClause ::= 'LET' Variable ':=' Expr
   | LetClause ',' Variable ':=' Expr
WhereReturnClause ::= WhereClause? ReturnClause
WhereClause ::= 'WHERE' Expr
ReturnClause ::= 'RETURN' QuiltValue

/* For now, a node constructor is an element constructor.
   In the future we will add processing instructions and comments. */
NodeConstructor ::= ElementConstructor
ElementConstructor ::= StartTag ExprList? EndTag
   | EmptyElementConstructor
StartTag ::= '<' TagName AttributeList? '>'
TagName ::= QName
   | Variable
AttributeList ::= (AttributeName '=' ArithExpr)*
AttributeName ::= QName
   | Variable
EndTag ::= '</' TagName '>'
EmptyElementConstructor ::= '<' TagName AttributeList? '/>'

/* A name test is a Qname where "*" serves as a wild card. */
NameTest ::= QName
   | NamePrefix ':' '*'
   | '*' ':' LocalPart
   | '*'
NodeType ::= 'NODE'
   | 'TEXT'
   | 'COMMENT'
   | 'PROCESSING_INSTRUCTION'
QName ::= LocalPart
   | NamePrefix ':' LocalPart
NamePrefix ::= Identifier
LocalPart ::= Identifier
CompareOp ::= '=' | '<' | '<=' | '>' | '>=' | '!='

The terminal symbols of this grammar (other than keywords and special symbols) are:
   Variable   (example: $x)
   Identifier   (example: x)
   StringLiteral   (example: "x")
   IntegerLiteral   (example: 5)
   FloatLiteral   (example: 5.7)

As in XPath, many Quilt operators are overloaded and can be applied to values of various types. For example, A = B where A and B are sets is true if and only if there exists an element a in A and an element b in B such that a = b. The detailed semantics of these operators will be provided as part of a more complete language specification.

The Quilt core function library includes the following:

1. The functions of the XPath core function library[4]
2. The "aggregation functions" of SQL that operate on a collection and return a scalar result: sum, count, avg, max, and min.
3. Additional functions such as the following (partial list):
   document(string) returns the root node of a named document
   empty(collection) returns True if its argument is empty
   distinct(collection) removes duplicates from its argument
   name(element) returns the name (generic identifier) of an element
   shallow(element) strips an element of its subelements
   coalesce(set(set(element))) converts a set of sets into a single set that is the union of its members

References

1. World Wide Web Consortium. *Extensible Markup Language (XML) 1.0.* W3C Recommendation, Feb. 10, 1998. See http://www.w3.org/TR/1998/REC-xml-19980210

2. World Wide Web Consortium. *XML Schema, Parts 0, 1, and 2.* W3C Working Draft, April 7, 2000. See http://www.w3.org/TR/xmlschema-0, -1, and -2.

3. World Wide Web Consortium. *XML Query Requirements.* W3C Working Draft, Jan. 31, 2000. See http://www.w3.org/TR/xmlquery-req

4. World Wide Web Consortium. *XML Path Language (XPath) Version 1.0.* W3C Recommendation, Nov. 16, 1999. See http://www.w3.org/TR/xpath.html

5. J. Robie, J. Lapp, D. Schach. *XML Query Language (XQL).* See http://www.w3.org/TandS/QL/QL98/pp/xql.html.

6. Alin Deutsch, Mary Fernandez, Daniela Florescu, Alon Levy, and Dan Suciu. *A Query Language for XML.* See http://www.research.att.com/~mff/files/final.html

7. International Organization for Standardization (ISO). *Information Technology—Database Language SQL.* Standard No. ISO/IEC 9075:1999. (Available from American National Standards Institute, New York, NY 10036, (212) 642-4900.)

8. Rick Cattell et al. *The Object Database Standard: ODMG-93, Release 1.2.* Morgan Kaufmann Publishers, San Francisco, 1996.

9. Serge Abiteboul, Dallan Quass, Jason McHugh, Jennifer Widom, and Janet L. Wiener. The Lorel Query Language for Semistructured Data. *International Journal on Digital Libraries,* 1(1):68-88, April 1997. See http://www-db.stanford.edu/~widom/pubs.html

10. S. Cluet, S. Jacqmin, and J. Simeon. *The New YATL: Design and Specifications.* Technical Report, INRIA, 1999.

11. Jonathan Robie, Don Chamberlin, and Daniela Florescu. Quilt: an XML Query Language. Graphic Communications Association, *Proceedings of XML Europe*, June 2000.

12. World Wide Web Consortium. *XML Query Data Model*. W3C Working Draft, May 11, 2000. See http://www.w3.org/TR/query-datamodel.

13. World Wide Web Consortium. *XSL Transformations (XSLT)*. W3C Recommendation, Nov. 16, 1999. See http://www.w3.org/TR/xslt.

14. World Wide Web Consortium. *XML Pointer Language (XPointer)*. W3C Working Draft, Dec. 6, 1999. See http://www.w3.org/TR/WD-xptr.

15. World Wide Web Consortium. *Namespaces in XML*. W3C Recommendation, Jan. 14, 1999. See http://www.w3.org/TR/REC-xml-names.

Theme-Based Retrieval of Web News

Nuno Maria and Mário J. Silva

DI/FCUL
Faculdade de Ciências
Universidade de Lisboa
Campo Grande, Lisboa
Portugal
{nmsm, mjs}@di.fc.ul.pt

Abstract. We introduce an information system for organization and retrieval of news articles from Web publications, incorporating a classification framework based on Support Vector Machines. We present the data model for storage and management of news data and the system architecture for news retrieval, classification and generation of topical collections. We also discuss the classification results obtained with a collection of news articles gathered from a set of online newspapers.

1 Introduction

The number of publications and news articles published on the Web had a dramatic increase over the last years. Existing keyword query-driven search engines cannot cope with this ever-growing mass of information. Readers often want to access news articles related to a particular subject such as sports or business. Many electronic publications on the Web already separate their articles into a set of categories, but classification criteria are not uniform, leading to a poor satisfaction of reader's information needs.

Our project involves the creation of a framework to define Web services that let users see published news on the Internet sites organized in a common category scheme. To achieve this, specialized information retrieval and text classification tools are necessary. The Web news corpus suffers from specific constraints, such as a fast update frequency, or a transitory nature, as news information is "ephemeral." In addition information availability is also uncertain. As a result, traditional Information Filtering/Retrieval systems are not optimized to deal with such constraints.

A successful information filtering system sharing common goals, SIFTing Netnews [11], disseminates customized news reports through email, matching profiles to documents through common IR techniques. However, SIFTing Netnews did not apply classification techniques for information filtering. Other research of relevance to our work is broadly available. In the automatic text categorization field, detailed examinations on the behavior of statistical learning methods and performance comparisons are periodically available [10]. Bayesian probabilistic approaches, nearest neighbor, decision trees, inductive rule learning, neural networks and support vector machines are some techniques applied to this domain. However, and according

D. Suciu and G. Vossen (Eds.): WebDB 2000, LNCS 1997, pp. 26–37, 2001.

to several recent experiments [3, 4, 10], support vector machines appear as the most efficient technique available. Its efficiency and accuracy are only compared with nearest neighbor learning approaches, and between these two and the others there is a big gap.

Recent work on topic detection and tracking (TDT) and document clustering is also available [1, 12]. These fields are studying automatic techniques for detecting novel events from streams of news stories, and track events of interest over time. However, these topics are recent research and many questions remain open.

In our work, we are addressing some of these problems applying advanced information retrieval and classification techniques to the physical world of Web publishing as we gather, index and classify the major Portuguese news publications available online.

The Web news environment is very unstable: news information quickly becomes obsolete over time and is discarded by publishers. In addition, text categorization applied to news information is also a complex task, given the information's subjective and heterogeneous nature.

In our research, we have identified the following main problems associated with automatic retrieval of theme-based news:

- In general, news articles are available on the publisher's site only for a short period of time. Many Publications do not give access to their archive of previous editions and a database of references becomes easily invalid.
- Many news Web sites are built dynamically, often showing different information content over time in the same URL. This invalidates any strategy for incremental gathering of news from these Web sites based on their address.
- Direct application of common statistical learning methods to automatic text classification raises the problem of non-exclusive classification of news articles. Each article may be classified correctly into several categories, reflecting its heterogeneous nature. However, traditional classifiers are trained with a set of positive and negative examples and typically produce a binary value ignoring the underlying relationships between the article and multiple categories;
- It is necessary to validate the classification models created with the trained examples from our local digital library of news information. As each publication has a different classification scheme, manual labeling of validating test examples is sometimes necessary;
- Accuracy of the classification activity: the classification system must measure classification confidence and prevent misclassifications, as they have a strong negative impact in the reader. In Web news, good values for classification accuracy obtained in research environments (over 90%) may be insufficient. A reader that detects semantic incoherence will probably distrust the system and stop using it;
- News clustering, which would provide easy access to articles from different publications about the same story, is another risky operation. The automatic grouping of articles into the same topic requires very high confidence, as mistakes would be too obvious.
-

To address the above presented problems we believe that it is necessary to integrate in a global architecture a multiple category classification framework, including a data model for information and classification confidence thresholds.

We present the design of a prototype of a system that addresses the above introduced requirements. We have used it to study how classifiers behave as the time distance between the date of news articles in the training set and evaluated news increases. We measured how they lose accuracy as new topics and vocabulary are added and strong weight features are discarded.

2   Support Vector Machines

Support Vector Machines - SVMs are a new learning method introduced by Vapnik [9], but only recently they have been gaining popularity in the learning community. In its simplest linear form, an SVM is a hyperplane that separates a set of positive examples from a set of negative examples with a maximum margin. Figure 1 illustrates this scheme.

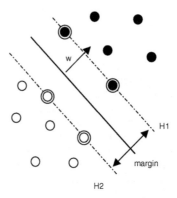

Fig. 1. Linear separating hyperplanes. The support vectors are circled

The formula for the output of a linear SVM is $u = \vec{w} \cdot \vec{x} - b$, where $\vec{w}$ is the normal vector to the hyperplane, and $\vec{x}$ is the input vector. In the linear case, the margin is defined by the distance of the hyperplane to the nearest of the positive and negative examples. Maximizing the margin can be expressed as an optimization problem: minimize $\frac{1}{2} \| \vec{w} \|^2$ subject to $y_i (\vec{w} \cdot \vec{x}_i - b) \geq 1, \forall i$ where x_i is the ith training example and y_i is the correct output of the SVM for the ith training example.

SVMs have been shown to yield good generalization performance in a variety of classification problems, including handwritten character recognition, face recognition and more recently text categorization [4]. The simplest linear version of the SVM provides good classification accuracy, is fast to learn and fast classifying new instances.

3   Theme-Based News Retrieval System

Our system integrates a set of built or customized software components for retrieval and classification of text documents and a shared database of news articles. Figure 2 presents our architecture for retrieval and classification of Web news. It has the following main components:

Retrieval Service: This Service was implemented as a modified version of the Harvest Information Discovery and Access System [2]. On a higher abstraction level, we view the service as a provider of a continuous stream of news articles retrieved from news Web sites.

Classification Service: This Service was built on SVM^{ligth}, a package written for automatic text classification using support vector machines [5]. This enables the classification of the gathered news articles into a reduced, but uniform, set of categories based on train examples from pre-classified news. In our prototype the examples were taken from an existing publication that acted as our classifier reference [8].

Topic Collection Index Generators: Together the two components presented above load a common database with the indexed and classified news articles. From this database, specific topic collection index generators can be built to provide updates to topical Web portals (also known as vertical portals).

The remainder of this section presents the components of our news information management system in detail.

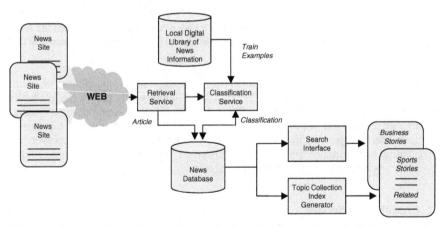

Fig. 2. Architecture for retrieval and classification of news articles. The Retrieval Service collects articles from news sites distributed over the Web. These articles are sent to the Classification Service for classification on a common scheme according to train examples provided by a Local Digital Library. Classified articles are then stored in a News Database, ready to use by custom publications. Topic Collection Index generators update vertical Web portals

3.1 Retrieval Service

Figure 3 details the Retrieval Service behavior. Multiple gathering agents retrieve and index news Web sites. To deal with different periodicity of publications, several queues are created and managed expressing different update priorities and different gathering schedules (Q_{D1} for daily publications, Q_{W1} for weekly editions, etc.).

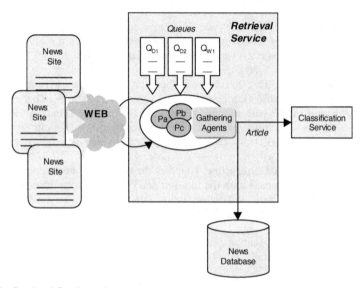

Fig. 3. The Retrieval Service sub-components. Articles are retrieved and indexed from the Web by gathering agents, according to a pre-defined periodicity queue. New articles are stored in the Database

In general, as we are only interested in indexing the current edition of each publication site, gathering agents can be configured to index only part of the available information in the site. This capacity allows the scalability of our solution, avoiding indexing or re-indexing of past news or irrelevant information, despite the fact that a simple header comparison in some cases would prevent re-indexing. However, in some cases, news articles are dynamic Web pages built on demand, which would invalidate any header information in our database.

3.2 Classification Service

Figure 4 details the Classification Service sub-components and their behavior. As articles arrive from the stream provided by the Retrieval Service, they are automatically converted into a vector format according to a pre-defined vocabulary.

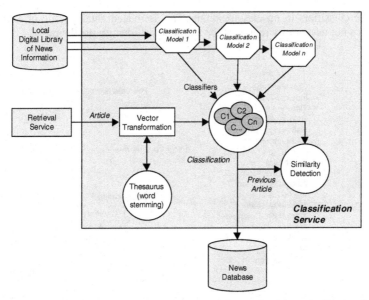

Fig. 4. The Classification Service sub-components. Articles received from the Retrieval Service are converted to a vector format according to a predefined vocabulary. This enables classification based on the models defined for each category. Classification results are loaded in the News Database. Upon insertion, each new article is compared with a set of recent articles checking possible similarities

Actual classification, based on pre-defined classification models, one for each category, is performed with this vector format. The models are built with trained examples prepared from the news corpus provided by the local news library. In our implementation this corpus is taken from a daily newspaper containing articles manually classified by their editors.

Once the Classifier processes one article, the resulting classification confidences are loaded in the News Database. We store the article's confidence level, returned from the classifier for each model, and information about possibly related articles. A Similarity Detection mechanism is run to quantify proximity between each new article and recently processed articles. If similarity is detected, then the article is grouped with other articles on a related cluster.

3.3 News Database

Figure 5 presents the data model for the news articles database. Each loaded article has the common attributes shown in the Figure 5. Some attributes of this set are extracted with heuristics, as the document structure of the target publication is unknown. This is the case of "article-bodytext." It is important that the article text, delivered to Classification Service, is clean from navigation bars or headers commonly found in the HTML of Web news information. These act as noise that can induce the classifiers in misclassifications. This is indeed data specific of each site, which does not necessarily represent the features that identify the themes.

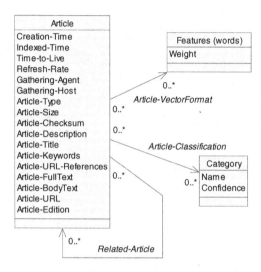

Fig. 5. Data model for the article database. News articles are catalogued with the set of attributes shown. Its vector format is stored with the association to Features and the article's classification is stored with the confidence level for each category. Articles can also be related to other articles

In our data model, we also store each article's vector format as associations to the Features class. The weights of the features (words) in a document are calculated with the Inverse Document Frequency - IDF based on the vocabulary defined by the trained examples. The weights are also normalized. This format is used in the Similarity Detection mechanism to determine possible relations with other articles through a similarity function. If similarity is detected, then an association with other articles is stored creating a cluster of related news.

The article classification activity is not exclusive: an article may belong to several categories. Each classification model expresses an absolute confidence value for the article. So, for each article, multiple associations with categories and confidence values are stored.

3.4 Theme-Based Portals Generator

Figure 6 presents an overview of the access methods to the News Database.

The database can be accessed through an advanced search interface where the user can customize the query with restrictions according to the data model. The interface enables search and retrieval of news articles from selected news Web sites filtered by category or edition. The entity that handles submitted queries is an application server that in turn uses the Glimpse search engine from the Harvest system [7]. This search engine uses a simple query format but handles complex and advanced queries efficiently and scales well.

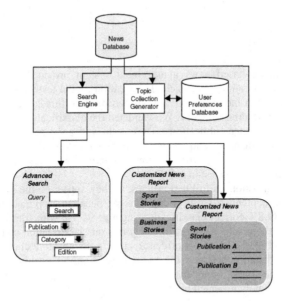

Fig. 6. Interface to the News Database search engine. Users may submit advanced queries specifying multiple restrictions or access customized news reports, built according to stated personal preferences

The News Database can also be used to generate customized news reports. These are dynamically built with preferences supplied by the users. Preferences are stored in an autonomous database that associates each user with a list of rules. These define the format for a personalized publication containing a list of potential highly relevant references to the user's information interest. The Topic Collection Generator also uses Glimpse as the search engine in the News Database.

3.5 Classifiers Training Strategies

Selection of the appropriate training information is crucial in our system, as it determines the classifiers' efficiency and accuracy.

The news articles used in training are previously filtered. Filtering consists in cleaning new Web pages from HTML tags and all other noise that they may have related to formatting and navigation.

The selected articles were picked from a reference newspaper and have publication dates uniformly distributed along the last year. We have observed that this approach minimizes the negative effects of cyclic events.

Our classifiers use the maximum number of features available, as the SVM-based classification mechanism scales well and we do not suffer the performance degradation of traditional classification algorithms.

4   Results

The developed theme-based news management system provides a framework for multi-category classifications. For each classification model tested, if the confidence value returned by each model is above a defined positive threshold, we classify the article in the corresponding category. We validated the classification models from our local library against other publications. These achieved good accuracy, 94,5% with non-exclusive classification and using contents filtering. This precision was accomplished with a sample of articles from six publications representing one day of news (approximately one thousand articles).

We tested classification on full-text articles, as they appear on the publishers' sites (N/Filt.), and with contents filtering (Filt.). The gap between each method precision is about 5% (only 89,8% correct classifications against 94.5% with filtering strategies). Figure 7 presents the results for a set of categories on classification confidence using these two different methods. The confidence value is the absolute classification score representing the distance between the hyperplane dividing positive from negative examples and the point represented by the article (regarding SVM theory). Confidence is ultimately reflected in classification precision.

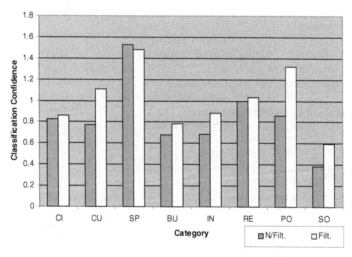

Fig. 7. Comparison of the confidence in classifications on test examples with a limited set of categories. (Categories: CI: Science, CU: Culture, SP: Sports, BU: Business, IN: International Politics, RE: Regional News, PO: Politics, SO: Society)

Filtering of format elements and navigation bars, generally present in Web documents, is performed by applying a set of heuristics specific of scanned news sites. Degradation in classification confidence of unfiltered news is more evident in general themes such as 'Society', 'Politics' or 'Culture'. However, in more specific categories, like 'Sports', 'Business' or 'Regional', accuracy does not improve significantly with filtering.

In the extremely dynamic environment of Web news we also must be aware of the degradation of the classifiers' accuracy in time. Figures 8 e 9 present the behavior of four category classifiers with two distinct training strategies. In the first experiment, we built models with articles from January and classified news dated from the following months. In the second strategy we built models with selected articles from all the months of the year.

With the first strategy, the efficiency of the classifier decreased tracking seasonality of the news events. This behavior is more apparent in dynamic categories such as 'Sports' or 'Politics'. In more static domains, such as 'Culture' or 'Business', classifiers have shown to be more stable.

The decreasing efficiency tendency is not visible using the second strategy, where classifiers, built with a higher number of articles spread along the year, present more stable levels of accuracy.

The degradation of accuracy, measured by the confidence on positive classification, obtained by linear regression of the average behavior with the first strategy is however, minimized with our classifier building strategies, which do not force any feature selection. On the other hand, the above results have been obtained for a reduced number of wide scope categories. For a more specialized collection of categories we can expect a sharper degradation.

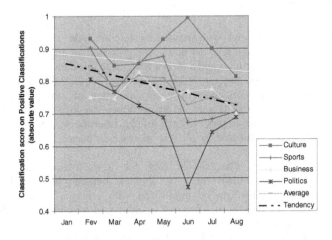

Fig. 8. The classification score on positive examples in time, obtained with models trained with articles from January. In topics with low seasonality such as culture, confidence is higher, but in other topics, like politics, confidence may decrease sharply

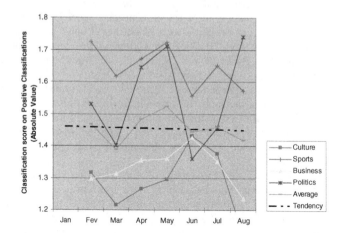

Fig. 9. The classification score on positive examples in time, obtained with models trained with articles of a full year. Confidence in classifications is significantly higher than with the previous strategy. Although some variations are visible the overall behavior is more stable in time

We are now finishing the similarity detection mechanism. Once completed, we will measure the accuracy of the used clustering techniques.

5   Conclusions

The increasing number of news Web sites on the Internet today demands specialized services to efficiently manage relevant news. We proposed an architecture to gather, retrieve and classify news articles and a model to manage this data.

Our classifiers, based on Support Vector Machines, presented good performance when applied to the categorization of news (accuracy of approximately 94%), confirming the ability of SVM's to build accurate and efficient classifiers. To accomplished this result we preprocess each article, filtering presentation noise with specific heuristics. We estimated in 5% the increase in accuracy when filtering is applied.

Our experiments have also shown that for news classification, accuracy degradation in time is minimal for some themes, but can be very high when seasonality is present. This can be minimized with criterious selection of train examples, sampled from a long time interval to compensate for the seasonality of the topics and periodic retraining of the classifiers.

The news retrieval and classification system, discussed in this paper, is now under user evaluation. We have re-implemented and incorporated it as part of the LinXs [6], a news search engine for the community of Portuguese news readers.

References

1. Allan, J., Papka, R. and Lavrenko V.. On-line New Event Detection and Tracking. In Proceedings of the 21th Ann Int ACM SIGIR Conference on Research and Development in Information Retrieval (SIGIR'98), pages 37-45, 1998.
2. Bowman, C., Danzig, P., Hardy, D., Manber, U. and Schwartz, M.. The Harvest Information Discovery and Access System. In Proceedings of the Second International WWW Conference. pp.763-771, 1994.
3. Dumais, S., Platt, J., Heckerman, D. and Sahami, M., Inductive Learning Algorithms and Representations for Text Categorization. Proceedings of the Seventh International Conference on Information and Knowledge Management, 1998.
4. Joachims, T., Text categorization with support vector machines: Learning with many relevant features. In Proceedings of the Tenth European Conference on Machine Learning - ECML, 1998.
5. Joachims, T., Making large-Scale SVM Learning Practical. Advances in Kernel Methods - Support Vector Learning, B. Schölkopf and C. Burges and A. Smola (ed.), MIT-Press, 1999.
6. LinXs Web Site. http://linxs.pt, 2000.
7. Manber, U., and Wu, S.. Glimpse: a tool to search through entire file systems. In Proceedings of the USENIX Winter Conference, pages 23-32, 1994.
8. Maria, N., Gaspar, P., Grilo, N., Ferreira, A. and Silva M. J.. ARIADNE - Digital Library Architecture. In Proceedings of the 2nd European Conference on digital Libraries (ECDL'98), pages 667-668, 1998.
9. Vapnik, V. N.. The Nature of Statistical Learning Theory. Springer, New York, 1995.
10. Yang, Y. and Liu X.. A re-examination of text categorization methods. In Proceedings of the 22th Ann Int ACM SIGIR Conference on Research and Development in Information Retrieval (SIGIR'99), pages 42-49, 1999.
11. Yan, T. and Garcia-Molina, H.. SIFT – A Tool for Wide-Area Information Dissemination. In Proceedings of the 1995 Usenix Technical Conference, pages 177-86, 1995.
12. Yang, Y., Carbonell, J., Brown, R., Pierce, T., Archibald B. T. and Liu X.. Learning approaches for Detecting and Tracking News Events. IEEE Intelligent Systems: Special Issue on Applications of Intelligent Information Retrieval, Vol. 14(4), pages 32-43, July/August 1999.

Using Metadata to Enhance Web Information Gathering

Jeonghee Yi[1], Neel Sundaresan[2], and Anita Huang[3]

[1] Computer Science
University of California, Los Angeles
405 Hilgard Av. LA, CA 90095, USA
jeonghee@cs.ucla.edu
[2] NehaNet Corp.
2533 Paragon Dr. Suite E, San Jose, CA 95131, USA
neel@nehanet.com
[3] IBM Almaden Research Center
650 Harry Rd. San Jose, CA 95120, USA
anhuang@almaden.ibm.com

Abstract. With the web at close to a billion pages and growing at an exponential rate, we are faced with the issue of rating pages in terms of quality and trust. In this situation, what other pages say about a web page can be as important as what the page says about itself. The cumulative knowledge of these types of recommendations (or the lack thereof) can be objective enough to help a user or robot program to decide whether or not to pursue a web document. In addition, these annotations or metadata can be used by a web robot program to derive summary information about web documents that are written in a language that the robot does not understand. We use this idea to drive a web information gathering system that forms the core of a topic-specific search engine.

In this paper, we describe how our system uses metadata about the hyperlinks to guide itself to crawl the web. It sifts through useful information related to a particular topic to eliminate the traversal of links that may not be of interest. Thus, the guided crawling system stays focused on the target topic. It builds a rich repository of link information that includes metadata. This repository ultimately serves a search engine.

1 Introduction

The World Wide Web (web) today contains close to a billion pages and is growing at an exponential rate [13,14]. As the number and complexity (in terms of the scripts, graphics, animations) of pages grow, to study and rate these pages based upon their content can become expensive and complex. As an alternative, it is possible to look at the pages that point to a page and to rate whether or not the page is of interest based on what other pages say about it. In this way, it is possible to learn from other people's experience.

D. Suciu and G. Vossen (Eds.): WebDB 2000, LNCS 1997, pp. 38–57, 2001.

Typical web crawlers crawl the web indiscriminately, paying little attention to the quality of search information. The goal of these crawlers is to get to as many pages as possible. Topic-directed crawlers have a different objective. Their goal is to get to all the pages related to their topic of interest as fast as possible without deviating to unrelated pages.

HITS[10] is a pioneering work that uses the link structure in hypertext documents to identify highly reference pages to discover high quality pages. HITS introduces the notion of authoritative pages and hub pages. Hub pages *point to* authority pages, and authority pages are *pointed to by* hub pages. This system has been extended to build an automatic classifier [4] and a focused web crawler [5].

We start with the HITS premise and enhance it with descriptive information around hyperlinks to identify the most appropriate metadata. We use a scheme that assigns weights to the edges in the link topology based upon the occurrences of certain topic words in the metadata to rate pages. We also use metadata to enhance abstracts and, among other things, to decide on recrawl strategies.

The Organization of the Paper

The rest of the paper is organized as follows: Section 2 presents the architecture of our web gathering system, called Grand Central Station. Section 3 gives an introduction to hyperlink metadata in Web pages, describes how we extract it, and presents the results of our analysis of it. Section 4 discusses how we use this hyperlink metadata to enhance topic-specific gathering. Section 5 reviews related work, and section 6 draws conclusions.

2   The Web Gatherer Environment

The experiments in this paper were conducted using the Grand Central Station (GCS) web gathering system[8]. GCS provides an information discovery infrastructure that aims to deliver useful information to users regardless of the location and the format of the information source. GCS has been used to build a number of domain-specific search engines, which include *jCentral*[1] (a search engine specific to Java-related information) and *xCentral*[2] (an XML-specific search engine).

The GCS architecture consists of sets of distributed gatherers and summarizers that target, collect, and summarize data. This architecture is extensible to handle virtually any protocol (e.g., HTTP, NNTP, etc.) and to summarize virtually any content-type (e.g., HTML, Java, XML, etc.). Moreover, it is programmable to use custom crawling strategies. The algorithms described in this paper were used to build the *xCentral* search engine.

Figure 1 shows GCS's extensible architecture, which consists of two main components—a *gatherer* and a *summarizer*—and an additional component for topic-specific crawling— a *topic expander*.

---

[1] *jCentral* at http://www.ibm.com/developer/java/
[2] *xCentral* at http://www.ibm.com/developer/xml/

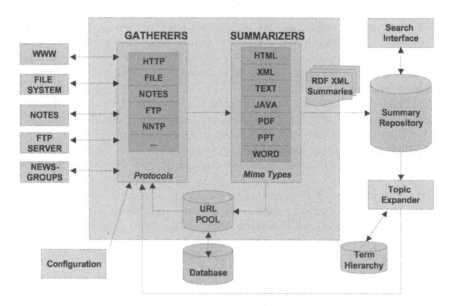

Fig. 1. System Architecture. The *gatherer* visits web pages and the *summarizer* produces metadata on the links and the content of the pages. *Topic expander* identifies and extends relevant topic terms to the given topic on the basis of the metadata.

The *gatherer* component of GCS systematically finds data to be parsed and summarized by the *summarizer* component. New protocol handlers, content summarizers, and crawl algorithms may be implemented in the GCS system by writing Java classes that use GCS-defined APIs. The gatherer loads and plugs-in the appropriate classes, using the Java reflection mechanism, according to an input specification file (based on eXtensible Markup Language (XML)[2] syntax). The configuration file informs the system of the specific protocol handlers, content-summarizers, and crawling algorithms to use. Currently, the GCS system can gather data from an extensive number of protocols, including HTTP, NNTP, FTP, and file systems, and can summarize data for a wide range of content-types, including HTML, XML, text, PDF, Word, Java source code and Java class files. Moreover, it is able to use various topic-specific crawl strategies (as described in this paper), as implemented through custom URL pools.

The GCS *summarizers* produce metadata descriptions of the gathered data using Resource Description Framework (RDF) [12,3]—the W3C recommendation for storing data about data. Each metadata summary takes the form of an RDF metadata graph serialized as XML. In addition to RDF, each summary uses *SumML*[18], an extensible schema architecture provided by GCS. The GCS system indexes the metadata summaries to serve a front-end search engine. The advantage of producing RDF metadata is that it retains structure. Most typical search engines, such as AltaVista[3],Infoseek[4], or Hotbot[5], limit themselves to simple boolean or structurally static queries. GCS's RDF metadata summaries, on the other hand, allow our search engines to respond to structurally dynamic queries. For example, the RDF metadata summary for a Java program will contain structural information, such as abstract information, class names, imported classes, inherited classes and interfaces, method names with signatures, and exceptions thrown. Keeping the structure enables our search engine to respond to structured queries such as "show me all Java classes that implement the XML notation interface and are written by Kento Tamura".

Finally, the GCS *topic expander* is used to enhance topic-specific crawling. The topic-expander incrementally expands a topic definition as web crawling proceeds. It thereby refines the gatherer's definition of the topic to be used to determine the relevance of specific resources. Typically, a target topic consists of many subtopics. For example, the topic XML, according to the the Yahoo! [6] hierarchy (November 1999), consists of three subtopics: XSL (Extensible Stylesheet Language), SVG (Scalable Vector Graphics), and Software. In addition to subtopics, the target topic also consists of related topics that share relevant properties but do not fall under the hierarchy. For example, topics relevant to but not subtopics of XML include SGML (Standard Generalized Markup Language), DTD (Document Type Definition), and XML Namespace. Exploiting hyperlink annotations, the topic expander learns of these relevant topics as the crawling proceeds. The *topic expander* is presented in detail in [21].

3   Metadata in Web Documents

Hyperlink metadata, or simply *metadata*, is the information about a referenced document provided by the attributes of and the text around its hyperlink. As an analogy, consider the information about a research paper provided by its citation in another paper. In addition to the fact that the research paper was cited in the other paper, the citing paper offers the reader information about the cited paper. For example, the citing paper might provide a critique of the cited paper in its review of related works. In web documents, citations are in the form of hyperlinks. In this paper, we concentrate on the hyperlink metadata in HTML documents (on which our experiments were run).

This section gives an overview of the hyperlink metadata found in HTML documents. It also describes our analysis of this metadata to determine the best types for use in a topic-specific gathering environment.

---

[3] AltaVista at http://www.altavista.com/

[4] Infoseek at http://www.infoseek.com/

[5] Hotbot at http://www.hotbot.com/

[6] Yahoo! at http://www.yahoo.com/

3.1 HTML Metadata

In HTML documents we find four kinds of hyperlinks:

- anchor(<A>) tags
- Image(<IMG>) tags
- Map and Area tags
- Frame and iFrame tags

Anchor tags are the most commonly used. They have several attributes associated with them. The main attributes include name, title, alt, on-mouse-over, and href. Image tags have other attributes such as name, alt, src, dynsrc, lowsrc, onabort, onload, and onerror. Map and Area tags have similar attributes to anchor tags. Some of these attributes are browser-specific but most are browser-independent. In addition to considering these attributes for use as hyperlink metadata, we also extract and examine information from text surround the tags, from text contained inside the tags, and from text at the parent level of the tags.

We consider parent-level text because it often provides a summary of a group of links within a list. For example, when a page lists outgoing links using a set of <li> tags within a list structure (like ul or ol), the overall summary of these <li> elements is often found at the parent level. Figure 2 shows an example of this pattern in a web page that categorizes publications by subject area. The example is an excerpt from a publication web page of IBM Almaden Research Center[7]. Here all the papers related to "Association Mining" are listed together with a common metadata element (an <H3> tag) and all the papers related to "Classification" are listed together under a different metadata element.

The goal is to identify the attributes and text that are most appropriate for the purpose of hyperlink metadata. In order to do so, we treat the HTML tags as structured XML elements, extract the relevant attributes and text from them, and identify the most suitable ones to be used as hyperlink metadata.

3.2 Metadata Extraction

In order to extract metadata for hyperlinks from an HTML document, we first convert the HTML document to a well-formed XML document. Most HTML browsers tend to be very forgiving and accept and display documents that are poorly formed HTML. We have an *XML Filter* that converts the HTML documents to well-formed XML documents, which performs extensive error recovery in the case of poorly formed HTML documents. Once we have a well-formed XML document, we check the document for elements with element names corresponding to the hyperlink elements (i.e., A for anchor tags, IMG for image tags, and so on) and extract their attribute values. In order to identify the surrounding text, we identify XML elements of type PCDATA which are left and right siblings of these tags. For text contained inside a hyperlink tag, we look for PCDATA inside the HTML tags. For parent-level text, we pick the text data at the ancestral level where the closest sibling of a previous ancestor is a text node.

---

[7] http://www.almaden.ibm.com/cs/quest/publications.html

```
<H3> <a name=associations> Associations Mining: </a> </H3>
<ul>
  <li> R. J. Bayardo Jr. and R. Agrawal,
       <a href="http://www.almaden.ibm.com/.../kdd99.ps.Z">
       "Mining the Most Interesting Rules"</a>
       In <em> Proc. of the 5th ACM SIGKDD Int'l Conf. on
       Knowledge Discovery and Data Mining</a></em>, 145-154,
       August 1999.
       ....
  <li> R. J. Bayardo Jr., R. Agrawal, and D. Gunopulos.
       <a href="http://www.almaden.ibm.com/.../icde99.ps.Z">
       "Constraint-Based Rule Mining in Large, Dense Databases".</a>
       <em> Proc. of the 15th Int'l Conf. on Data Engineering</a></em>,
       188-197, Sydney, Australia, March 1999.
       ....
  <li> ....
  ....
</ul>
<H3>  <a name=classification> Classification: </a> </H3>
<ul>
  <li> M. J. Zaki, C. T. Ho, R. Agrawal,
       <a href="papers/de99_smp.ps"> "Parallel Classification
       for Data Mining on Shared-Memory Multiprocessors"</a>,
       <em> Proc. of the 15th Int'l Conf. on Data Engineering</a></em>,
       198-205, Sydney, Australia, March 1999.
       ....
  <li> ....
  ....
</ul>
```

Fig. 2. The excerpt of publication web page of Quest project at IBM Almaden Research Center (http://www.almaden.ibm.com/cs/quest/publications.html). The text at the parent level of the anchor tags provides the overall summary of these <li> elements. I.e., the anchor text "Association Mining" describes the subject of the papers listed underneath, and so does the anchor text "Classification".

3.3   Metadata Analysis

We studied a sample set of 20,000 HTML pages, which was collected by recursively visiting all hyperlinked pages from a given set of seed pages. We discovered over 206,000 hyperlink references from the sample set. Some of these hyperlinks pointed to pages within the sample set, while others pointed to pages outside the sample set. Using this sample set, we measured the frequency and quality of the various attributes/text associated with the hyperlinks.

Table 1 lists several characteristics of various metadata types. It can be seen that, second to HREF, anchor text is the most common metadata type. To determine the quality of the metadata types, we tested them in our data mining experiments for topic discovery, as described in [21]. The quality of each metadata-type was determined based on the number of relevant topic terms discovered by its use during mining. In addition, we determined the absolute and relative reliabilities of each metadata-type. To do so, we determined the accuracy of what the metadata said about the page that it pointed to by determining what the page actually contained. This reliability measurement also accounted for outdated and expired references. From these experiments, we found that anchor text, HREF, and surrounding text, in that order, provide the highest quality hyperlink metadata.

In the experiments discussed in this paper, we limit the hyperlink metadata to anchor text because it is the most frequently occurring and the most reliable metadata type. Alternative schemes, such as choosing weighted averages of different metadata types, could also be applied.

Table 1. This table lists various attributes associated with a hyperlink. The numbers in the column "Hyperlinks" measures the number of hyperlinks (and the percentage) which are referenced with a particular metadata type. The column "Pages" gives the number of pages which contains at least one particular metadata type.

Metadata Type	Hyperlinks	Pages
HREF	176,412 (85 %)	16313 (87 %)
Anchor Text	147,745 (72 %)	14320 (76 %)
NAME	5,487 (27 %)	779 (4.1 %)
Surrounding Text	49,138 (24 %)	8424 (45 %)
ONMOUSEOVER	9,383 (4.5 %)	1523 (8.1 %)
ALT Tag	1,890 (0.9 %)	281 (1.5 %)
Title	885 (0.4 %)	249 (1.3 %)

4   Enhancing Topic-Specific Information Gathering Using Metadata

This section demonstrates the utility of hyperlink metadata for topic-specific information gathering. We utilize metadata information

i) for guiding crawlers to gather topic relevant pages efficiently,
ii) for making recrawl decisions, and
iii) for producing rich metadata summaries of web pages.

This section begins with a brief review of the metadata database of our gathering system. It then presents the set of algorithms that we use, which exploit hyperlink metadata, to guide the crawler. Finally, it outlines some metadata-based recrawl strategies and concludes with a discussion of cumulative metadata in web page summaries.

4.1   The Metadata Database

Our gathering system is multi-threaded and distributed, which means that crawlers run on multiple machines with tens of threads on each individual machine. A small group of machines share URL information through a relational database (DB/2). As the crawl progresses, the database grows into a rich repository of URL link and metadata information. Hence, the gathering system provides a scalable solution where multiple groups of such machines communicate with each other during a crawl through a distributed messaging system. For the results shown in this paper, we used a set of four machines sharing information through a single relational database.

As a crawler visits a page it extracts all the links (with their metadata) in the page and adds them to the URL database. The URL database maintains, for each URL, the URL itself, its crawl history information, and other information useful for future visits of a URL. In addition, it creates a table of link metadata information consisting of (URL, parent-URL, metadata) triples.

The URL database and metadata tables are used to rank the URLs according to relevance to the target topic. The URLs with higher ranks will have higher crawl priority than URLs with lower ranks. While the crawler adds all URLs that it encountered into the database, it visits the URLs based on their ranking. Hence, the gatherer is able to pick up pages with higher relevance sooner than pages with lower relevance to the topic. The ultimate goal is to maximize the visits to the most relevant pages while minimizing visits to irrelevant pages.

The summarizer component also uses the URL database tables to produce RDF metadata for the page. The summarizer generates a description of a page that includes what other pages say about the given page and what the given page says about the pages it points to. The summarizer uses RDF, the W3C language for describing *metadata* (data about data), to capture this hyperlink metadata information. With its XML serialization syntax, these RDF structures can be incorporated into query systems that understand XML.

4.2   Topic-Directed Crawling Algorithms

Good pages for topic-specific information gatherers are the pages that pertain to the target topic. We developed various algorithms for guiding topic-specific gatherers on the basis of hyperlink metadata in order to crawl the topic relevant pages with highest priority. In general, the topic-specific gatherer crawls a page, w, if the relevance of the page to the topic, $\Theta(w)$, is greater than the relevance threshold, c, given by the user. The actual computation of $\Theta(w)$ varies depending on the topic-directed crawling algorithms. For each of the algorithms that we developed, this computation relies either heavily or entirely on hyperlink metadata.

We first describe a crawling algorithm based purely on hyperlink connectivity (i.e., which does not use hyperlink metadata): Hyperlink Induced Topic Search (HITS). We describe this algorithm because we use it as a basis for comparison for the performance of the other algorithms. Next, we describe each of the four algorithms that exploit hyperlink metadata for topic-specific crawling:

---

1. Let P be a set of web pages.
   Let $E = \{(p_1, p_2) \mid$ Page p_1 has hyperlink to another page $p_2, p_1, p_2 \in P\}$.
2. For every page p in P, let $H(p)$ be its hub score and $A(p)$ its authority score.
3. Initialize $H(p)$ and $A(p)$ to 1 for all p in P.
4. While the vectors H and A have not converged:
5.   - For all p in P, $A(p) = \sum_{(p',p) \in E} H(p')$
6.   - For all p in P, $H(p) = \sum_{(p,p') \in E} A(w')$
7.   - Normalize the H and A vectors.

Fig. 3. Hypertext Induced Topic Search (*HITS*)

- Simple Heuristics (SH)
- Relevance Weighting (RW)
- Relevance Weighting with Boosting (RWB)
- Hypertext Induced Topic Search with Relevance Weighting (HITS-RW)

After presenting these algorithms, we analyze their performance for crawling relevant pages. In sum, the experimental results demonstrate that each of the hyperlink metadata-based algorithms outperforms HITS. Moreover, based on metadata only, these algorithms discover relevant pages with as much as 90% of the accuracy. Of note, the hyperlink metadata approach achieves this accuracy without having to download irrelevant pages and, thereby, significantly improves the crawl performance.

1. ***HITS* - Kleinberg's Algorithm**
   HITS (Hypertext Induced Topic Search) [10] provides a weighting mechanism based on structural linking relationships among web pages. An *authoritative* web page is a highly referenced web page, and a *hub* page is a web page that references many authority pages. In general, a page is a good authority if many good hub pages point to it. Conversely, a page is a good hub if it points to many good authority pages. The intuition is as follows: A page which points to many others is a good hub, and a page that many pages point to is a good authority. Transitively, a page pointing to many good authorities is an even better hub, and similarly a page pointed to by many good hubs is an even better authority.
   HITS computes hub($H(p)$) and authority($A(p)$) scores of a page, p, as shown in figure 3. As proven by Kleinberg [10], the H and A vectors ultimately converge. In the crawling experiments, the system assigns hub and authority scores after iterating about n times (with n at times as low as 5). The crawler assigns priority according to the authority score of each page. Authoritative assignment ultimately does not affect which pages will be crawled; rather, it determines only the order of the crawl, serving to build a high-quality collection of URLs in the early stages of the crawl. This type of crawl order is important when a system has limited resources to conduct the crawl. Moreover, for the Web which has more pages than what typical web gathering systems can deal with, this practically means that only the highly authoritative pages will be crawled.

2. **Simple Heuristics (*SH*)**

Simple Heuristics, or *SH*, first gives the highest crawl priority to those URLs that contain a predetermined set of relevant topic terms in their HREF metadata (i.e, the URL itself). For example, SH will prioritize URLs that contains the terms XML, DTD, or XSL for an XML crawl. After prioritizing according to topic terms, *SH* prioritizes URLs based on recursion depth (the depth away from the seed set at which the URL was discovered). Using the *SH* algorithm, the crawler ultimately crawls all URLs that contain the topic terms in the URL:

$$\Theta_{SH}(w) = \begin{cases} 1 \text{ , if url}(w) \text{ contains a topic term} \\ 0 \text{ , otherwise} \end{cases}$$

SH is designed to exploit the web page organization convention adopted by many web masters: groups of web pages that contain similar content are often assigned URLs that begin with a similar URL prefix. This trend in URLs reflects the organization within a directory hierarchy. The prefix also often reflects the page content. For example, web pages that have URLs that start with the prefix `http://www.ibm.com/java` have a high probability of containing content that is related to the topic "Java".

Topic terms include the *sub-topics* or *relevant topics* of the given target topic. A formal description of relevant topics and their discovery is out of the scope of this paper. We refer the interested reader to [21] for a detailed discussion of this data mining process.

3. **Relevance Weighting (*RW*)**

Relevance Weighting, or *RW*, prioritizes pages on the basis of the relevance of its hyperlink metadata. The crawler selects pages to crawl based on this relevance score and prunes pages for which the metadata relevance score does not meet some threshold value. Using *RW*, crawlers will not visit a page unless the hyperlink metadata for the page looks promising, i.e., is relevant enough to the topic.

$\Theta_{RW}(w)$, the *RW* relevance score of a page, *w*, is computed as follows:

$$\Theta_{RW}(w) = \begin{cases} max(\Theta(t)_{t \in M(w)}) \text{ if } \max(\Theta(t)_{t \in M(w)}) \geq c \\ 0 \qquad\qquad\qquad\qquad \text{otherwise} \end{cases}$$

where $\Theta(t)$ denotes the relevance of a term t to the target topic [20,19]. $M(w)$ is the hyperlink metadata of the in-link of w. c is a user defined threshold for relevance.

4. Relevance Weighting with Boosting (RWB)

Relevance Weighting with Boosting, or RWB, is similar to RW but deliberately increases the relevance score of some pages where these pages fail to meet the relevance threshold. To be specific, among the pages of which RW score is lower than c, RWB selects pages using a random boosting factor, R_1, and recalculates the relevance of these selected pages based on the entire page content (rather than just the hyperlink metadata). Hence, this algorithm includes relevant pages that would otherwise have been pruned in RW. In addition to boosting pages based on the entire page content, among the pages of which content failed to be relevant, RWB also selects pages using a second random probability, R_2, and boosts the relevance scores of the selected pages whether or not they qualify under either metadata or content relevance calculations.

$\Theta_{RWB}(W)$, the RWB relevance score of a page (w), is computed as follows:

$$
\Theta_{RWB}(w) = \begin{cases} \Theta_{RW}(w) & \text{if } \Theta_{RW}(w) > c \\ & \text{or } R_1 < b \\ max(\Theta(t)_{r \in w}) & \text{if } R_1 \geq b \\ & \text{and } max(\Theta(t)_{t \in w}) \geq c \\ R_2 & \text{if } R_1 \geq b \\ & \text{and } max(\Theta(t)_{t \in w}) < c \end{cases}
$$

where R_1 and R_2 are random variables with uniform distribution, and b is a user-defined boosting factor.

RWB is designed to overcome the potential stagnation by RW that results from aggressive pruning of URLs on the basis of the link metadata only. By deliberately increasing the score of some pages that fail to meet the relevance threshold, RWB allows the crawler to visit pages beyond the current local cluster.

The web page, `http://ala.vsms.nottingham.ac.uk/analog.html`, for instance, as illustrated in figure 4, has the hyperlink metadata, "Site Access Statistics." This metadata is provided by a parent page, with the URL `http://ala.vsms.nottingham.ac.uk`. The actual page content of the sample page does not appear to be relevant. It includes a hyperlink of which the metadata, 'vsms/catalog.html', does not seem to be relevant. Though, the link is not appealing, the page has a hyperlink through which one can reach many topic-related websites. The page `http://www.vsms.nottingham.ac.uk/`
`vsms/java/index.html` leads to numerous good XML sites. In other words, the page is a bridge between the two good local clusters of XML related sites. There are over 2600 bridge links like this, in the sample URLs under the experiments, which directly link one XML cluster to another.
RWB algorithm overcomes the drawback of RW on bridge links by consulting the web pages and/or by visiting unqualified pages to reach to other

Fig. 4. A bridge page that connects two clusters of relevant web pages though itself does not exhibit any relevant content. *RWB* is a useful tool to visit pages across the bridge.

clusters relevant to the target concept. This boosting allows the crawler to visit pages even though the hyperlink is not described using the topic terms. Also boosting enables crawling other web communities that are not immediately connected.

5. *HITS* with *RW* (*HITS-RW*)

HITS with Relevance Weighting, or *HITS-RW*, assigns a relevance weight using the *RW* metric, $\Theta(w)$, to each link. After adding this adjustment, the computation of authority scores of pages follows *HITS* as in figure 3. Ultimately, each in-link contributes different weights to the relevance measure of the page.

The *HITS* algorithm is known to drift from the target topic [9,1] because the algorithm is purely based on the link topology of web pages and does not take into account the relevance of each page. *HITS* initially assigns the same weight for every link. Consequently, a page with a large number of *irrelevant* in-links may obtain a higher authority score than a page with a relatively smaller number of *relevant* in-links. *HITS-RW* compensates for this behavior by adjusting link weights with the relevance of the hyperlink's metadata, instead of using the uniform link weights of *HITS*. With *HITS-RW*, an incoming link of a web page that has a higher relevance score for the topic lifts the *authority* score of the page more than the other links with lower scores. Ultimately, *HITS-RW* priori- tizes web pages based on the relevance scores of the pages that point to them.

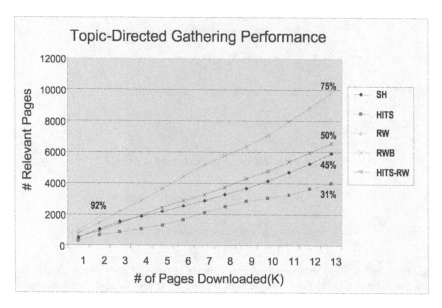

Fig. 5. Quality of Crawling. The graph shows the total number of relevant pages discovered by each algorithm as the crawl progresses. The percentages of relevant pages crawled by *HITS*, *SH*, *RW*, RWB, and *HITS-RW* are 31%, 45%, 50%, 75%, and 92%, respectively. *RW* achieves highest accuracy: 92% of pages crawled by *RW* are topic relevant. However, it stopped crawling after gathering about 3K pages due to the stagnation problem. RWB performs next best in accuracy, 75%. Moreover, it does not suffer from stagnation. By relevance edge weighting, the performance of *HITS* is improved from 31% (*HITS*) to 50% (*HITS-RW*). Yet the improvement is still marginal in comparison to the performance of RWB.

Topic-Directed Crawling Results

Figure 5 shows the effectiveness of the various crawling techniques: *HITS*, *SH*, *RW*, *RWB*, and *HITS-RW*. The performance is measured by the total number of relevant pages identified by each technique as the crawl progresses. The effectiveness of Kleinberg's *HITS* is shown for the purpose of comparison. The percentages of relevant pages crawled by *HITS*, *SH*, *RW*, RWB, and *HITS-RW* are 31%, 45%, 50%, 75%, and 92%, respectively.

RW gathers the highest quality web pages by avoiding unpromising hyperlinks, as expected. 92% of the web pages collected by *RW* were related to the target topic. In other words, decisions based on anchor-text metadata were accurate 92% of the time. The result was achieved without page lookups, i.e., downloading the pages. However, *RW* runs out of pages to crawl quickly because it over-prunes potential URLs to crawl.

Overall, the *RWB* technique performs the best considering both the rate of relevant pages harvested and degree of crawling reliability without stagnation. *RWB* overcomes the over-pruning problem that *RW* suffers from. The reason is that it visits pages, with random probability, even if the metadata shows no promise. While this deliberate introduction of noise reduces the relevance of the crawled pages, it allows the crawler to visit pages even if the metadata does not show immediate relevance or if the system is unable to decipher the relevance easily. In addition, *RWB* allows the crawler to discover new clusters that are linked by pages that do not contain relevant content by themselves. It thus increases the scope of relevant resources. The quality is lower than *RW* because the noise pages are added deliberately. Despite the noise, RWB does not extensively chase irrelevant links, in contrast to both *SH* and *HITS*, which do.

In general, the *HITS* performs the worst. In the early phases of the crawl, *HITS* discovers, as expected, good authoritative sites (such as the site http://www.yahoo.com). These pages, however, pertain to multiple topics. Hence, to prioritize these pages leads the crawler to topic-irrelevant pages, pages that are authorities for other, unrelated topics. Ultimately, the *HITS* algorithm causes the crawler to drift away from the target topic. This behavior confirms that a crawling algorithm based on static link structure alone does not suffice as an effective strategy for a topic-sensitive search engine. Results in [1] also support this fact. On the other hand, this result also confirms that *HITS* is able to locate important centers of link structures. In this way, the method might serve well when applied to order the search results of a query on the basis of the quality, i.e., authority.

HITS-RW weights the hyperlinks based on metadata relevance. By doing so, *HITS-RW* improves the relevance of crawled pages of *HITS* from 31% to 50%, a 65% increase in accuracy. This result validates the utility of metadata for topic-specific crawling. However, *RWB* still surpassed *HITS-RW* by a wide margin, 50% vs. 75%. At the moment, we tentatively conclude that the semantic weighting of hyperlinks is not enough to compensate for the influence of irrelevant references to the page. We expected that *HITS-RW* would perform superbly with the combination of link and semantic weighting. Further investigation into this problem might further enhance the remedy. Also, a hybrid algorithm, such as *HITS-RW*, that considers both semantic relevance and link connectivity might be useful for topic-specific crawling with slightly different objectives. For example, if the objective of the crawl is to crawl relevant and authoritative pages, the hybrid algorithm will likely perform better.

SH crawls 45% of relevant pages. It performs much better than *HITS* even with the simplistic heuristic. Perhaps, this heuristic can be applied to fine tune the boosting algorithm of *RWB* as the URL of a page itself provides additional evidence to better anticipate the potential relevance of a page.

These results support the use of hyperlink metadata for relevance measures. This behavior confirms that topic-directed crawling should take into account the page relevance and hyperlink metadata as an inexpensive estimation tool for measuring the relevance.

4.3 Recrawling

We use several different strategies to recrawl the web pages efficiently. The idea is to recrawl pages close enough to their time of change so that the search results are as up to date as possible. This means not recrawling pages that do not change and recrawling pages that change quickly, fast enough. In addition, given a choice between pages whose change frequency is unknown, we recrawl those that can result in pages with better content.

In the context of our discussion of metadata, we recrawl the hub pages more often because the chances of discovering new links from these pages is quite high. Since the hub pages are known to point to authority pages, if and when they change, they would probably add relevant links. Also, given a choice between two hub pages with the same relevance measure, we pick the one with the highest density of pointers to authority pages. Probabilistically, the chance of such a page adding a new authority page is higher than the one with a lower density of pointers to authority pages.

4.4   Cumulative Metadata

The cumulative metadata for a web page includes the metadata that the page provides about the pages that it points to, the metadata that the pages that point to it provide about it, and a summary of the content of the page. It is not possible, at the time a page is crawled, to obtain exhaustive and up-to-date hyperlink metadata provided by other pages. The reason is that some of the pages that point to the crawled page might not yet have been visited.When we recrawl a page, however, even if its content has not changed, the metadata for the page will improve if more pages that point to the page have been crawled. Hence, the link metadata repository gets richer as we continue to crawl, and the cumulative metadata for a page continues to be updated even without revisiting the page.

Example:
Suppose an HTML page, `http://www.xml.com/xpat`, has in-bound and out-bound links as illustrated in figure 6. As seen in this figure,

  i The page points to two other pages: `http://www.xml.com/SAXprocessor` and `http://www.xml.com/XML-press`

  ii The page is pointed to by two other pages: `http://www.xmlauthority1.org` and `http://www.xmlauthority2.org`.

  iii The in-bound link, `http://www.xmlauthority1.org`, has the anchor tag `<A HREF="http://www.xml.com/xpat">Fast XML Parser</A>`

  iv The in-bound link, `http://www.xmlauthority2.org`, has the anchor tag `<A HREF="http://www.xml.com/xpat">Yet another SAX based XML Processor</A>`.

The summary for the page `http://www.xml.com/xpat` in XML-encoded RDF is in figure 7.

To summarize, the **parent-annotations** property gives a list of metadata annotations by the pages that point to the summarized page. The **annotations** property gives the list of metadata annotations by the summarized page about

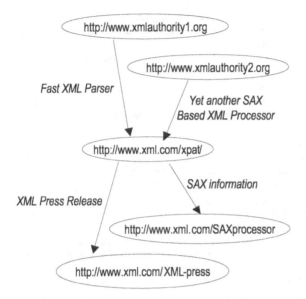

Fig. 6. A hypothetical web page `http://www.xml.com/xpat` and its link connectivity: the page has two in-bound links, `http://www.xmlauthority1.org` and `http://www.xmlauthority2.org`, and two out-bound links, `http://www.xml.com/SAXprocessor` and `http://www.xml.com/XML-press`.

the URLs that it points to. This information is indexed and fed to the search engine enhancing it in multiple ways. A good page that would not normally qualify under a search request might qualify because of its metadata. Alternatively, a page may be disqualified from the search result because it does not have strong enough annotative recommendations. The search engine also uses the metadata to enhance the abstracts of the search result entries.

The example shown here just shows plain text metadata. Our system defines a class hierarchy of metadata types. For instance, the metadata itself can be an XML fragment. The target search can be enhanced with support for RDF schemas [3] that understands the different metadata types.

5   Related Work

HITS[10] introduces a novel mechanism to rate web documents based on hyperlink structure. This algorithm identifies authoritative resources based on hyperlinks. *HITS* has given rise to subsequent work based on it in the fields of classification [4], focused crawling [5], and web trawling for identifying micro-web communities [11]. Our system also begins with the *HITS* premise and enhances it using hyperlink metadata, particularly in the HITS-RW algorithm.

Cho *et al.* [7] discusses a system that ranks pages according to both content and link similarity in order to prioritize the pages in a crawl. The system stores

```
<rdf:RDF xmlns:rdf=http://www.w3.org/schemas/rdf-schema
         xmlns:gcs="http://w3.almaden.ibm.com/gcs/summ1-schema"/>
  <rdf:Description
    <!- attributes related to the web gatherer information ->
    resource="http://www.xml.com/xpat/">
  <rdf:Description>
    <parent-annotations>
      <!- annotations by the pages pointing to this page ->
      <rdf:Bag>
        <rdf:LI>
          <rdf:Description
            annotator="http://www.xmlauthority1.org"
            annotation="Fast XML Parser"/>
        </rdf:LI>
        <rdf:LI>
          <rdf:Description
            annotator="http://www.xmlauthority2.org"
            annotation="Yet another SAX based XML Processor"/>
        </rdf:LI>
      </rdf:Bag>
    </parent-annotations>
    <annotations>
      <!- annotations by this page about the URLs it is pointing to ->
      <rdf:Bag>
        <rdf:LI>
          <rdf:Description
            annotatee="http://www.xml.com/SAXprocessor"
            annotation="SAX information"/>
        </rdf:LI>
        <rdf:LI>
          <rdf:Description
            annotatee="http://www.xml.com/XML-press"
            annotation="XML Press Release"/>
        </rdf:LI>
      </rdf:Bag>
    </annotations>
    <!- other information from the web page being summarized ->
    .......
  </rdf:Description>
</rdf:RDF>
```

Fig. 7. Cumulative metadata of figure 6

important pages in a separate queue and visits these pages first. The similarity measure is based on the occurrence of a topic word in the content of the page. Our system is similar in that it prioritizes its crawling based on page ranking. By contrast to Cho *et al.*, however, our system focuses on exploiting hyperlink metadata to determine page relevance. Hence, our system provides a mechanism that minimizes the visitation and processing of irrelevant pages.

The *focused crawler* (*FC*) [5], which is based on *HITS*, guides crawlers to seek out pages relevant to a topic. It gives the crawler a set of seed pages to be used to determine topic relevance for other pages. *FC* uses a *classifier* to evaluate the relevance of crawled pages compared to the seed pages. It also uses a *distiller* to identify hub pages linked to authoritative source pages and helps *FC* to overcome stagnation. For *FC*, the estimation of relevance of child pages solely depends on the relevance of parent pages. In other words, *FC* crawls all child pages if a parent page is relevant, even though the child page may not be relevant. This property, together with the behavior of the *distiller* (which prefers hub pages) contributes to the relatively low precision of *FC*.

Cora [15] is a search engine for research papers in computer science. It uses reinforcement learning methods to gather computer science papers in postscript format, starting at the homepages of computer science departments. After gathering the papers, it analyzes their titles, authors, and cross reference information to increase the power of the search. Cora uses techniques to search for papers in postscript format. A postscript document can be identified through its URL. Hence, the problem of guiding crawlers to target documents with a specific format (i.e., postscript) is more straightforward than guiding crawlers to target documents that pertain to a particular topic. To guide crawlers in this broader domain, as our system does, requires strategies for more intensive learning.

Similar to our system, various other works focus on the use of metadata. Chen *et. al.* [6] refines the techniques of utilizing metadata for information retrieval. SPHNIX[16] builds web-site specific and customizable crawlers by using a classifier that annotates pages and links with various types of metadata. ParaSite[17] exploits link information (not just hyperlinks) to build applications like finding personal homepages, expired pages, and moved pages.

6   Conclusions

In this paper we described our work on using hyperlink metadata to build the topic-specific search engine, *xCentral*. The hyperlink metadata includes information that other pages provide about a given page. We exploit this information to direct our crawler to find pages that pertain to a particular topic of interest. The crawling strategies that utilize this hyperlink metadata significantly improves the relevance of the gathered pages. Using the *RW* algorithm, more than 92% of the web pages that the crawler gathered were relevant to the topic but the crawler suffered from stagnation. Using the *RWB* algorithm, over 75% of the web pages that the crawler gathered were relevant, and the the crawler did not suffer from stagnation. Of note, these results were achieved without having to download irrelevant pages, an extra cost to algorithms that do not exploit hyperlink metadata. Hence, this approach significantly improved crawl performance. In all cases, metadata based algorithms outperformed purely hyperlink connectivity based algorithm.

Moreover, the hyperlink metadata of the crawled pages were described in XML-encoded RDF graphs. This metadata information is augmented with weighted measures of authority pages. This metadata was included as part of the page summary to be indexed by the search engine. Hence, the metadata was used to enhance search results and enrich the abstracts of the search results.

References

1. Bharat, K., Henzinger, M: Improved Algorithms for Topic Distillation in Hyper-linked Environments. The 21st Int. ACM SIGIR Conference. Melbourne, Australia, (1998)
2. Bray, T., Paoli, J., Sperberg-McQueen, C.M.: Extensible Markup Language (XML) 1.0, W3C Recommendation. W3C. (1998), *http://www.w3.org/TR/1998/REC-xml-19980210*
3. Brickley, D., Guha, R.B.: Resource Description Framework (RDF) Schema Specification 1.0. W3C Candidate Recommendation. Mar., 2000, *http://www.w3.org/TR/PR-rdf-schema*
4. Chakrabarti, S., Dom, B., Raghavan, P., Rajagopalan, S., Gibson, D., Kleinberg, J.: Automatic Resource Compilation by Analyzing Hyperlink Structure and Associated Text. The 7th Int. World Wide Web Conference. Brisbane, Australia, (1998)
5. Chakrabarti, S., van den Berg, M., Dom, B.: Focused Crawling: A New Approach to Topic-Specific Web Resource Discovery. The 8th Int. World Wide Web Conference. Toronto, Canada, (1999)
6. Chen, H., Chung, Y.M., Ramsey, M., Yang, C.C.: A Smart Itsy Bitsy Spider for the Web. Journal of American Society of Information Science. **49(7)** (1998) 604–618
7. Cho, J., Garcia-Molina, H., Page, L.: Efficient Crawling through URL Ordering. The 7th Int. World Wide Web Conference. Brisbane, Australia, (1998)
8. Eichstaedt, M., Ford, D., Kraft, R., Lu, Q., Niblack, W., Sundaresan, N.: Grand Central Station. IBM Research Report. IBM Almaden Research Center, (1998)
9. Gibson, D., Kleinberg, J., Raghavan, P.: Inferring Web Communities from Link Topology. The 9th ACM HyperText. Pittsburgh, PA, (1998)
10. Kleinberg, J.: Authoritative Sources in a Hyperlinked Environment. The 9th ACM-SIAM Symposium on Discrete Algorithms. (1997)
11. Kumar, R., Raghavan, P., Rajagopalan, S., Tomkins, A.: Trawling the Web for Emerging Cyber-Communities. The 8th Int. World Wide Web Conference. Toronto, Canada, (1999)
12. Lassila, O., Swick, R.R.: Resource Description Framework (RDF) Model and Syntax Specification W3C Recommendation. (1999), *http://www.w3.org/TR/REC-rdf-syntax/*
13. Lawrence, S., Giles, L.: Searching the World Wide Web. Science, **280**, (1999) 98–100.
14. Lawrence, S., Giles, L.: Accessibility and Distribution of Information on the Web. Nature. **400**, (1999) 107–109
15. McCallum, A., Nigam, K., Rennie, J., Seymore, K.: Building Domain-Specific Search Engines with Machine Learning Techniques. AAAI Spring Symposium. (1999)
16. Miller, R., Bharat, K.: SPHNIX: A Framework for Creating Personal, Site-Specific Web Crawlers. The 7th Int. World Wide Web Conference. Brisbane, Australia, (1998)

17. Spertus, E.: ParaSite: Mining Structure Information on the Web. The 6th Int. World Wide Web Conference. Santa Clara, CA, (1997)
18. Sundaresan, N., Ford, D.: An architecture for summarizing the web, Int. Conference on Metadata. Montreal, Canada (1998)
19. Yi, J., Sundaresan, N., Huang, A.: Automated Construction of Topic-specific Web Search Engines with Data Mining Techniques. IBM Research Report. IBM Almaden Research Center. (2000)
20. Yi, J., Sundaresan, N., Huang, A.: Metadata Based Web Mining for Topic-Specific Information Gathering. The 1st Int. Electronic Commerce and Web Technologies Conference. *forthcoming*. London, UK, (2000)
21. Yi, J., Sundaresan, N.: Metadata Based Web Mining for Relevance. Int. database Engineering and Applications Symposium, *forthcoming*. Yokohama, Japan, (2000)

Architecting a Network Query Engine for Producing Partial Results

Jayavel Shanmugasundaram[1,3], Kristin Tufte[1,2], David DeWitt[1],
David Maier[2], Jeffrey F. Naughton[1]

[1] Department of Computer Sciences
University of Wisconsin-Madison, Madison, WI 53706, USA
{jai, dewitt, naughton}@cs.wisc.edu
[2] Department of Computer Science
Oregon Graduate Institute, Portland, OR 97291, USA
{tufte, maier}@cse.ogi.edu
[3] IBM Almaden Research Center
650 Harry Road, San Jose, CA 95120, USA

Abstract. The growth of the Internet has made it possible to query data in all corners of the globe. This trend is being abetted by the emergence of standards for data representation, such as XML. In face of this exciting opportunity, however, existing query engines need to be changed in order to use them to effectively query the Internet. One of the challenges is providing partial results of query computation, based on the initial portion of the input, because it may be undesirable to wait for all of the input. This situation is due to (a) limited data transfer bandwidth (b) temporary unavailability of sites and (c) intrinsically long-running queries (e.g., continual queries or triggers). A major issue in providing partial results is dealing with non-monotonic operators, such as sort, average, negation and nest, because these operators need to see all of their input before they can produce the correct output. While previous work on producing partial results has looked at a limited set of non-monotonic operators, emerging hierarchical standards such as XML, which are heavily nested, and sophisticated queries require more general solutions to the problem. In this paper, we define the semantics of partial results and outline mechanisms for ensuring these semantics for queries with arbitrary non-monotonic operators. Re-architecting a query engine to produce partial results requires modifications to the implementations of operators. We explore implementation alternatives and quantitatively compare their effectiveness using the Niagara prototype system.

1 Introduction

With the rapid and continued growth of the Internet and the emergence of standards for data representation such as XML [1], exciting opportunities for querying data on the Internet arise. For example, one might issue queries through web browsers rather than relying on semantically impoverished keyword searches. An important and chal

D. Suciu and G. Vossen (Eds.): WebDB 2000, LNCS 1997, pp. 58–77, 2001.

lenging research issue is to architect query engines to perform this task. Some of the main issues in designing such query engines are to effectively address (a) the low network bandwidth that causes delays in accessing the widely distributed data, (b) the temporary unavailability of sites and (c) long running triggers or continual queries that monitor the World Wide Web. An elegant solution to these problems is to provide partial results to users. Thus, users can see incomplete results of queries as they are executed over slow, unreliable sites or when the queries are long running (or never terminate! [2]).

A major challenge in producing partial results is dealing with non-monotonic operators, such as sort, average, sum, nest and negation. Since the output of these operators on a subset of the input is not, in general, a subset of the output on the whole input, these operators need to see all of their input before they produce the correct output. Previous solutions to the problem of producing partial results proposed by Hellerstein et al. and Tan et al. present solutions for specific non-monotonic aggregate operators, such as average [3,7], and thus do not extend to non-monotonic operators such as nest and negation that are becoming increasingly important for network query engines. Further, the previous solutions do not allow non-monotonic operators to appear deep in a query plan. Thus, for example, a query that asks for all BMW cars that do not appear on salvage lists and that cost less than 10% of the average price of cars in its class is a query that cannot be handled by previous techniques. Neither could a query that requests an XML document where books are nested under author, and authors are nested under state, and states are further nested under country. (The non-monotonic operators in the first query are "not in" and "average" while the non-monotonic operators in the second query is "nest").

A main contribution of this paper is the development of a general framework for producing partial results for queries involving any non-monotonic operator. A key feature of this framework is that it provides a mechanism to ensure consistent partial results with unambiguous semantics. The framework is also general enough to allow monotonic and non-monotonic operators to be arbitrarily intermixed in the query tree (as in the examples above), i.e., monotonic operators can operate on the results of a non-monotonic operator and vice-versa. It is important to note that the framework by itself does not stipulate any particular implementation of non-monotonic operators but merely identifies some abstract properties that operator implementations need to satisfy (indeed, much of the generality of the framework is precisely due to this). Interestingly, these properties affect both monotonic and non-monotonic operator implementations. Another contribution of this paper is the identification of implementations for operators that satisfy the desired properties and a performance evaluation of the various alternatives using our prototype system.

1.1 Relationship to Other Work

As mentioned above, most of the previous research by Hellerstein et al. and Tan et al. on partial results has been in the context of particular aggregate functions such as sum and average [3,7]. Further, they deal with at most one level of nesting of non-monotonic operators [7]. The main focus of this paper is to provide a general framework whereby queries with arbitrary non-monotonic operators appearing possibly deep in the query tree can produce partial results. Thus, techniques developed for specific cases, such as aggregates fit in easily in our framework and can exploit the general system architecture. For instance, it would be possible to integrate the methods for relaying accuracy [3] into our system. The added flexibility is that the operators can appear anywhere in the query tree, mixed with other monotonic and non-monotonic operators (see Section 3.3).

There has been some work on non-blocking implementations (i.e., implementations that produce some output as soon as they see some input) of monotonic operators so that results can be sent to the user as soon as they are produced. Urhan and Franklin have proposed a non-blocking implementation of join [8]. Ives et al. describe an adaptive data integration system that uses non-blocking operators to address issues including unpredictable data arrival [5] and have also proposed an operator, x-scan, for incrementally scanning and parsing XML documents [4]. There has also been work on modifying the query plans so that network delays can be (partially) hidden from the user [9]. These approaches, while partially addressing the problem of low network bandwidth and unavailable sites, do not address the general problem because a query may require non-monotonic operators, such as nest and average. In these cases, unless we provide partial results, the query execution has to block until all the data is fetched.

1.2 Roadmap

The rest of the paper is organized as follows. Section 2 formally defines the semantics of partial results and identifies some key properties that query engine operator implementations need to satisfy in order to produce complete and meaningful partial results. Section 3 proposes a system architecture that produces consistent partial results and Section 4 identifies alternative operator implementation techniques. Section 5 provides a performance evaluation of the various operator implementation strategies and Section 6 concludes the paper and outlines our ideas for future work.

2 Partial Results and Implications for Operator Implementations

In the previous section, we illustrated the need for producing partial results for queries having arbitrary non-monotonic operators appearing deep in the query plan. Having such a general notion of partial results does not come without associated challenges. The following questions immediately come to mind: What are the semantics of partial results? Can we use traditional query engine architectures and associated operator implementations to produce partial results? If not, then what are the modifications that need to be made? This section is devoted to the above questions. We begin by briefly outlining the structure of traditional query engines. We then formally define the semantics of partial results and identify key properties of operator implementations, not supported by traditional query engine architectures, which are crucial for partial result production. These properties lay the foundations for designing operator implementations capable of producing correct, maximal partial results.

2.1 The Traditional Query Engine Architecture

A common way of executing a query is to structure it as a collection of operators, each of which transforms one or more input streams terminated by an End of Stream (EOS) element and produces one or more output streams, also terminated by an EOS element. Thus an operator defines the transformation that input streams undergo in order to produce the output stream. Typical operators include Select, Project, Join and Group-by. The query execution can be represented as a directed graph, where each operator is a node and each stream is represented as a directed edge from the operator writing into the stream to the operator reading from the stream.

As an example, consider a query that asks for the details of all cars priced less than 10% of the average price of cars of the same model. Figure 1 shows a graphical representation of an operator tree for this query. The replicate operator produces two identical output streams containing the car information. The replication captures the fact that the car information is a common sub-expression used in two places. The first output stream of the replicate operator feeds to the average operator, which computes the average selling price for each model of cars. The second output stream of the replicate operator feeds to the join operator that relates a car's price to the average price of cars of that model.

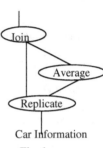

Fig. 1

Each operator in a query graph potentially has many implementations. Each implementation defines a particular mechanism to achieve the transformation specified by the operator. For example, a join operator can have nested-loops and hash-based implementations, while an average operator can have both sort-based and hash-based implementations. Each operator implementation again operates on input streams and produces output streams. The output of an operator implementation is well defined even on input streams not terminated by an EOS element because it represents the output of the operator implementation on seeing the input streams "so far", at the current point in time. On the other hand, there is no notion of "time" for operators, and so their output is well defined only on input streams terminated by an EOS element.

The relationship between operators and their implementations is formalized below. For ease of exposition, the formal discussion is restricted to unary operators. It is easy to generalize to n-ary operators based on later descriptions of operator implementations. We begin by defining stream and sub-stream.

Definition D1: A **stream** is a sequence (ordered collection) of data elements. A **sub-stream** is a contiguous sub-sequence of the original stream sequence.

Definition D2: An operator implementation, O, is an **implementation** *of* an operator, Oper, if for all input streams I not having an EOS element, Oper(I.EOS) = O(I.EOS).

The previous definition just says that an operator implementation (O) should produce the same output as the operator it implements (Oper) at the point in time when all the inputs have been seen (i.e., the point in time when the input stream has been terminated by an EOS element). However, this definition requires nothing about what the implementation emits before the EOS. Traditionally the input stream(s) and output stream of each operator implementation are monotonically increasing, i.e., data is only added to the streams, never updated or removed. Thus, operator implementations and streams are structured to consume and produce only additions. This restriction limits traditional query engine architectures for producing partial results. To see why this is the case, we need to first formally define the semantics of partial results and understand the behavior of operators and their implementations. We will then be in a position to identify the properties, not satisfied by traditional query engines, that nevertheless need to be satisfied by operator implementations in order to produce maximal and correct partial results.

2.2   Preliminaries: Partial Results, Operators, Operator Implementations

We begin by defining the notion of a partial result of a query.

Definition D3: Let Q be a query with input I and let Q(I) represent the result of the query Q on input I. A ***partial result*** of a query Q, given an input I, is Q(PI), where PI is a sub-stream of I.

Intuitively, a partial result of a query on an input stream is the result of the query on a (possibly) different input stream such that the new input stream is a sub-stream of the original input stream. We proceed to formally define monotonic and non-monotonic operators and blocking and non-blocking implementations and provide a theorem connecting the concepts of monotonicity and blocking.

Definition D3: An operator Oper is a ***monotonic operator*** if for all input sub-streams I, J not having an EOS element, if I is a sub-stream of J, then Oper(I.EOS) is a sub-stream of Oper(J.EOS). An operator is a ***non-monotonic operator*** if it is not a monotonic operator.

Intuitively, a monotonic operator is one that given additional input produces additional output without needing to modify previously produced output. As an illustration, consider the average operator in the example in Figure 1. This operator takes an input stream having (car-model, car-price) pairs and computes the average car-price for each car-model. The output of this operator on the input I1 = ("Toyota", 10000).EOS is O1 = ("Toyota", 10000).EOS. Its output on the input I2 = ("Toyota", 10000).(Toyota, 20000).EOS is O2 = ("Toyota", 15000).EOS. Since I1 is a sub-stream of I2 but O1 is not a sub-stream of O2, the average operator is not monotonic.

Select and join operators are examples of monotonic operators. For example, consider a select operator that selects all (car-price) tuples that have a car-price less than 10000. Its output on the input I1 = (5000).(10000).EOS is the output O1 = (5000).EOS. Its output on the input I2 = (5000).(10000).(7000).EOS is the output O2

= (5000).(7000).EOS. Here I1 is a sub-stream of I2 and O1 is a sub-stream of O2. In general, operators such as the select and join operators always add more data to the output when they see more data on their inputs. They are thus monotonic.

An interesting case is the nest or group-by operator. Formally, a monotonic function, f, on inputs x, y, is a function such that $x \leq y \Rightarrow f(x) \leq f(y)$. Traditionally, a database operator, Oper, is considered monotonic if $I \subseteq J \Rightarrow \text{Oper}(I) \subseteq \text{Oper}(J)$ where I and J are sets. In this case, "less than (or equal to)" is interpreted as subset. The extension to nested structures is, however, not straightforward. Consider a query that nests (CarMake, CarModel) pairs on CarMake to produce (CarMake, {Set of Car Model}) pairs. The table below shows possible initial and subsequent inputs and results for the query.

Initial Input	Initial (Partial) Result
(Toyota, Camry)	(Toyota, {Camry})
(Honda, Accord)	(Honda, {Accord, Prelude})
(Honda, Prelude)	
Subsequent Input	**Subsequent Result**
(Toyota, Corolla)	(Toyota, {Camry, Corolla})
	(Honda, {Accord, Prelude})

At issue is whether Initial Result is "less than" Subsequent Result. Depending on your viewpoint, it may or may not be. The real question is how to extend "less than" to nested structures such as XML documents (or sequences of such structures). There are two obvious possibilities:

1. "Less than" is interpreted as "subset" – Oper(A) ≤ Oper(B) means that all the elements (pairs) in Oper(A) are in Oper(B).
2. "Less than" is interpreted as "substructure" – Oper(A) ≤ Oper(B) means that all the elements (pairs) in Oper(A) are sub-structures of some element (pair) in Oper(B). Here, sub-structure is a "deep" (recursive) subset relationship.

Under the first interpretation listed above, Initial Result is not "less than" Subsequent Result and nest would not be considered monotonic. Under the second interpretation, Initial Result is "less than" Subsequent result and nest would be considered monotonic. Both interpretations of "less than" are valid; the interpretation chosen should be determined by the query processing framework and how that framework interprets nested structures. We use the first interpretation since our system does not support nested updates.

Definition D4: An operator implementation O is a ***non-blocking operator implementation*** if for all input sub-streams I not having an EOS element, O(I.EOS) = O(I).EOS. An operator implementation is a ***blocking operator implementation*** if it is not non-blocking.

Intuitively, a non-blocking operator implementation is one that does not "block" waiting for the EOS notification to produce results. The EOS notification on its input stream can cause it only to send an EOS notification on its output stream. As an illustration, consider a hash-based implementation of the average operator in Figure 1.

This implementation, on seeing an input (car-model, car-price) pair, hashes on the car-model to retrieve the node in the hash table that stores the number of tuples and the sum of the car-prices in these tuples, for the given car-model. It increments the number of tuples by one, and adds the new car-price to the running sum, and then proceeds to process the next input tuple. On seeing an EOS element, it divides the sum of the car-prices for each car-model by the number of cars seen for that car-model and writes the (car-model, avg-car-price) pairs to the output stream. This operator implementation is blocking because it does not produce any output until it sees an EOS element.

On the other hand, consider an implementation of a select operator that selects all (car-price) tuples that have a car-price less than 10000. This implementation looks at each tuple and adds it to the output stream if the car-price value is less than 10000. On seeing the EOS element in the input, it just adds the EOS element to the output. This is thus a non-blocking operator implementation of the select operator.

The following theorem relates monotonic operators and non-blocking operator implementations. We use the notation O(I/J) to denote the output of an operator implementation O on the input I when it has already seen (and output the results corresponding to) the input sub-stream J.

Theorem T1: An operator Oper is monotonic if and only if Oper has a non-blocking operator implementation O.

Proof: (If Part) Consider a non-blocking operator implementation O of Oper. We must prove that for all input streams I, J not having an EOS element, if I is a sub-stream of J then Oper(I.EOS) is a sub-stream of Oper(J.EOS). Consider any two input sub-streams I, J not having an EOS element such that I is a sub-stream of J. There exists a input sub-stream K such that I.K = J. Now:

Oper(I.EOS) = O(I.EOS)	(by definition D1)
= O(I).EOS	(because O is non-blocking)
is a sub-stream of O(I).O(K/I).EOS	(by definition of sub-streams)
is a sub-stream of O(I.K).EOS	(by definition of O(K/I))
is a sub-stream of O(I.K.EOS)	(because O is non-blocking)
is a sub-stream of O(J.EOS)	(because I.K = J)
is a sub-stream of Oper(J.EOS)	(by definition D1)

(Only If Part) Consider a monotonic operator, Oper. Now consider the operator implementation O that works as follows. Let PrevI denote the input stream seen so far. On a new input element e that is not an EOS element in the input stream, the output of O, i.e. O(e/PrevI), is the sub-stream J such that PrevOpt.J = CurrOpt. Here PrevOpt is the output stream Oper(PrevI.EOS) without the EOS element, and CurrOpr is the output stream Oper(PrevI.e.EOS) without the EOS element. Such a J always exists because Oper is monotonic. When O sees an EOS, it simply puts an EOS element to the output stream. It is easy to see that O is an operator implementation of Oper. Also, by the definition of O, O(I.EOS) = O(I).EOS for all input streams I. Thus, O is a non-blocking operator implementation of Oper. *(End of Proof)*

We are now in a position to study the properties that operator implementations need to satisfy in order to produce partial results.

2.3 Desirable Properties of Operator Implementations

Theorem T1 has important implications for the production of partial results. These are best brought out by means of an example. Consider the query in Figure 1 that asks for all cars that cost less than 10% of the average price of cars of the same model. The average operator is non-monotonic because the average cost for a given model potentially changes as more inputs are seen. The join operator, on the other hand, is monotonic because no future input can invalidate the join between two previous inputs.

Consider a scenario where the query plan has been running for a few seconds and car information for a few cars has been sent as input to the query processor, but the query processor is still waiting for more inputs over an unreliable network channel. If the user now desires to see the partial results for the query, then the average operator implementation must output the average "so far" for each car model seen so that the join operator implementation can join the average price for each model with the cars seen "so far" for that model. The only way the user will automatically see the partial results is if all the operators in the query graph have been implemented with non-blocking implementations. However, from Theorem T1, we know that average does not have a non-blocking implementation. In order to produce partial results, the blocking implementation for average has to be able to produce the result "so far" on request. In general, in order to produce partial results, all blocking operator implementations for non-monotonic operators need to be structured in such a way that they can produce the result "so far" at any time. We refer to this as the *Anytime* property for blocking operator implementations.

The fact that blocking operator implementations for non-monotonic operators need to produce results "so far" at any time has other implications. In our example, the average price transmitted per model is potentially wrong because there can be more inputs for a given model, which can change the model's average price. When more inputs are seen and the average price per model changes, this change must be transmitted to the join operation above (which needs to transmit it to the output). In general, the fact that an operator is non-monotonic implies that the result "so far" transmitted to higher operators can be wrong. Therefore, there needs to be some mechanism to "undo" the wrong partial outputs (change the average price for a given model, in our example). In other words, operator implementations need to be capable of producing non-monotonic output streams (as in the case of the average operator implementation) and processing non-monotonic input streams (as in the case of the join operator implementation). Note that both blocking and non-blocking operators need to handle non-monotonic input and output streams as they can be arbitrarily placed in the query graph. We refer to this as the *Non-Monotonic Input/Output* property for operator implementations. We now turn our attention to another property of operator implementations that is useful for producing partial results.

Intuitively, the *Maximal Output* property requires that operator implementations produce results as soon as possible. That is, the operator implementation puts out as much of the result as it can without potentially giving a wrong answer. This property is useful for producing partial results because the user can see all the correct results that can possibly be produced, given the inputs seen so far. For example, consider the non-monotonic operator "outer join." Operator implementations for this operator can output the joining results as soon as they are produced, without having to wait for the end of its inputs. The ***Maximal Output*** property is formally defined below.

Definition D5: Let Oper be an operator and O an implementation of Oper. Let I be a stream of elements in the domain of Oper. O satisfies the ***Maximal Output*** property if O(I).EOS is the maximal stream such that it is a sub-stream of Oper(I.K.EOS), for every K, where K is a stream of elements from domain of Oper.

It is easy to see that all non-blocking operator implementations automatically satisfy the Maximal Output property. It turns out that, in fact, there is a stronger relationship between these two properties, as exemplified by the following theorem.

Theorem T2: An operator implementation O of an operator Oper is non-blocking if and only if Oper is monotonic and O satisfies the Maximal Output property.
Proof: (If Part) Assume Oper is monotonic and O satisfies the Maximal Output property. We must prove that for all input sub-streams, I, not having EOS, O(I).EOS = O(I.EOS). Since Oper is monotonic, by definition D3, Oper(I.EOS) is a sub-stream of Oper(I.J.EOS) for all J. Since O satisfies the Maximal Output property, O(I).EOS is the maximal sub-stream of Oper(I.K.EOS), for all K. We can thus infer that O(I).EOS = Oper(I.EOS) which implies that O is non-blocking.
(Only If Part) Assume O is a non-blocking operator implementation. Since non-monotonic operators cannot have non-blocking operator implementations (Theorem T1), O must be an implementation of a monotonic operator, Oper. It remains to be shown that O satisfies the Maximal Output property. For every K, a stream of elements from the domain of Oper, we know that Oper(I.EOS) is a sub-stream of Oper(I.K.EOS) because Oper is monotonic. By the definition of a non-blocking operator implementation, we have O(I).EOS = Oper(I.EOS). This implies that O(I).EOS is the maximal sub-stream of Oper(I.K.EOS), for all streams K in the domain of Oper. Hence O satisfies the maximal output property. *(End of Proof)*

The theorem above essentially states that for operator implementations of monotonic operators, the maximal output property and the non-blocking property are the same thing. Thus ensuring that all operator implementations satisfy the maximal output property automatically ensures that all monotonic operators will have non-blocking operator implementations.

A final operator implementation property that is useful for producing partial results is what we call the ***flexible input*** property. This property essentially states that operator implementations should not stall on a particular input stream if there is some input available on some other input stream. The motivation behind this property is that in a network environment, traffic delays may be arbitrary and data in some input streams may arrive earlier than data in other input streams, and it may be impossible to determine this information a priori. Thus, in order to provide up-to-date partial results at any time, operators need to be able to process information from any input stream, without stalling on any particular input stream. Many traditional operator implementations do not satisfy this property. Consider, for example, typical implementations of the join operator. The nested loops join operator implementation requires all the tuples of the inner relation to be present before it can process any tuple in the outer relation. Similarly, the hash join operator implementation requires the whole inner relation (to build the hash table) before it can process the outer relation. Symmetric hash join [10] and its variants [8,4] are the only join operator implementations that satisfy this property. In order to provide partial results effectively, traditional implementations will have to give way to the "flexible input" variants.

To summarize, in this section we formally defined the semantics of partial results and developed the notions of monotonic and non-monotonic operators and blocking and non-blocking operator implementations. We then identified certain key properties, namely the Anytime, Non-monotonic Input/Output, Maximal Output and Flexible Input properties, that operator implementations need to satisfy in order to provide partial results.

Before we turn our attention to the design of operator implementations satisfying the above properties, let us pause for a moment to ask whether these properties in isolation are sufficient to ensure the semantics of partial results as defined above. It turns out that while the above properties are sufficient to produce partial results upon user-request, they are not sufficient to ensure that the partial results are consistent. The next section is devoted to studying this problem and proposing a solution. We tackle the issue of designing operator implementations in Section 4.

3 Consistency of Partial Results and Its Implications for a Query Engine Architecture

As mentioned in Section 2.1, the query execution graph can be represented as a graph with the nodes representing operators and the edges representing streams. In general, this graph is not a tree but a Directed Acyclic Graph (DAG), as shown in Figure 1. This form is due to the presence of common sub-expressions in a query (in our example, the car information is the common sub-expression, which is replicated along two separate paths). The fact that the operator graph can be a DAG has important implications for the architecture of a system designed to produce partial results. The definition of partial results requires that the partial output be the result of executing the query on a subset of the inputs. This requirement implies that any data item that is replicated must contribute to the partial result along *all* possible paths to the output or not contribute to the output at all (along any path). This condition is necessary to avoid anomalies such as selecting cars below the average price, without the car's price being used to compute the average (see Figure 1). Note that this issue does not arise when constructing only final results because each operator then produces results based on all of the inputs it sees. This potential inconsistency is because of our desire to interrupt input streams in order to produce partial results.

A related issue also arises when an operator logically produces more than one output data item corresponding to a single input data item. This situation might arise, for instance, in a join operator when a single tuple from one input stream joins with more than one tuple from the other input stream and produces many output tuples. Another example where this can arise is while projecting many set sub-elements (say employees) from a single element (say department) in XML documents. In these cases again, we need to ensure that the partial query result includes the effects of all or none of the output data items that correspond to a single input data item.

3.1 Synchronization Packets

We now show how the notion of *synchronization packets* can be used to ensure the consistency of partial results. Conceptually, these packets are inserted in the input streams of the query plan whenever a partial result is desired as is shown in Figure 2. These synchronization packets are replicated whenever a stream is replicated and their main function is to "synchronize" input streams at well-defined points so that operator implementations see consistent partial inputs. More precisely, each operator uses all the data "before" the synchronization packets in the production of partial results. In the example above, the join operator implementation uses all the data before the synchronization packets in the production of partial results. This ensures that every data item reaching the join directly from replicate is also reached through average (and vice versa). The problem now is to determine how the synchronization information is to be propagated up the operator graph. We propagate synchronization packets up the operator graph by following the rules below:

1. If there is a synchronization packet received through an input stream of an operator implementation, then no further inputs are taken from that input stream until synchronization packets are received through all input streams

2. Once synchronization packets are received from all input streams of an operator implementation, the operator implementation puts its partial results (in the case of a blocking operator implementation) and synchronization packets into its output stream(s). It is important to note that the Anytime property of blocking operators is used here for partial result production and synchronization packet propagation.

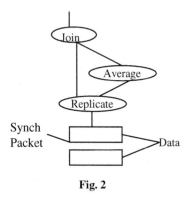

Fig. 2

The following theorem shows that these rules are sufficient to guarantee consistent partial results. We assume that all common sub-expressions have a replicate operator that produces many output streams, as in Figure 1.

Theorem T3: If the synchronization packets are inserted into the input streams when partial results are desired, the synchronization rules guarantee that the partial results produced are consistent.

Proof Sketch: Since the operator graph is a DAG, there exists a topological ordering of the operators in the graph such that each operator in the graph appears before all the operators reachable from it. The proof uses induction on the position of operators in the topological ordering to prove that for the implementation of each operator, its partial output is based on all and only the data of the input streams occurring before the synchronization packets (and is hence consistent). Thus implying that the top-level operator implementation's output (the query's output) is consistent.

3.2 Partial Request Propagation and Generation

In the previous section, we assumed that synchronization packets are inserted into input streams when partial results are required. Typically, however, the user or application has access only to the output stream of the top-level operator because the operators of the query plan can be distributed at various sites in the network. Thus, user and application requests must be propagated down the operator graph. This can be achieved by propagating control messages from the user or application to the base of the operator graph. Once the partial result request control messages reach the base of the operator graph, they must be intercepted and synchronization control messages must be inserted into the input streams. "Partial" operators provide this functionality.

Partial operators are added to the base of the operator graph and perform two simple functions: (a) propagate the data from the input stream unchanged to the output stream and (b) on receiving a partial result request from an output stream, they send a synchronization packet to their output streams. Thus partial operators provide an automatic way of handling synchronization packets.

Using partial operators to handle synchronization packets allows us to explore algebraic equivalences between partial operators and other operators. These equivalences can be used to move partial operators up in the operator graph (and even merged) under certain conditions. This "transformation" of the operator graph is likely to lead to better response times because synchronization packets travel less far down the operator graph and because operators below the partial operators do not have to be synchronized. We plan to study these equivalences in more detail as part of future work.

To summarize this section, we outlined consistency anomalies that can arise while producing partial results and proposed solutions using the notions of synchronization packets and partial operators. Together with the operator implementation extensions discussed in Section 2, they extend the traditional query engine architecture to support the generation of consistent partial results. A key part of the puzzle, however, remains to be solved – the design of operators satisfying the properties outlined above. We turn to this issue next.

4 Operator Implementation Alternatives

We explore two alternatives, Re-evaluation and Differential, for modifying existing operator implementations so that they satisfy the desired properties for producing partial results outlined in Section 2.3. The Re-evaluation approach retains the structure of existing operator implementations but requires the re-execution of all parts of the query plan above the blocking operators. Alternatively, the Differential approach processes changes as part of the operator implementation, similar to the technique used in the CQ project [6], and avoids re-execution. There is thus a trade-off between the complexity of the operators and their efficiency: Re-evaluation implementations are easier to add to existing query engines, while Differential implementations are more complex and require changes to the tuple structure, but are likely to be more efficient.

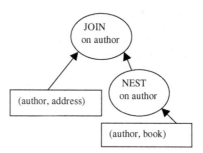

Fig. 3

The Re-evaluation and Differential approaches are similar in that, for monotonic operators, they use existing non-blocking and flexible input operator implementations where possible. For example, joins are implemented using symmetric hash join [10] and symmetric nested loops join algorithms (or their variants [4,8]). The algorithms in this section extend such non-blocking and flexible input operator implementations to satisfy the non-monotonic input/output property and further, identify blocking operator implementations satisfying all four desirable properties.

4.1 Re-evaluation Approach

In order to satisfy the Non-monotonic Input/Output property, we must determine what form partial results produced by blocking operators take and how updates to those results are communicated. The Re-evaluation approach handles this decision straight-forwardly by having blocking operator implementations transmit their current result set when a partial result request is received. If there are multiple partial result requests, the same results will be transmitted multiple times. Note that all operator implementa-tions above a blocking operator implementation must re-evaluate the query each time a partial result request is issued; hence the name Re-evaluation approach.

Consider the query execution graph in Figure 3 which shows a nest operator read-ing (author, book) pairs from an XML file on disk (or any non-blocking operator im-plementation), nesting the pairs on author and sending its output to a join operator implementation. The nest implementation is blocking; the join implementation is non-blocking. Upon receipt of a partial result request, the nest operator implementation transmits all (author, <set of books>) groups it has created so far to the join. At this point, the join implementation must ignore all input it has previously received from nest, and process the new partial result as if it had never received any input from nest before. We describe the re-evaluation implementations of join and nest below. Descriptions of other operator implementations are omitted in the interest of space.

Re-evaluation Join: The Re-evaluation join implementation functions similar to a symmetric hash join implementation except that when the Re-evaluation join implementation is notified that a new partial result set is beginning on a particular input stream, it clears the hash table associated with that input stream. In addition, special techniques are used to deal with the case when an input contains a mixture of tuples that are "final" – produced by a non-blocking operator and will never be repeated and tuples that are "partial" – produced by a blocking operator (as part of a partial result set) and will be retransmitted at the start of the next partial result. The intermixing of partial and final tuples can occur if the input comes from a union operator implementation, which unions the output of a blocking and non-blocking operator implementation or from an operator such as outer join that produces final tuples before EOS and partial tuples upon request for a partial result.

Re-evaluation Nest: Similar to a traditional hash-based nest implementation, the Re-evaluation nest implementation creates a hash table entry for each distinct value of the grouping attribute (author in our example). When a partial result notification is received, the Re-evaluation nest implementation acts lazily and does not delete the hash table. Instead, the Re-evaluation nest implementation simply increments a partial result counter. Upon insert into the hash table, each book tuple is labeled with the current counter value. When an entry is retrieved during nest processing, all books having counter value less than the counter value of the operator are ignored and deleted. We utilize this lazy implementation because when the input consists of a mixture of partial and final tuples, they will be combined in the <set of book> entries in the hash table. Deleting all obsolete book tuples in an eager fashion would require retrieving and updating most of the hash table entries, which is too expensive.

4.2 Differential Approach

The Re-evaluation approach is relatively easy to implement, but may have high overhead as it causes upstream operators to reprocess results many times. The Differential approach addresses this problem by having operators process the changes between the sets of partial results, instead of reprocessing all results. Differential versions of traditional select, project and join are illustrated and formalized by Lin et al. [6] in the context of continual queries. Our system, however, handles changes as the query is being executed as opposed to that approach, which proposes a model for periodic re-execution of queries. This difference gives rise to new techniques for handling changes as the operator is in progress.

In Figure 3, in order for the join to process differences between sets of partial results, the nest operator implementation must produce the "difference" and the join operator implementation must be able to process that "difference." We accomplish this "differential" processing by having all operators produce and consume tuples that consist of the old tuple value and the new tuple value, as in Lin et al. [6]. Since the partial results produced by blocking operator implementations consist of differences from previously propagated results, each tuple produced by a blocking operator implementation is an insert, delete or update. In the interest of space, we describe only the differential join and nest operator implementations below.

Differential Join: The Differential join implementation is again based on the symmetric hash join implementation. A Differential join implementation with inputs A and B works as follows. Upon receipt of an insert of a tuple τ into relation B, τ is joined with all tuples in A's hash table and the joined tuples are propagated as inserts to the next operator implementation in the query execution graph. Finally τ is inserted into B's hash table for joining with all tuples of A received in the future. Upon receipt of a delete of a tuple τ from relation B, τ is joined with all tuples in A's hash table and the joined tuples are propagated as deletes to the next operator in the tree. Updates are processed as deletes followed by inserts.

Differential Nest: The Differential nest implementation is similar to the traditional hash-based nest implementation. Inserts are treated just as tuples are in a traditional nest operator implementation. For deletes, the Differential nest operator implementation probes the hash table to find the affected entry and removes the deleted tuple from that entry. For updates, if the grouping value is unchanged, the appropriate entry is pulled from the hash table and updated, otherwise, the update is processed as a delete followed by an insert. Changes are propagated upon receipt of a partial result request. Only the groups that have changed since the last partial request are propagated on receipt of a new partial request.

4.3 Accuracy of Partial Results

In the previous sections, we have concentrated on operator implementations that produce partial results. An important concern is the accuracy of the results produced. We believe that our framework is general enough to accommodate various techniques for computing the accuracy of partial results, such as those proposed for certain numerical aggregate operators [3,7]. These techniques can be incorporated into our framework if the desired statistics are passed along with each tuple produced by an operator. In addition, our framework allows non-monotonic operators (such as aggregates) to appear anywhere in the query tree. It is also important to address accuracy of partial results for non-numeric non-monotonic operators such as nest and except. Providing information about the accuracy of these operators is more difficult because we do not have notions such as "average" and "confidence intervals" in these domains. It is, however, possible to provide the user with statistics such as the percentage of XML files processed or the geographical locations of the processed files. The user may well be able to use this information to understand the partial result.

5   Performance Evaluation

This section compares the performance of the Re-evaluation and Differential approaches for implementing operators. We begin by describing the experimental set up in Section 5.1 and outline our performance results in Section 5.2.

5.1   Experimental Setup

Our system is written in Java and experiments were run using JDK 1.2 with 225MB of memory on a Sun Sparc with 256MB of memory. Our system assumes that the data being processed is resident in main memory. Though we expect this assumption to be acceptable for many cases given current large main memory sizes, we plan to explore more flexible implementations that handle spillovers to disk in the future.

We used three queries to evaluate the performance of the Re-evaluation and Differential approaches. The first query (Q1) contains a join over two blocking operators. The input is two XML documents, one having flat (author, book) pairs and the other having flat (author, article) pairs. It produces, for each author, a list of articles and a list of books written by that author. Q1 is executed by nesting the (author, book) and (author, article) streams on author and (outer) joining these streams on author to produce the result. Finally, a construct operator is used to add tags. The number of books (articles) for each author follows a Zipfian distribution.

The second query (Q2) is similar to Q1 except that the inputs are (author, book-price) and (author, article-price) pairs and the blocking operators are average, in contrast to nest in Q1. Q2 produces the average prices of books and articles written by an author. This query was modeled after Q1 to study the effect of the size of the result of blocking operators on performance (average returns a small, constant size result compared to the potentially large, variably sized result of nest). The number of books (articles) per author follows a Zipfian distribution.

Query 3 (Q3) is similar to the query in Figure 1 and has a DAG operator graph. The data consists of tuples with car model, dealer, price and color information. The query returns all cars that meet a selection criterion and which are priced less than the average price of cars of the same model. To execute Q3, the car information is replicated: one leg of this information goes to the average and then to the join; the other leg goes through a selection and then to the join. The number of cars for a given model follows a Zipfian distribution.

The parameters varied in the experiments are (a) the Zipfian skew, (b) the Zipfian mean, (c) the number of partial result requests issued during query execution, (d) the number of tuples ((author, book) or (author, article) pairs for Q1, (author, bookprice) or (author, articleprice) pairs for Q2, number of cars for Q3), in the base XML data files and (e) percentage of cars selected (Q3 only). The default parameters are shown in Figure 4. In addition, we explore the case where the input is ordered on the nesting or averaging attribute (author for Q1, Q2 and model for Q3) because it corresponds to some real world scenarios where, for example, each XML file contains information about an author, and because it illustrates the working of the differential algorithm.

Skew of Zipfian Distribution: 1
Mean of Zipfian Distribution: 10
Number of partial result requests: 10
Number of Tuples: 10000
Selectivity (Q3 only): 10%

Fig. 4: Default Parameters

5.2 Performance Results

Figure 5 shows a breakdown of the execution time for Q1 using the default parameters. For reference, the graph shows a point for the query evaluation time in the absence of any partial result calculation (No Partial). There were 10 partial result requests, each returning about 9% of the data, and a final request to get the last 9% of
the data. The data points show the cumulative time after the completion of each partial
result. The overhead of parsing, optimization, etc. is contained in the time for the first
partial result.

For the first 45% of the input, the Differential and Re-evaluation algorithms perform similarly. After that point, the differential algorithm is better. In fact, for the
complete query, the Differential algorithm reduces the overhead of partial result calculation by over 50%. An interesting observation from the graph above is that if a user
issues only a limited number of partial result requests, the Re-evaluation algorithm
may be adequate because the extra overhead of the differential algorithm more than
offsets the reduction in retransmission.

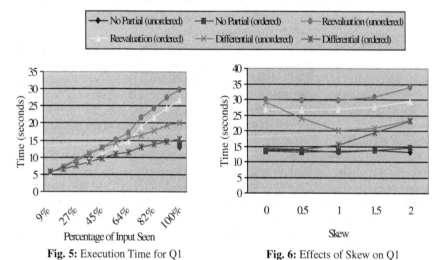

Fig. 5: Execution Time for Q1   **Fig. 6:** Effects of Skew on Q1

The difference between Differential (ordered) and No Partial is exactly the over-head of the Differential tuple processing. The 25% difference in total execution time between the ordered and unordered versions of Differential is the overhead caused by tuple retransmission and reprocessing (Differential reduces retransmission, it does not eliminate it.) Finally, though the behavior of Re-evaluation and No Partial is insensi-tive to order we notice improvement on ordered input, which may be due to processor cache effects.

Figure 6 shows the effect of skew on the different algorithms for Q1. Skew has the effect of changing the size of the groups. The interesting case is the unsorted Differ-ential graph where we see a decrease in execution time followed by an increase. The cost of the Differential algorithm is directly related to the number of tuples that have to be retransmitted. At a skew of 0, there are 1000 groups each with approximately 10 elements. If a group has changed since the last partial result request, the whole group must be retransmitted and reprocessed by the join operator. With a group size of 10 and 10 partial result requests, most groups will change between partial result sets limiting the ability of Differential to reduce retransmission. As skew increases, we see the presence of many very small (2-5 element) groups and a few medium size groups. Very small groups are good for the performance of the Differential algorithm because a group can not be transmitted more times than it has elements. As the skew increases further, the presence of a few very large groups begins to hurt performance. When the skew is 2, there is one group of size approximately 6000. This group changes with almost every partial result request and therefore many elements in this group must be retransmitted many times.

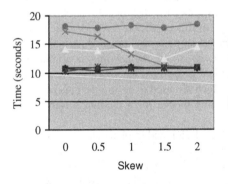
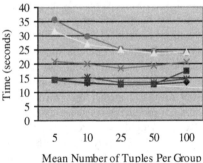

Fig. 7: Effects of Skew on Q2   **Fig. 8:** Varying Mean No. of Tuples – Q1

In contrast to Q1, increasing skew for query Q2 (Figure 7) does not adversely affect the performance of the Differential algorithm. At high skews, the partial result for each group is still small for Q2, unlike the large nested values for Q1, and hence has a very low retransmission overhead. This result suggests that finer granularity imple-mentations for large partial results, whereby changes to groups rather than entire groups are retransmitted, can make the Differential algorithm more effective.

Figure 8 shows the affect of changing the mean number of tuples per group (mean of the Zipfian distribution) for Q1. As the mean number of tuples increases, the number of groups decreases since the number of tuples is fixed. The decrease in the number of groups helps the Re-evaluation algorithm because it reduces the size of the join. The Differential algorithm also sees this advantageous affect, but as the mean group size increases, the Differential algorithm suffers because it does more retransmission, as discussed before. Note that when there is only one group, Differential is identical to Re-evaluation and when all groups have size 1, Differential is identical to the case when no partial result requests are issued.

The results from varying the number of tuples (not shown) indicated that the performance of both algorithms scales linearly with the number of tuples. Varying the selectivity for Q3 (not shown) produced predictable results; the Differential approach always performed better than the Re-evaluation approach and the difference increased with decreasing selectivity. We ran experiments with simulated network delays wherein we inserted an exponential delay after every 100 input tuples during query execution. The results (not shown) showed that with increasing delay, the overhead of partial results production decreases. This reduction is due to the overlap between the partial result computation and time spent waiting for data over the slow network.

6 Conclusion and Future Work

Querying the web is creating new challenges in the design and implementation of query engines. A key requirement is the ability to produce partial results that allows users to see results as quickly as possible in spite of low bandwidth, unreliable communication media and long running queries. In this paper, we have identified extensions to the traditional query engine architecture to make this possible. A main extension is the design of operator implementations satisfying the anytime, non-monotonic input/output, maximal output and flexible input properties. Another extension is synchronization packets and partial operators, which are used to ensure the consistency of partial results. Together they form the building blocks for a flexible system that is capable of producing consistent partial results.

Generalizing the operator properties leads to design and implementation challenges. One approach is to stay close to the traditional operator implementation and make as few changes as possible, thus reusing operator code and structure. This choice is embodied in our Re-evaluation approach. Another approach is to design operators to handle the changes intrinsic to the production of partial results. This Differential approach requires more extensive rewrite to the operators, but is more suited to the task of producing partial results. Our quantitative evaluation shows that the Differential approach is successful in reducing partial result production overhead for a wide variety of cases, but also indicates that there are important cases where the Re-evaluation approach works better. In particular, for the cases where the user kills the query after just two or three early partial results, the overhead of the differential approach more than offsets the gain in performance. Another interesting conclusion from the experiments is that the size of the results of blocking operators has a significant bearing on the performance of the Differential approach – Differential performs better for "small" aggregate results because the cost of retransmission is less. As expected, the overhead of partial result production reduced with increased communication delays because partial result processing is overlapped with the delays.

There are many threads to follow in the scope of future research. The good performance of the Differential approach suggests that handling changes at granularities finer than tuples is likely to lead to further improvements. Studying fine granularity changes in the context of heavily nested XML structures would be very useful for efficiently monitoring data over the Internet. In terms of providing accuracy and consistency for arbitrary queries, there is the open issue of providing accuracy bounds for general non-monotonic operators. Optimizing the placement of partial operators in the operator graph and generalizing the consistency model to handle weaker and stronger forms of consistency is another area for future investigation.

Acknowledgement. Funding for this work was provided by DARPA through NAVY/SPAWAR Contract No. N66001-99-1-8908 and by NSF through NSF award CDA-9623632.

References

1. T. Bray, J. Paoli, C. M. Sperberg-McQueen, "Extensible Markup Language (XML) 1.0", http://www.w3.org/TR/REC-xml.
2. J. Chen, D. DeWitt, F. Tian, Y. Wang, "NiagaraCQ: A Scalable Continuous Query System for Internet Databases," Proceedings of the SIGMOD Conference, Dallas, Texas (2000).
3. J. M. Hellerstein, P. J. Haas, H. Wang, "Online Aggregation", Proceedings of the SIGMOD Conference, Tuscon, Arizona (1997).
4. Z. G. Ives, D. Florescu, M. Friedman, A. Levy, D. S. Weld, "An Adaptive Query Execution System for Data Integration", Proceedings of the SIGMOD Conference, Philadelphia, Pennsylvania (1999).
5. Z. G. Ives, A. Y. Levy, D. S. Weld. Efficient Evaluation of Regular Path Expressions on Streaming XML Data. Technical Report UW-CSE-2000-05-02, University of Washington.
6. L. Liu, C. Pu, R. Barga, T. Zhou, "Differential Evaluation of Continual Queries", Proceedings of the International Conference on Distributed Computing Systems (1996).
7. K. Tan, C. H. Goh, B. C. Ooi, "Online Feedback for Nested Aggregate Queries with Multi-Threading", Proceedings of the VLDB Conference, Edinburgh, Scotland (1999).
8. T. Urhan, M. J. Franklin, "XJoin: Getting Fast Answers from Slow and Bursty Networks", University of Maryland Technical Report, UMIACS-TR-99-13 (1999).
9. T. Urhan, M. J. Franklin, L. Amsaleg, "Cost Based Query Scrambling for Initial Delays", Proceedings of the SIGMOD Conference, Seattle, Washington (1998).
10. A. N. Wilschut, P. M. G. Apers, "Data Flow Query Execution in a Parallel Main Memory Environment", International Conference on Parallel and Distributed Information Systems (1991).

Argos: Efficient Refresh in an XQL-Based Web Caching System*

Luping Quan, Li Chen, and Elke A. Rundensteiner

Department of Computer Science
Worcester Polytechnic Institute
Worcester, MA 01609, USA
{lupingq|lichen|rundenst}@cs.wpi.edu

Abstract. The Web has become a major conduit to information repositories of all kinds. Web caches are employed to store web views to provide an immediate response to recurring queries. However, the accuracy of the replicates in web caches encounters challenges due to the dynamicity of web data. We are thus developing and evaluating a web caching system equipped with an efficient refresh strategy. With the assistance of a novel index structure — the Aggregation Path Index (APIX), we built Argos, a web caching system based on the GMD XQL query engine. Argos achieves a high degree of self-maintenance by diagnosing irrelevant data update cases. It hence greatly improves the refresh performance of the materialized web view. We also report preliminary experimental results assessing the performance of Argos compared to the state-of-the-art solution in the literature.

Keywords: XQL Query Engine, Web Caching, View Maintenance, Indexing, XML, Data Update.

1 Introduction

The advent of the web has dramatically increased the proliferation of information of all kinds. XML [22] is rapidly becoming popular for representing web data as it brings a finely granulated structure to the web information and exposes the semantics of the web content. In web applications including electronic commerce and intelligent agents, view mechanisms are recognized as critical and are being widely employed to represent users' specific interests. To compute an integrated web view, web information that resides at sites without query capabilities may need to be shipped over to the web view site to be queried against. Such a

---

* This work was supported in part by several grants from NSF, namely, the NSF NYI grant #IRI 94-57609, the NSF CISE Instrumentation grant #IRIS 97-29878, and the NSF grant #IIS 97-32897. Dr. Rundensteiner would like to thank our industrial sponsors, in particular, IBM for the IBM partnership award. Li Chen would like to thank IBM for the IBM corporate fellowship.

D. Suciu and G. Vossen (Eds.): WebDB 2000, LNCS 1997, pp. 78–91, 2001.

transmission of a large volume of data across the network can be costly. Hence the view results are oftenly cached locally for recurring queries instead of being re-computed on the fly.

However, the cached view results may become stale due to the flux of the content or the structure of the underlying web sources. With many applications requiring an up-to-date content of the web view at all times, two alternative web view materialization strategies, namely, materialized or materialized on-demand can be adopted [14]. While this work in [14] evaluates the two strategies in terms of their trade-off of whether to materialize a web view and when to refresh it, we aim at improving the refresh efficiency of a materialization strategy. In other words, we present an efficient web view *maintenance* technique designed to minimize the delay of keeping a web view consistent with its updated data sources. This efficiency of the view adaptation to changes, as indicated from the view maintenance techniques studied in the conventional database context [8,9,12,17,20], is very critical especially in the era of electronic commerce. For example, a bid site allows its users to post queries in a watch list for goods of interest to them. For a certain period, users expect to be notified of any changes to the view results in their watch list. The efficiency of the notification will effect the customers' business decisions and hence is critical.

It is observed that not all updates affect cached view results. Therefore recent research efforts [6,1,24] study self-maintenance by utilizing auxiliary information piggybacked during the initial view computation phase. Along the same direction, we have developed a materialized web view cache system with an efficient refresh capability by employing a novel index structure [4]. It can be utilized to discover many self-maintenance cases and thus to eliminate unnecessary accesses to base web sources.

In this paper, we describe the web caching system called Argos that adopts this novel refresh technique. Argos is based on the query capability of XQL [16], which is the first XML-based query language under full implementation. We describe the architecture of the Argos system, its index structure and maintenance strategy. We also present the preliminary experimental results of comparing the Argos approach with the naive maintenance approach and with the most recent solution to web view maintenance proposed in literature [1] the *RelevantOid* approach.

2   Argos System Framework

We assume a distributed environment with multiple web sources registered at the site where the view cache maintained by Argos will reside (see Figure 1). We consider data sources that contain XML documents. They are parsed once and stored in the binary form of persistent DOMs (PDOM) [10,21], which from then onwards are accessible to DOM operations without the parsing overhead.

The workflow of the Argos system consists of three phases. First, given a specific XQL query defining the request of a web view, the initial web view results are computed by shipping the remote PDOMs over to the local site and

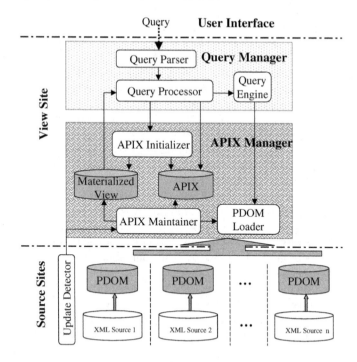

Fig. 1. System Framework of Argos

then processing the query against these sets of PDOMs using the GMD XQL query engine [10]. In the Argos system, we built an auxiliary index structure called the Aggregate Path IndeX (APIX) [4] to reflect the structural pattern of the query. During the web view computation, maintenance relevant data is piggybacked to fill in the APIX structure so that it can later be utilized for future self-maintenance. When an update is detected at any registered web source, the notification is sent to the view site. Then the *APIX Manager* will diagnose whether it is an irrelevant update by performing self-maintenance tests with the help of the cached objects in the APIX structure. If it is a self-maintenance case, the web view is maintained locally without access to web sources. Otherwise, the third phase of maintenance follows. Namely, the *APIX Maintainer* submits a partial query against the web source to extract relevant information needed for view compensation. In this phase, the *APIX Manager* is able to limit the web source re-access to its minimal scope. Lastly, the web view is compensated by the additional query results.

As shown in Figure 1, the main part of the Argos system sits in the view site consisting of two main modules: *Query Manager* and *APIX Manager*. The former is further decomposed into a *Query Parser*, which accepts a specified query in XQL and parses it into an abstract syntax tree, and a *Query Processor* based on the GMD XQL query engine. Within the *APIX Manager*, the *APIX*

Initializer module is responsible for the initialization of the APIX structure [4] for a given query and the generation of the materialized web view according to the query processing results. Once the *APIX Maintainer* is notified by the *Update Detector* of an update to a web source, the *APIX Maintainer* performs view maintenance with the help of *APIX*. In Setction 3, we will describe the APIX structure and its maintenance algorithms in detail.

3   Argos Maintenance Strategy

Given a data update, a *naive* algorithm simply refreshes the web view by re-computing it from scratch. This is as costly as the initial web view computation over all its XML sources [1] since it may involve uploading and processing queries against each of them. Therefore, given a materialized web view at the view site, recent research work [6,1] is striving to provide an efficient maintenance strategy to minimize the refresh delay of the web view.

The incremental view maintenance approach proposed by Abiteboul et. al [1] utilizes an auxiliary index structure called *RelevantOid* at the view site, which stores all the objects that are relevant to a given query. For example, if the given XQL query is like "/publisher/book/author", then all the *publisher, book* and *author* elements in the XML sources will be kept in the RelevantOid index. When an update happens to an author element *au1*, this maintenance approach needs to query against all PDOMs and process all *publisher* and *book* elements before it proceeds to the *author* element type and binds only *au1* to it. Using this approach, an object is kept in the RelevantOid index as long as it is bound to some query variable. Therefore the size of the RelevantOid index tends to be large and the self-maintenance test is not efficient.

We are inspired by the Satisfiability Indicating Multi-Index (SMX) approach [13,18,19] in the multiview Object-Oriented database view project [17], which is an indices organization proposed to facilitate the incremental maintenance of path query views in the OODB context. We then propose a novel index scheme, called Aggregate Path IndeX (APIX) [4], to address the indexing needs of maintaining the materialized web view, besides that of supporting the query process. During the initial web view computation phase, APIX is populated with a collection of qualified objects with respect to the query path or pattern. An object is "qualified" when it has the children elements of the required types. Together with each of these objects it also stores the statistics information about the support of the pattern and an indicator (true/false boolean value) about whether it leads to a leaf object satisfying the query predicates. Such information can be utilized during the maintenance phase to determine whether an update would effect the instantiations that fulfill a given query criteria by looking forward most small necessary steps. APIX can also be used to diagnose many more irrelevant update cases than the RelevantOid approach. Figure 2 illustrates the basic idea of the Argos maintenance strategy using APIX.

---

[1] In our experimental study, only the PDOM instead of the XML document is shipped to avoid the parsing overhead.

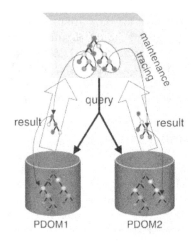

Fig. 2. Illustration of the APIX Maintenance

3.1   APIX Structure

Unlike the data structure summary in the Lore [15] system called DataGuide [7], which is subject to change upon updates on the base data, the structure of an empty APIX reflects the structural pattern of a given query and hence is stable.

Given an example XML document (see Figure 3 for its content and Figure 4 for its parsed DOM representation), we assume the XQL query below gives the specification of the web view to be maintained.

$$//entry[@quantity=2]/product[@maker=\text{``BSA''}\,and@price\leq\text{``20''}]$$

The semantics of this XQL query is to obtain all products whose immediate parent *entry* has an attribute *quantity* with the value of 2, and the product is made by "BSA" and its price is less than or equal to 20. The notations "/" and "//" denote the path operators for immediate children and for arbitrary depth descendants respectively. The symbol "@" is added as prefix to attribute names. These symbols together with the element or attribute names immediately following them specify the navigation paths, along each step of which an intermediate search context (a set of objects) is obtained. The partial query within "[ ]" denotes a filter specifying what to further select from the left-side search context for the next step navigation.

By decomposing a given query into parts, each of which is a set of partial queries, we capture the overall navigational pattern in a tree-like structure (see Figure 5). Each node represents a query variable (assigned for an element or attribute name) with its outgoing labels denoting the set of partial queries aggregated. For example, the only partial query related to the root object of the given example XQL is *"//entry"*. *"./@quantity"* and *"./product"* are the partial queries starting from the variable *entry*.

```
<?xml version="1.0"?>
<invoicecollection>
<invoice>
  <customer> Wile Scott, San Jose, CA </customer>
  <annotation> Guaranteed Quality </annotation>
  <entries n=2>
    <entry quantity=2 total_price="134.00">
      <product maker="ACME"
        prod_name="screwdriver" price="80.00"/>
    </entry>
    <entry quantity=1 total_price="20.00">
      <product maker="ACME"
        prod_name="power wrench" price="20.00"/>
    </entry>
  </entries>
</invoice>
<invoice>
  <customer> Camp Mertz </customer>
  <entries n=2>
    <entry quantity=2 total_price="80.00">
      <product maker="BSA"
        prod_name="book" price="40.00"/>
    </entry>
    <entry quantity=2 total_price="26.00">
      <product maker="BSA"
        prod_name="pen" price="13.00"/>
    </entry>
  </entries>
</invoice>
</invoicecollection>
```

Fig. 3. An Example XML Document

3.2   APIX Initialization

Argos initially fills in the APIX structure with objects satisfying their query path patterns (the detailed APIX initialization is described in the Path Evaluation procedure in [4]). The resulting content of APIX is depicted in Figure 6.

The number of the objects stored in APIX is much smaller compared to the RelevantOid index structure [1] due to its strict structural requirements on the data to be indexed. These objects are considered critical for maintenance.

We now continue to evaluate the value constraints on the leaf objects in the APIX structure and then propagate the results from bottom up to compute truth values for the non-leaf objects (see Figure 7). The truth value for an object

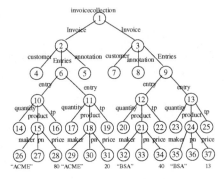

Fig. 4. DOM Tree of the Example XML Document

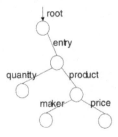

Fig. 5. Tree Structure Representation of Query

is set to be true iff: *For each set of its children objects that are reached by the same outgoing label, there exists at least one true-valued object.*

View results are derived from APIX by selecting only the true-valued objects along the paths. When an update occurs, it may affect the truth values in APIX and hence the view results. But in many cases, APIX and the view results can be self maintained without requiring any access back to the remote XML sources.

3.3   View Maintenance Using APIX

With the locally cached APIX nodes and their truth values, we can conduct a set of self-maintenance checks before any uploading of remote base data becomes necessary. Our self-maintenance tests are more effective than those proposed by [23] in the sense that more updates can be diagnosed by our APIX approach as being maintenance irrelevant. We define an update to be maintenance irrelevant if it falls into one of the following four cases: 1) The new truth value of a leaf object is the same as that before its content value got modified. 2) For an *insert* or *delete* operation, the variable of the affected object is not an APIX node. 3) For a *delete* case, either the parent object or the object to be deleted is not

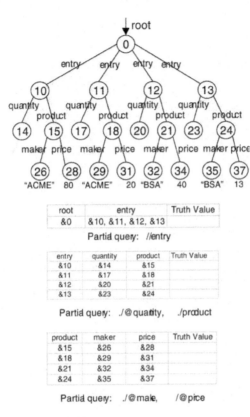

root	entry	Truth Value
&0	&10, &11, &12, &13	

Partial query: //entry

entry	quantity	product	Truth Value
&10	&14	&15	
&11	&17	&18	
&12	&20	&21	
&13	&23	&24	

Partial query: ./@quantity,   ./product

product	maker	price	Truth Value
&15	&26	&28	
&18	&29	&31	
&21	&32	&34	
&24	&35	&37	

Partial query: ./@maker,   /@price

Fig. 6. The Initialized APIX

cached in APIX. 4) The parent object of a value-changed leaf node is not in APIX.

Even if the self-maintenance test fails, APIX can compute the view patch either on APIX itself at the view site or by accessing a restricted scope of source data. For example, if the truth value of an APIX object is changed from *true* to *false* due to the deletion of one of its children objects, it may or may not affect the truth value of its parent object in APIX. APIX can help to propagate such an effect properly upwards until no further propagation is needed. On the other hand, an *insertion* may result in remote access to the source data. However, the scope of data to be re-evaluated is restricted to the subtree of the highest ascending object that is not in APIX yet. The detailed maintenance algorithms for the insertion, deletion and change updates can be referred to in the technical reports [5,3].

We now illustrate how to maintain APIX and update the materialized view. Assume three value change operations occur: a) The value of object &17 is

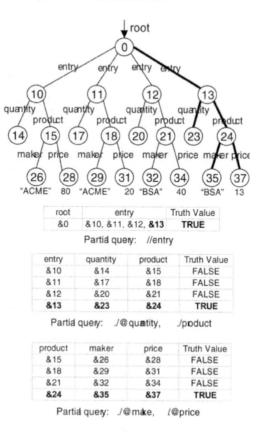

Fig. 7. APIX with Truth Values

changed from 1 to 2, b) The value of object &19 is changed from 20 to 40, c) The value of object &29 is changed from "ACME" to "BSA".

For the first case, the truth value associated with object &17 is changed to be *true*. Thus it triggers a recomputation of the truth value of the label associated with object &17 and a propagation up to object &11. There the propagation stops since its truth value won't change because of the *false* of the other child object &18. For the second case, object &19 is not cached in APIX and it thus is an irrelevant update. For the third case, the truth value of object &29 is changed. It further causes that of its parent object &18 and grandparent &11 to be examined via propagation.

By computing the delta view objects based on the changed truth values in APIX, the materialized view can be easily maintained in all three cases (see to [5,3]).

4   System Implementation

The Argos system has been developed on the Windows/NT platform using java. The implementation of the XQL parser is based on the Antlr [11] compiler toolsuite. Its query facility is based on the GMD-IPSI XQL engine with persistent DOM capability.

Argos is implemented as a client-server system. XML sources at multiple remote servers are registered at the client site where the user specifies the web view. Argos implements an id mechanism for each PDOM object so that the view caching strategy can identify updates at the granularity of individual XML elements (and not just complete XML documents) and can refer to them uniquely in its index. The APIX index [4] and its manager module co-exist with the materialized web view at the local view site. Partial queries, filtering mechanisms and truth value propagation functions associated with APIX nodes collaborate to maintain the materialized web view and to minimize the search scope if loading of base data is inevitable.

We implemented the compute-from-scratch (Naive) algorithm, which does not materialize the view result at all and repeats the query every time when an update occurs. We also implemented, in the same experimental environment as Argos, the *RelevantOid* maintenance mechanism that has been proposed by Abiteboul et. al [1].

5   Experimental Evaluation

Experimental Setup: Experimental tests are conducted to compare the refresh delay time of Argos to the naive recomputation approach and to the *RelevantOid* approach [1]. We use a large test dataset distributed at different sites. We are experimenting on a collection of Shakespeare plays [2] (the overall data size is about 7.5M bytes and the maximum document depth is 7) and the width of the query structure is 2. This test data set is in either XML documents or XML PDOMs.

For all the experiments, we keep the query fixed and vary the overall data size, the type and the loction of updates.

In the first experiment, we compare the refresh delay time of Argos to the *RelevantOid* approach for each type of update in 50 different cases. We design and control these update cases to have 20% query relevancy by varying the location they occur. Then we run each case 10 times, and take the average time (in millisecond) as the maintenance cost for each type of update. For the naive approach, it re-computes the view every time when an update occurs. Given a fix sized document, its refresh time is always the same since it is irrelevant of the type of update. We observe from the experimental result (Figure 8) that the APIX approach always wins significantly over the *RelevantOid* approach especially in the *delete* and *update* situations (in Figure 8, the Chg_Apix and Del_Apix bars are almost invisible due to their very low maintenance cost values). This is because that a *deletion* or a *change* usually only involves the propagation

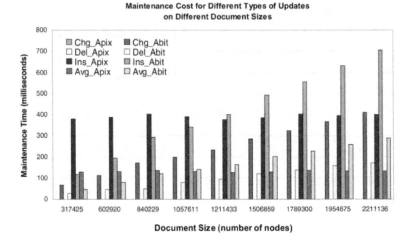

Fig. 8. Different Types of Updates for Different Document Sizes

of the changed value evaluation result or the dropping of object tuples at the local APIX site and thus tends to be much less costly (faster in refresh) than the alternative approach.

For the *insert* update cases, the APIX approach takes more time than the *RelevantOid* approach to refresh the view result from querying a small document. However, APIX starts to perform better than the latter approach when the document size is reasonably large (in our testing environment, when the document has more than 1.2M nodes). We can easily explain this first-lose-then-win phenomenent. First, the APIX approach is relatively more complicated than the *RelevantOid* approach, and such computation cost becomes the dominant factor when the document size is small. As the document increases, the APIX index space cost would become significantly smaller than the *RelevantOid* index space (as shown in Figure 9 from the second experiment). Therefore, even if the average computation cost for each APIX index node is larger than that for the *RelevantOid*, the total maintenance cost for all APIX nodes would become smaller than that for the *RelevantOid* index nodes.

This experiment also shows that, in the average case of all three possible update types being equally likely, the APIX approach starts to outperform the *RelevantOid* approach when the document size has more than 1M nodes, which is a reasonable size to expect for web documents.

In the second experiment, we vary the document size and compare the space cost for building APIX to that for setting up the *RelevantOid* index. The third line is showing that the recomputation-from-scratch approach doesn't need to build any index and hence its space cost is always 0. Figure 9 shows that APIX always costs less space than the *RelevantOid* index. Especially when the document size increases, the space cost for APIX scales much better than the alternative *RelevantOid* index space.

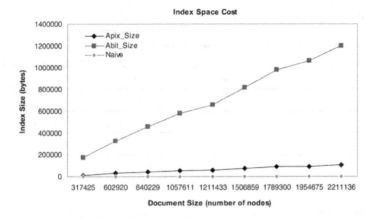

Fig. 9. Index Space Costs for Different Document Sizes

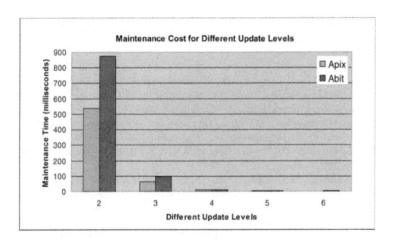

Fig. 10. Different Levels of Updates

In the third experiment, we use a fixed document size (about 1.5M in nodes) and then control the updates to happen at a certain level (varying the level from the second level up to the sixth level. We compare the maintenance cost for the APIX approach to that for the *RelevantOid* approach. Figure 10 shows that the maintenance costs for both approaches decrease when the updates occur at deeper levels. Especially for an insertion case, if an update occurs closer to the root object, it is more likely to introduce a larger subtree and hence to cause a bigger insertion cost for the index maintenance.

6   Conclusion

In this paper, we have presented the Argos client/server framework aiming to minimize the refresh delay of the materialized web view with the help of a locally cached index structure – APIX. We designed and implemented the Argos caching system based on the GMD-IPSI XQL engine. We also present in this paper the preliminary experimental results showing advantage of the APIX approach over the state-of-the-art approach in literature [1] in terms of the web view maintenance efficiency.

ACKNOWLEDGMENT. The authors would like to thank students in the Database Systems Research Group at WPI for their interactions and feedback on this research.

References

1. S. Abiteboul, J. McHugh, M. Rys, V. Vassalos, and J. Wiener. Incremental Maintenance for Materialized Views over Semistructured Data. In *Int. Conference on Very Large Data Bases*, pages 38–49, August 1998.
2. J. Bosak. Shakespeare 2.00. http://metalab.unc.edu/bosak/xml/eg/shaks200.zip.
3. L. Chen and E. A. Rundensteiner. Aggregate Path Index for Incremetnal Web View Maintenance. Technical Report WPI-CS-TR-99-33, Worcester Polytechnic Institute, 1999.
4. L. Chen and E. A. Rundensteiner. Aggregate Path Index for Incremetnal Web View Maintenance. In *The 2nd Int. Workshop on Advanced Issues of E-Commerce and Web-based Information Systems, San Jose*, June 2000.
5. L. Chen and E. A. Rundensteiner. APIX: An Efficient Approach to Maintain Web Views. Technical Report WPI-CS-TR-00-08, Worcester Polytechnic Institute, 2000.
6. D. Gluche, T. Grust, C. Mainberger, and M. H. Scholl. Incremental Updates for Materialized OQL Views. In *The 5th International Conference on Deductive and Object Oriented Databases (DOOD), Switzerland*, pages 52–66, Dec. 1997.
7. R. Goldman and J. Widom. DataGuides: Enabling Query Formulation and Optimization in Semistructured Databases. In *the 23rd Int. Conf. on Very Large Databases (VLDB), Athens, Greece*, pages 436–445, Aug. 1997.
8. A. Gupta and I. S. Mumick. Maintenance of Materialized Views: Problems, Techniques, and Applications. In *Bulletin of the Technical Committee on Data Engineering, 18(2)*, pages 3–18, June 1995.
9. A. Gupta, I. S. Mumick, and V. S. Subrahmanian. Maintaining Views Incrementally. In *Proceedings of the 1993 ACM SIGMOD International Conference on Management of Data, Washington, D.C., May 26-28, 1993*, pages 157–166, 1993.
10. G. Huck and I. Macherius. GMD-IPSI XQL Engine. http://xml.darmstadt.gmd.de/xql/, 1999.
11. J. Inc. ANTLR: Complete Language Translation Solutions. http://www.antlr.org/.

12. A. Kawaguchi, D. F. Lieuwen, I. S. Mumick, and K. A. Ross. Implementing Incremental View Maintenance in Nested Data Models. In *In Proceedings of the Workshop on Database Programming Languages*, pages 202–221, August 1997.

13. H. A. Kuno and E. A. Rundensteiner. Incremental Maintenance of Materialized Object-Oriented Views in MultiView: Strategies and Performance Evaluation. 10(5):768–792, Sept/Oct. 1998.

14. A. Labrinidis and N. Roussopoulos. On the Materialization of WebViews. In *The Workshop on the Web and Databases (WebDB'99), Philadelphia, USA*, pages 79–84, June 1999.

15. J. McHugh, S. Abiteboul, R. Goldman, D. Quass, and J. Widom. Lore: A Database Management System for Semistructured Data. In *SIGMOD Record 26(3)*, pages 54–66, Sep. 1997.

16. J. Robie, J. Lapp, and D. Schach. XML Query Language (XQL). http://www.w3.org/TandS/QL/QL98/pp/xql.html, Sep. 1998.

17. E. A. Rundensteiner, H. A. Kuno, Y. Ra, and V. CrestanaTaube. The MultiView Project: Object-Oriented View Technology and Applications. In *Proceedings of the ACM SIGMOD International Conference on Management of Data*, page 555, June 1996.

18. E. A. Rundensteiner, H. A. Kuno, and J. Zhou. Incremental Maintenance of Materialized Path Query Views. In *Object-Oriented Information Systems (OOIS'98)*, Sept. 1998.

19. E. A. Rundensteiner, H. A. Kuno, and J. Zhou. Experimental Evaluation of the SMX Strategy for Incremental Materialized Path View Maintenance. *Int. Journal of Computer Systems, Science and Engineering, Special Issue on Selected Papers from Object-Oriented Information Systems (OOIS'98) Conference, G. Grosz (Guest Editor*, 14(6):331–342, Nov. 1999.

20. M. H. Scholl, C. Laasch, and M. Tresch. Updatable Views in ObjectOriented Databases. In *Proceedings of the 2nd International Conference on Deductive and ObjectOriented Databases (DOOD), Munich, Germany*, pages 189–207, December 1991.

21. W3C. Document Object Model (DOM). http://www.w3.org/TR/REC-DOM-Level-1/, 1998.

22. W3C. XML^{TM} . http://www.w3.org/XML, 1998.

23. Y. Zhuge and H. GarciaMolina. Self-Maintainability of Graph Structured Views. In *Technical Report, Computer Science Department, Stanford University*, pages 116–125, October 1998.

24. Y. Zhuge and H. G. Molina. Graph Structured Views and Their Incremental Maintenance. In *Proceedings of the 14th International Conference on Data Engineering, Orlando, Florida*, pages 116–125, February 1998.

Active Query Caching for Database Web Servers

Qiong Luo, Jeffrey F. Naughton, Rajasekar Krishnamurthy, Pei Cao *, and
Yunrui Li **

Computer Sciences Department
University of Wisconsin-Madison
Madison, WI 53706, U.S.A.
{qiongluo, naughton, sekar}@cs.wisc.edu,
cao@cisco.com,yuli@us.oracle.com

Abstract. A substantial portion of web traffic consists of queries to
database web servers. Unfortunately, a common technique to improve
web scalability, proxy caching, is ineffective for database web servers
because existing web proxy servers cannot cache queries. To address this
problem, we modify a recently proposed enhanced proxy server, called
an active proxy, to enable *Active Query Caching*. Our approach works by
having the server send the proxy a *query applet*, which can process simple
queries at the proxy. This enables the proxy server to share the database
server workload as well as to reduce the network traffic. We show both
opportunities and limitations of this approach through a performance
study.

Keywords: Active query caching, proxy caching, database web servers,
query containment.

1 Introduction

Many web sites are constructed using back-end database systems and provide
form-based interface for users to submit queries. We call this kind of system a
database web server. With the rapid growth of user accesses to the Web, database
web servers encounter very heavy workloads and produce a growing percentage
of network traffic.

Web caching proxies are today's main solution to improve web performance,
share server workload, and reduce wide area network traffic. However, queries
and responses of database web servers are uncacheable by existing web proxies,
which cache only static files. This motivates us to investigate the problem of how
to answer queries efficiently at a web proxy.

In this paper, we propose a new collaboration scheme between an *active
proxy* (an experimental enhanced web proxy server [4]) and a database web
server. In our approach, the web server passes a simple query processing ability

---

* Currently at Cisco Systems, Inc., 230 West Tasman Drive, San Jose, CA 95134,
U.S.A.
** Currently at Oracle Corporation, 500 Oracle Parkway, Redwood Shores, CA 94065,
U.S.A.

D. Suciu and G. Vossen (Eds.): WebDB 2000, LNCS 1997, pp. 92–104, 2001.

to the proxy when needed, through a *query applet*. The proxy can then not only answer queries that are an exact match to cached queries, but also queries whose results are contained in the cached results of more general queries. This increases the cache hit ratio of the proxy, and further decreases the number of trips to the database web server. In turn, this reduces network traffic as well as the load on the server, which allows the system to scale with the addition of multiple proxies.

Our approach is inspired by the following three observations. First, despite the high volume of user queries on the web, one interesting aspect is that these queries are usually very simple from the web proxies' point of view. This is because the queries that database web servers allow users to submit are typically form-based. If we consider a form to be a single table view and the blanks to be filled in as the columns of the single table view, queries on the form can then be treated as simple selection queries with conjunctive predicates over this single table view. For example, although the back-end database of an on-line bookstore may have a complex schema, queries submitted through the on-line form of the bookstore are just selections with some title, author, publisher and price range predicates on a single table view "books".

Secondly, among these simple queries submitted to a database web server, a significant portion of them further concentrate on some hot regions of data. In the previous example of the on-line bookstore, there might be many similar questions on the best sellers in a day's sale. Studies on search engine query traces [14,16] also report that web user queries to these search engines show excellent locality on the data they access.

Finally, a common query stream pattern of individual users is refinement. Typically users first ask a general query. Having viewed some results, they then decide to refine the query with more restrictive conditions, and keep asking a series of queries. The query refinement feature of our university on-line library is a good example. When a set of initial query results on books comes back to the user, a "refine your search" button also shows up so that the user can refine the queries on publishing year, campus library locations, and other parameters. These series of refining queries certainly provide temporal locality for query caching.

The rest of the paper is organized as follows. Section 2 introduces the proxy caching background of our work. Section 3 presents the system overview, and Sect. 4 describes active query caching in more detail. Section 5 shows performance results, Sect. 6 discusses related work, and finally conclusions are drawn in Sect. 7.

2   Background

Caching proxies are widely deployed in several places: at the network boundaries to serve local users, in the network infrastructure to reduce wide area network traffic, or in front of server farms to share server workload (called reverse proxies, or httpd accelerators).

One major limitation of current caching proxy servers is the lack of collaboration with original content providers. This causes a large amount of web traffic to be uncacheable to web proxies. Recent studies [3,12,19] have shown that the percentage of uncacheable requests is growing over time and that two major reasons are queries (URLs that include question marks) and response status (the server response code does not allow a proxy to cache the response) [19].

Unlike other proxy caching schemes, which only cache non-executable web objects, the Active Cache scheme [4] allows servers to associate a piece of Java code (called a *cache applet*) with a document. An *active proxy* (a proxy that supports the Active Cache scheme) can cache these cache applets from web servers, along with the associated documents. For efficiency or security concerns, the active proxy has the freedom of not invoking a cache applet but directly forwarding a request to the server. However, if the proxy regards a request as a hit in its cache, it will invoke the corresponding cache applet to do some processing rather than just sending the cached document to the user.

Cache applets get their name because of their similarity to Java applets, which are lightweight, originate from a server, and can communicate with the server. Our query applet is an extension to the generic cache applet. A straightforward function of the query applet would be to cache the query results at the proxy and return the results to users when they ask queries that are identical to a cached query. We call this *passive query caching*. To further reduce the workload on the server, we have added two more functions to the query applet – query containment checking and simple selection query evaluation. Having these two functions, the query applet can perform *active query caching*, where the proxy not only answers queries that are identical to a cached query, but also answers queries that are more restrictive than a cached query.

3   System Overview

We have developed a prototype system consisting of a database web server and an active proxy with the active query caching capability. The system architecture, along with the handling process is shown in Fig. 1. The shaded parts represent the components we implemented.

In this system, we used a modified version of the active proxy [4], which was originally developed on the CERN httpd code base [20]. The modifications included allowing CGI requests with query strings in GET or POST methods to be cached, and loosening certain security inspections and resource limits on cache applets. We also used a CERN httpd as the web server. The database server was the IBM DB2 Universal Database Server V5.2 with a JDBC driver.

As illustrated in Fig. 1, the three components we have implemented are the query front-end, the query applet, and the query back-end. They reside on the client side, the proxy (after the proxy gets the applet from the server), and the web server.

When a user submits a query to the query front-end, the front-end program will convert the user query into an HTTP request and send it to the proxy. The proxy then examines the URL to see if it is a cache hit at the proxy. If it is a cache hit and the server form URL has a corresponding query applet in the proxy, the proxy will invoke the query applet. Otherwise, the proxy will forward the request to the web server.

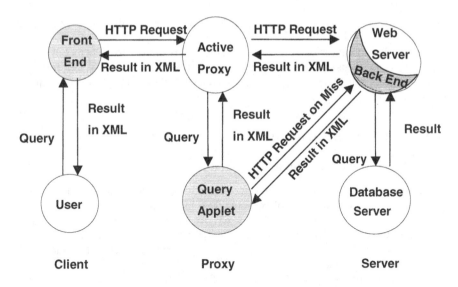

Fig. 1. System architecture

On the web server, the query back-end program transforms an HTTP request into a SQL query and sends it through JDBC to the back-end database. The query back-end program then retrieves result tuples from the database server, wraps them into an XML file with an XML representation of relational data proposed by Bos [2], and sends the XML file to the proxy. If the server decides to send a query applet to the proxy, the query back-end program will send a query applet header along with the query result.

If a query applet header is sent to the proxy along with the document, the proxy will obtain the applet from the server and associate it with the server form URL. The next time the proxy receives a request to the server form URL with a query, it will invoke the corresponding query applet.

The query applet maintains a mapping between the cached queries and their corresponding results. When the query applet is invoked upon a request, it extracts the query from the request parameters and examines its own cache. If the new query is the same as a cached query, the cached result will be returned; if the new query is more restrictive than a cached query, it is then evaluated on the result of the cached query, and new query results are generated and sent back to the user. Otherwise, the query applet forwards the request to the web server and caches the query and result from the server before passing the result to the client.

Note that in practice one HTTP request may be transformed into several SQL queries or involve more complex operations at the server side. However, the proxy does not need to know about this because all it sees is single table views expressed by forms. Also, in our implementation we only deal with XML files, not HTML files. This scenario is possible in automatic business data exchange applications. If HTML pages are needed, servers can modify the query applet code to generate the HTML.

In our implementation each query applet corresponds to a form URL at a web server, so it answers all the queries submitted to that form. When multiple query applets are present at the proxy, each of them manages its own query cache.

4   Active Query Caching

4.1   Query Caching Scheme

We chose caching at the query level rather than at the table level or semantic region level for a number of reasons. The most prominent reason is its low overhead, which is crucial to a web proxy. As discussed in Sect. 1, form-based queries at the proxy are treated as selection queries with simple predicates over a single table view. This greatly simplifies query containment checking and query evaluation at the proxy.

Moreover, the query level granularity fits well in the Web context. Firstly, each query corresponds to an individual user request so that later refinement queries from a user can be answered easily based on earlier queries. Secondly, if there are some hot queries during a period of time, many queries can be answered from the results of these hot queries.

In contrast, table level caching does not seem to apply naturally for proxy caching. It requires the proxy to get the base data (usually large), store all of it, translate simple form queries into complex queries on base data, and evaluate them at the proxy. This is undesirable in terms of resource consumption, efficiency, and proxy autonomy. To take advantage of the dynamic nature of caching, we chose query level caching, which seems more feasible and efficient than table level caching at this point.

Semantic region caching [7,8] has a finer granularity than query level caching and has the nice feature of non-redundancy. However, this advantage does not come for free. The expense of checking overlap among regions, coalescing regions, splitting queries among regions, and merging regions into the final query result is a lot more expensive than simple query containment checking and selection query evaluation. The small size of web query results causes region fragmentation and constantly triggers coalescence. Finally, it is complex to determine how "current" a coalesced region is in cache replacement.

4.2   Query Containment Checking

Query containment testing for general conjunctive queries is NP-complete [6]. However, there are polynomial time algorithms for special cases [17]. For our simple selection queries, which are a special case, we identify a sufficient condition to recognize subsumed queries efficiently. The worst-case time complexity of our query containment checking algorithm is polynomial in terms of the number of simple predicates in the Conjunctive Normal Form (CNF) query condition. The simple predicates we handle include semi-interval comparison predicates (e.g.,

Field1 > 5, Field2 <= 3) and SQL string "LIKE" predicates (e.g., Field3 LIKE '%Java Programming%').

Table 1. Two simple selection queries

Query1	Query2
SELECT List1	SELECT List2
FROM Table1	FROM Table2
WHERE WhereCondition1	WHERE WhereCondition2

Given the above two queries, Query1 and Query2, whose where-conditions have been transformed into CNF, we recognize that Query1 is *contained* in Query2 (we call Query1 a *subsumed query* of Query2 and Query2 a *super-query* of Query1) if all of the following conditions are satisfied:

- Table1 and Table2 are the same table (or view).
- Fields in List1 are a subset of the fields in List2.
- WhereCondition1 is *more restrictive than* WhereCondition2.
- If WhereCondition1 and WhereCondition2 are not equivalent, all fields that appear in WhereCondition1 also appear in List2.

In general the last condition is not a necessary condition. We specify it because eventually we need to evaluate a subsumed query on the query result of its super-query. Thus, we must guarantee that the result of the super-query contains all fields that are evaluated in the where-condition of the subsumed query. So we use the current sufficient condition for simplicity and efficiency. At this point, our query containment checking reduces to the problem of recognizing if one CNF where-condition is more restrictive than another CNF where-condition. The following two propositions further reduce the problem to testing if a simple predicate is more restrictive than another simple predicate.

Proposition 1. *Given*

$$WhereCondition1 = P_1 \ AND \ P_2 \ AND \ ...P_m,$$
$$WhereCondition2 = Q_1 \ AND \ Q_2 \ AND \ ...Q_n,$$

WhereCondition1 is more restrictive than WhereCondition2 if

$$\forall i, 1 \leq i \leq n, \exists k, 1 \leq k \leq m, P_k \text{ is more restrictive than } Q_i.$$

Proposition 2. *Given*

$$P_k = R_1 \ OR \ R_2 \ OR \ ...R_x,$$
$$Q_i = S_1 \ OR \ S_2 \ OR \ ...S_y,$$

P_k *is more restrictive than* Q_i *if*

$$\forall v, 1 \leq v \leq x, \exists u, 1 \leq u \leq y, R_v \text{ is more restrictive than } S_u.$$

Finally, given two simple predicates F1 op1 c1, F2 op2 c2, it is straightforward to test whether the former is more restrictive than the latter. Intuitively, F1 and F2 should be the same field, and the relationship among the two operators op1, op2, and the two constants c1, c2, should make the first predicate more restrictive than the second one. For example, "price <= 10" is more restrictive than "price < 20".

4.3   Query Cache Management

Since our cached query definitions use the CNF format, we transform user queries into CNF and store the AND-OR tree format at the proxy. The query cache consists of these query trees and their corresponding query results. A mapping table (called the *query directory*) is used to record the correspondence between queries and their results. Note that query definitions and their actual results are stored separately because query containment checking can be done by only comparing query trees and do not need the actual query results.

There is a choice about whether we should cache the query result of a subsumed query. One argument for caching it is that we may answer new queries faster on it because its result size is smaller than that of its super-query. The problem is the large redundancy between this query and its already cached super-query. Since web queries tend to return a small number of records per request, we chose not to cache any subsumed queries of a cached query. As a result, the cache hit ratio is improved because of less data redundancy in the cache.

There are three cache replacement schemes available in our implementation: LFU (Least Frequently Used), LRU (Least Recently Used), and benefit-based. The first two are straightforward. The third one is a combination of the other two in that it uses reference frequency and recency as parameters of the benefit. We define the benefit of a cached query as a weighted sum of the reference frequency and the recency. The heuristic behind the benefit metric is intuitive. If a query was used as a super-query for many new queries, it is likely that it will serve later queries also. This is a reflection of spatial locality – that the query covers a hot region of data. If a query was used as a super-query recently, we believe that it will probably be used as a super-query for subsequent queries soon if users are doing query refinement. This can be thought as temporal locality.

5   Experiments

5.1   On Excite Query Trace

Many web caching studies have used real traces [3,9,18] or synthetic web workloads [1]. However, these real traces or generated workloads usually do not include CGI script requests or queries. What we really needed was a trace that recorded user queries to a specific database web server. Fortunately we obtained a real query trace of around 900K queries [1] over one day from a popular search engine, Excite [10].

---

[1] In accordance with the notation in [14], a search engine query means a user's request of a specific page of the query results of a specific keywords sequence.

Search engines have their special features that may differ from other database web servers. The main differences include: their search forms conceptually have only one column (keywords), their query results are URLs, and these results are sent page by page upon user requests. Despite these differences, we feel that it is useful to investigate the effect of active query caching on search engine queries, because these queries represent web user query patterns to a popular class of web information sources.

A recent study [14] by Markatos has shown that 20-30% of the 900K queries in the Excite query trace can be answered directly from cache if the query results are cached. This caching is equivalent to what we called passive query caching. We set out our experiments to examine how much more opportunity exists for active query caching.

We transformed the search engine trace into a SQL query stream on two columns – keywords and page number and ran it through our query caching module. All experiments started from a cold query cache. The cache replacement policy was LRU.

We compared hit ratios of active query caching and passive query caching at various cache sizes. The legend "20KQ passive" in Fig. 2 means passive query caching using a cache of 20K queries. Other legends have similar meanings. If we use the assumption of 4KB per query result page [14], the query cache sizes of 20KQ, 50KQ, and 100KQ can be roughly translated into 80MB, 200MB, and 400MB correspondingly, while the cache sizes used in [14] vary between 500MB to 2GB.

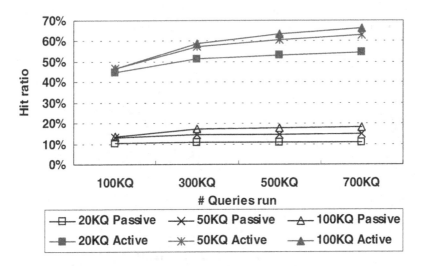

Fig. 2. Query cache hit ratios on Excite query trace

From Fig. 2 we can clearly see that there is much more opportunity for active query caching than passive query caching. The whole trace of 900K queries has

29% non-unique queries, which is the upper limit of the cache hit ratio of passive query caching with a sufficiently large cache. In contrast, we can achieve 45%-65% hit ratios in active query caching with a small to medium size cache. Notice that active query caching with a query cache size of 20K queries outperforms passive query caching with a cache size of 100K queries by a factor of three.

5.2   On Synthetic Data and Queries

No matter how high the cache hit ratios are, they are just part of the story. To identify the performance implications of our prototype system, we generated synthetic relational data and query streams for our experiments and measured actual query response times.

In the following experiments we ran the CERN httpd server and the active proxy on two Sun Ultra10 300Mhz machines with the SunOS 5.6 Operating System. The DB2 server was running on a Pentium Pro 200MHz PC with Windows NT Operating System. All machines are in our department local area network and query caches start cold.

First, we measured the response times of a query stream when the workload of the database server was varied. We used a stream of 100 queries to measure the response time when the database server was idle, when it had 6 other clients, and when it had 12 other clients. The measurements were made with R20, R40 and R60 query streams (RX reads that X% queries are subsumed queries). In this experiment, a cache size of 10 queries was sufficient to achieve the performance gain, since we generated subsumed queries immediately after their super-queries. In practice the cache size should be sufficiently large to ensure that the super-queries are in the cache when their subsumed queries arrive.

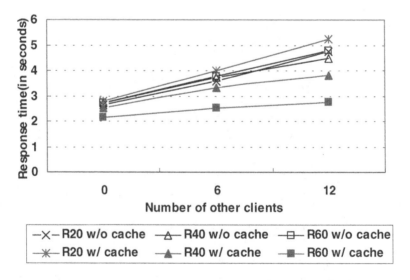

Fig. 3. Response time as server workload varies

The response time variation in Fig. 3 shows the impact of subsumed query distribution on response times with active query caching. Unlike the case without caching, the query response times with active query caching decrease when the percentage of subsumed queries increases. For the R40 and R60 query streams, the response time for the proxy with the cache is better than the case without the cache, which means these hit ratios offset the query applet overhead at the proxy. Although for the R20 query stream the response time with caching is slightly more than the response time without a cache, the proxy with caching can still share 20% of the workload with the server.

We then measured the breakdown of the time spent by a query at the various stages in a query applet. We considered the three cases – the new query could be identical to a query in the cache, be a subsumed query to a cached query, or need to be evaluated at the server. "Load + Save" refers to the time that the query applet takes to load the query directory from disk when it is invoked by the proxy plus the time taken for saving the query directory to disk before it finishes. "Check + Evaluate" includes the time that the query applet spends checking the query cache to see if the new query is subsumed by any cached query, and the time that the query applet spends evaluating the query from the cache. Finally, "Fetch from server" is the time spent sending the query to the server and waiting for the result back, if the query cannot be answered from the cache. The results are shown in Fig. 4.

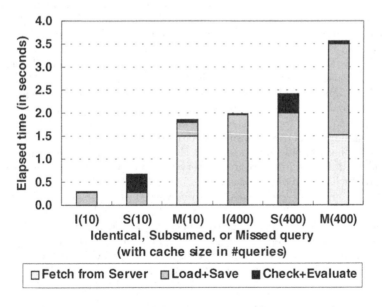

Fig. 4. Breakdown of the time spent in the query applet

The breakdown of the time spent at the various stages in the query applet shows that even in an intra-departmental network, the time taken to contact the server and get the result back is a major portion of the total time. From other experiments (not shown here) we observed that roughly 40% of the "Fetch from Server" time was spent at the database server and the remaining 60% was spent on the network. The time taken to evaluate the subsumed query from the result of the cached query is considerable. This time was also seen to be proportional to the size of the result file of the cached query as the file I/O of reading this file and writing the result back was seen to dominate this time. Within "Check + Evaluate" the portion of the time taken to check and find a super-query is quite small. Finally, we see that the time taken to load and save the cache directory is considerable. This time increases almost linearly with increase in cache size, and becomes comparable to the time taken to contact the server when the cache size is 400 queries. This cost would have been avoided if the query directory could be kept in memory in the active proxy. Unfortunately, this is not feasible in the current implementation of the active proxy.

6   Related Work

With the increase of dynamic content on the web, researchers have started studying the general problem of caching dynamic content from various aspects. Challenger et al. [5] have focused on how to efficiently identify and update obsolete pages in the web server cache. Florescu et al. [11] have proposed a customizable cache system at data-intensive web sites. Our approach complements these server-side techniques because it addresses the problem in the context of web proxies and aims at sharing the database web server workload and reducing network traffic. Furthermore, we focused on evaluating new queries on the cached results while the others just return the cached results on an identical query.

Caching dynamic content at proxies has also been studied in [15] by Smith et al. Their approach allows web content providers to specify result equivalence in generated documents so that the proxy can utilize the equivalence to return a cached result to a new request. However, they do not consider database query containment or evaluate subsumed query at the proxy. Compared with the declarative nature and limited scope of [15], the Active Cache scheme provides a simple and flexible interface to web servers at the price of a possible overhead associated with the mobile code.

Finally, our active query caching can be viewed as a special case of answering queries using views [13] if we consider cached queries to be materialized views. However, these views come and go dynamically because of the nature of caching. Moreover, as a first step of query caching at web proxies, we only consider answering a query using one view instead of multiple views and thus reduce the problem to simple query containment checking.

7   Discussion and Conclusions

In this paper, we have studied active query caching for database web servers. We have shown the opportunities that active query caching brings through a trace-driven simulation on real query traces and a prototype implementation. We have also identified the performance bottlenecks in the current implementation of the active proxy framework.

The active proxy made it possible for us to study active query caching at proxies for database web servers. Nevertheless, since the active proxy is in its prototype stage and active query caching is a brand-new application of the active proxy, we learned a few lessons from our experience. One major issue is that the active proxy does not provide any memory-resident structure for cache applets. This is not a limitation of the Active Cache protocol but is related to the CERN httpd proxy implementation. Two factors are involved. One is that the CERN proxy does not have memory-resident cache. The other is that CERN proxy forks one process per request and so the cache applet's memory structure cannot be directly passed back to the proxy. This limitation had a strong negative effect on our implementation's performance. Finally we note that Java in its current stage does have performance complications in spite of its attractive features of portability, security, and ease of implementation.

As the first step of active proxy query caching for database web servers, this prototype is a simple functional system rather than a mature one. There are many ways that our work can be extended. We are investigating ways of sharing memory structure between the proxy and the query applet to address the bottleneck. We plan to utilize indices on the query directory or other techniques to further reduce the time of query containment checking and query evaluation. We are also investigating other query caching schemes and cache replacement policies in this framework.

Acknowledgements. We would like to thank Jin Zhang for his technical support and helpful discussions on the active proxy prototype system, and Evangelos Markatos for his discussion on Excite search engine query trace. We would also like to thank Kevin Beyer, Jim Gast, and Chun Zhang for their comments.

Funding for this work was provided by DARPA through NAVY/SPAWAR contract No. N66001-99-1-8908 and NSF through NSF Award CDA-9623632.

References

1. P. Barford and M. E. Crovella. Generating Representative Web Workloads for Network and Server Performance Evaluation. Proc. Performance '98/ACM SIG-METRICS '98.
2. Bert Bos. XML representation of a relational database.
   http://www.w3.org/XML/RDB.html
3. Ramon Caceres, Fred Douglis, Anja Feldmann, Gideon Glass, and Michael Rabinovich. Web Proxy Caching: The Devil Is in the Details. In Workshop on Internet Server Performance, 1998.
4. Pei Cao, Jin Zhang, and Kevin Beach. Active Cache: Caching Dynamic Contents on the Web. Proc. IFIP International Conference on Distributed Systems Platforms and Open Distributed Processing (Middleware '98).
5. Jim Challenger, Arun Iyengar, and Paul Dantzig. A Scalable System for Consistently Caching Dynamic Web Data. Proc. IEEE INFOCOM 99.

6. Ashok K. Chandra and Philip M. Merlin. Optimal implementation of conjunctive queries in relational data bases. In Conference Record of the Ninth Annual ACM Symposium on Theory of Computing, May 1977, pages 77-90.
7. Boris Chidlovskii, Claudia Roncancio, and Marie-Luise Schneider. Semantic Cache Mechanism for Heterogeneous Web Querying. Proc. 8th World-Wide Web Conference (WWW8), 1999.
8. Shaul Dar, Michael J. Franklin, Bjorn T. Jonsson, Divesh Srivastava, Michael Tan. Semantic Data Caching and Replacement. VLDB 1996.
9. Fred Douglis, Anja Feldmann, Balachander Krishnamurthy, and Jeffrey Mogul. Rate of Change and other Metrics: a Live Study of the World Wide Web. In Symposium on Internet Technology and Systems. USENIX Association, December 1997.
10. Excite Search Engine. http://www.excite.com/
11. Daniela Florescu, Khaled Yagoub, Patrick Valduriez, Valerie Issarny. Caching Strategies for Data-Intensive Web Sites. INRIA Technical Report, INRIA, December 1999.
12. Steven D. Gribble and Eric A. Brewer. System design issues for Internet middleware services: Deductions from a large client trace. In Proc. of the USENIX Symposium on Internet Technologies and Systems, November 1997.
13. Alon Y. Levy, Alberto O. Mendelzon, Yehoshua Sagiv, Divesh Srivastava. Answering Queries Using Views. PODS, 1995 95-104
14. Evangelos P. Markatos. On Caching Search Engine Results. Technical Report 241, ICS-FORTH, January 1999.
15. Ben Smith, Anurag Acharya, Tao Yang, Huican Zhu. Caching Equivalent and Partial Results for Dynamic Web Content. Proc. of 1999 USENIX Symposium on Internet Technologies and Systems.
16. Craig Silverstein, Monika Henzinger, Hannes Marais, and Michael Moricz. Analysis of a Very Large AltaVista Query Log, SRC Technical note #1998-14.
17. Jeffrey D. Ullman. Principles of Database and Knowledge-Base Systems, Volume II. Computer Science Press 1989, pp. 877 - 907.
18. Craig E. Wills, and Mikhail Mikhailov. Examining the Cacheability of User-Requested Web Resources. In Proc. of the 4th International Web Caching Workshop, 1999.
19. Alec Wolman, Geoff Voelker, Nitin Sharma, Neal Cardwell, Molly Brown, Tashana Landray, Denise Pinnel, Anna Karlin, and Henry Levy. Organization-Based Analysis of Web-Object Sharing and Caching. In Proceedings of the 2nd USENIX Conference on Internet Technologies and Systems (USITS), October 1999.
20. W3C. http://www.w3.org/Daemon/.

Adding Relevance to XML

Anja Theobald and Gerhard Weikum

Department of Computer Science
University of the Saarland, Germany
WWW: http://www-dbs.cs.uni-sb.de
E-mail: {theobald, weikum}@cs.uni-sb.de

Abstract. XML query languages proposed so far are limited to Boolean retrieval in the sense that query results are sets of qualifying XML elements or subgraphs. This search paradigm is intriguing for "closed" collections of XML documents such as e-commerce catalogs, but we argue that it is inadequate for searching the Web where we would prefer ranked lists of results based on relevance estimation. IR-style Web search engines, on the other hand, are incapable of exploiting the additional information made explicit in the structure, element names, and attributes of XML documents. In this paper we present a compact query language, coined XXL for "flexible XML search language", that reconciles both search paradigms by combining XML graph pattern matching with relevance estimations and producing ranked lists of XML subgraphs as search results. The paper describes the language design, sketches implementation issues, and presents preliminary experimental results.

1 Motivation and Contribution

1.1 Reconciling XML Search and Information Retrieval Technologies

XML is the main driving force in the ongoing endeavor for data integration across the entire spectrum from largely unstructured to highly schematic data. In an abstract sense, all data is uniformly captured by a graph with nodes representing XML elements along with their attributes. A variety of query languages have been proposed for searching XML data (e.g., [ABS00, AQM+97, CCD+99, DFF+99, Ko99]). These languages essentially combine SQL-style logical conditions over element names, contents, and attributes with regular-expression pattern matching along entire paths of elements. The result of a query is a set of paths or subgraphs from a given graph that represents an XML document or document collection.

Although originally motivated by Web searching, the key target of XML query languages has shifted to searching over a single or a small number of federated XML repositories such as electronic shopping catalogs. In this setting, the focus on Boolean retrieval, where an XML path is either a query match or does not qualify at all, is adequate. In the Web, however, where the graph for an XML document is conceptually extended by following outgoing links to other sites, ranked retrieval remains the preferred search paradigm as it is practically impossible to compute

D. Suciu and G. Vossen (Eds.): WebDB 2000, LNCS 1997, pp. 105–124, 2001.

exhaustive answers for Boolean-search queries. Thus, traditional Web search engines, typically based on variations of the vector space model, remain the only viable choice for large-scale information retrieval on the Web. This well established technology, on the other hand, disregards the opportunities for more effective retrieval that arise from the fact that XML-based data makes more structure and semantic annotations (i.e., element and attribute names) explicit.

In this paper, we argue that XML query languages should be extended by information-retrieval-style similarity conditions, so that a query returns a ranked list sorted by descending relevance. We propose a concrete, simple language along these lines, which we have coined XXL for "flexible XML search language". To this end, we have adopted core concepts of XML-QL [DFF+99, XMLQL], and have extended them with similarity conditions on elements and their attributes. The relevance assessments, also known as "scores", for all elementary conditions in a query, are combined into an overall relevance of an XML path, and the result ranking is based on these overall relevance measures.

1.2 Related Work and Paper Outline

Related approaches that aim to exploit structural information in addition to textual content for better search quality have been pursued in the information retrieval community, especially in the context of hypertext data (e.g., [CSM97, BAN+97, FR98, MJK+98]). However, all this work predates XML, and lacks the clear structure and elegance of the recently developed XML query languages such as XML-QL. Furthermore, although an in-depth comparison is beyond the scope of this paper, it appears that this older work resulted in less expressive languages. In parallel to our work, [NDM+00] have proposed to combine XML querying with an IR search engine. However, the IR capabilities considered there are limited to simple containment predicates and seem to follow a Boolean retrieval paradigm (at least [NDM+00] does not mention anything about support for ranked retrieval).

The prior work that is closest to our approach is the WHIRL project [Coh98, Coh99]. This important work also introduced a text-oriented "semantic" similarity operator, denoted "~", as a basic building block for a relational query language, and used simple probabilistic reasoning to produce ranked search results. However, WHIRL did not consider the integration of such similarity comparisons into XML querying, which is our main contribution.

The rest of the paper is organized as follows. Section 2 presents an example scenario. Section 3 presents our language in more detail. Section 4 sketches a prototype implementation based on Oracle8i interMedia. Section 5 presents preliminary experimental results. We conclude with an outlook on ongoing and future work.

2 Example Scenario

As an example scenario, consider the following fragments of two XML documents about music CDs:

```
<cd_title> The Survivors' Suite
    <artist> Keith Jarrett </artist>
    <label> ECM </label>
    <track> Beginning
        <musician> Keith Jarrett
            <instruments>  piano, recorder, soprano saxophone
            </instruments>
        </musician>
        <musician> Dewey Redman
            <instruments> tenor saxophone </instruments>
        </musician>
        ...
    </track>
    ...
</cd_title>
```

```
<cd title="Full Force" label="ECM">
    <artist> Art Ensemble of Chicago </artist>
    <track title="Charlie M">
        <artist> Lester Bowie
            <plays> trumpet </plays>
        </artist>
        <artist> Roscoe Mitchell
            <plays> alto sax, baritone sax, piccolo </plays>
        </artist>
        ...
    </track>
    ...
</cd>
```

Obviously queries such as "who plays baritone saxophone on which tracks of CDs by the Art Ensemble of Chicago" are easily expressible in existing XML languages, for example, in the form (in our dialect XXL, with boldface keywords):

Q1: **Select** M, T
     From http://my.cdcollection.edu/allcds.xml
     Where (cd_title | cd) **As** C
      And C.#.artist **As** A
      And A="Art Ensemble of Chicago"
      And C.#.(track)? **As** T
      And T.(musician | artist) **As** M
      And M.# = "baritone saxophone"

where uppercase characters denote element variables that are bound to a node (i.e., element) and its attributes of a qualifying path (i.e., C, A, T, M in our example), # is a wildcard placeholder for arbitrary paths, ? indicates an optional element on a path, and dots stand for path concatenation. With a Boolean retrieval semantics, this query would return the empty set as far as the above XML data fragments are concerned, as there is no full match.

It is not too hard to introduce some more flexibility by allowing wildcard-enabled string comparisons for elementary conditions, for example, in SQL jargon something like "And M.# LIKE "baritone sax%"" with % denoting an arbitrary string inside an element's content or an attribute value. However, merely providing support for lexical string patterns is still way too limited. For example, it would not help at all if we wanted to search for musicians that play flutes and would intuitively expect to find Keith Jarrett playing recorder as well as Roscoe Mitchell playing piccolo. The key point is that we would actually prefer a *ranked search result*, once the search patterns becomes more elaborate and the probability of not finding an exact match approaches zero. For example, we would accept the track with Roscoe Mitchell playing baritone saxophone as an approximate match to a query for bass saxophones, with a relevance that is higher than that of the other track that features only soprano saxophone. Even more ambitiously, when searching for tracks with reed instruments, all the saxophones and flutes should qualify.

Obviously, all this requires combining XML querying with a text search engine that has some *ontological world knowledge* or, in more mundane terminology, a *thesaurus*. Once equipped with this kind of standard information-retrieval infrastructure, an XML search engine could easily infer similarity scores for the evaluation of elementary conditions and provide us with a relevance ranking for the entire search result. In our language, such queries can be expressed by means of an additional *similarity operator* "~" in the following style:

Q2: **Select** M, T
     From http://my.cdcollection.edu/allcds.xml
     Where ~cd **As** C
       And C.#.artist **As** A
       And A="Art Ensemble of Chicago"
       And C.#.(~track)? **As** T
       And T.~musician **As** M
       And M.# ~ "bass saxophone"

Here the similarity operator "~" is used for both element content (and also attribute value) comparisons, (i.e., in "M.# ~ "bass saxophone"") as well as approximate matching of element names (i.e., in "~cd", "~track", and "~musician").

3   XXL: A Flexible XML Search Language for Ranked Retrieval

3.1   A Simple Core Language

For the XXL search language we have adopted several concepts from XML-QL and similar languages as the core, with certain simplifications and resulting restrictions. Our design philosophy has been to support the common use cases in an easy-to-handle manner, and disregard rarely used high-end features.

We define the Where clause of a query as *the logical conjunction of path expressions*, where a path expression is a *regular expression over elementary conditions* and an elementary condition refers to the name or content of a single element or attribute. Regular expressions are formed by the operators "." for concatenation, "|" for union, and "*" for the Kleene star, all in combination with parentheses if necessary; in addition, the operator symbols "+", "?", "n", and "-n" with integers "n" are used to denote at least one, at most one, exactly n, or up to n occurrences of a pattern along a path. A common shortcut for the path expression "(%)*" is "#" which thus stands for an arbitrary path of elements. "#n" and "#-n" allows user-defined restriction of the length of a path in terms of number of elements along this path.

As for *elementary conditions*, we support the standard set of operators on strings and other simple data types, notably, equality "=", inequality "<>", other ordinal comparisons such as "<", "<=", etc., and string matching "LIKE" a la SQL. In addition we allow disjunctions and conjunctions of elementary conditions. All these conditions can refer to element names, element contents, or attributes of elements. Element attributes are denoted in the form "element.attribute".

Each path expression can be followed by the keyword "As" and a variable name that binds the end node of a qualifying path (i.e., the last element on the path and its attributes) to the variable. We use the syntactic convention to reserve single, uppercase letters for variables. In contrast to more general XML query languages, our dialect supports only *element variables* and no variables whose value domain includes entire paths. A variable is always bound to an element even if the qualifying path ends with an attribute; in this case the variable is bound to the element to which the attribute belongs. A variable can be used within path expressions, with the meaning that its bound value is substituted in the expression.

There are two special, reserved attribute names "NAME" and "CONTENT" to denote the part of an element, attribute, or element variable that a given condition refers to (e.g., "element.NAME = "%sax%"" for element names and "element.CONTENT = "%sax%"" for element contents). This is also helpful to define join conditions over element variables (e.g., A.NAME LIKE B.NAME). The default is CONTENT (e.g., in "element = "%sax%"", "element" stands for "element.CONTENT").

The wildcard symbols "%" (for an arbitrary string) and "_" (for an arbitrary character) can refer to both names and contents of elements and names and values of attributes including the special attributes NAME and CONTENT. This way we can easily specify conditions over names or contents without knowing whether certain data is represented as an element or as an attribute. An example for this convenient notation is "instrument%.% = "%sax%"", which would be matched by all elements whose name has the prefix "instrument" and contains the substring "sax" in its contents or any attribute or even in its name. A particular form of elementary condition is to specify simply an element name "string", possibly including wildcards; this is a shortcut for the condition "element.NAME LIKE "string"".

Section 2 has already given an example of our query language. As a second example for the same kind of XML data consider the query "which tracks of CDs from the label ECM feature both saxophone and trumpet". This can be expressed as follows:

Q3: **Select** C, T
     From http://my.cdcollection.edu/allcds.xml
     Where cd% **As** C
       And C.label="ECM"
       And C.#.track.(title)? **As** T
       And T.# LIKE "%sax%"
       And T.# LIKE "%trumpet%"

The semantics of such a query can be defined by structural induction over the query's constituents in a straightforward manner. The final query result is a set of pairs of

a)   a variable binding (i.e., a mapping of variables to nodes of the underlying XML data graph) and
b)   a subgraph that satisfies all elementary conditions of the query, with variable occurrences replaced by their bindings.

The full syntax of the XXL where clause is given in Appendix A.

3.2 Adding Similarity Conditions

So far we have merely described a simplified variation of concepts offered by most existing XML query languages. The key point of this paper is that our streamlined dialect can now be easily extended and made significantly more powerful by adding a new type of elementary conditions that capture relevance. We refer to such conditions as *similarity conditions*. At the level of name vs. content comparisons, we introduce a new, binary operator "~" that measures the similarity between a value of a node of the XML data graph and a constant or an element variable given by a query. The resulting score, which we assume to be normalized between zero and one, indicates the relevance of the node for the given constant as a search criterion. For example, the evaluation of the elementary similarity condition "instruments ~ "bass saxophone"" against our example data of Section 2 could return a relevance of 0.8 for the element whose contents contains "baritone sax", 0.6 for the element with "tenor saxophone", and 0.4 for the one with "soprano saxophone" (where the concrete relevance figures are made up for the example).

Within path expressions, the "~" symbol can also be used as a unary operator applied to an element (e.g., "~cd"). This is a shortcut for conditions of the form "element.NAME ~ constant". The same notational technique can be applied to attribute names; so prefixing an attribute name with the "~" symbol specifies that the attribute name should be matched as closely as possible. As an example, the query

Q4: **Select** T
     From http://my.cdcollection.edu/allcds.xml
     Where ~cd.#.~track **As** T
       And T.# ~ "bass saxophone"

should return both the track entitled "Charlie M" and the "Beginning" of "The Survivors' Suite", in this order of decreasing relevance.

It is important to note that such similarity conditions can be incorporated fairly easily into the language as they refer to elementary conditions. Of course, we do need a text retrieval mechanism for computing similarity scores, based on a thesaurus and other means. But this mechanism, which will be discussed in Section 4, can be invoked locally on a single XML element. This way we may even include special forms of linguistic similarity (e.g., testing for the same word stem) or phonetic similarity (i.e., similar pronounciation regardless of different spellings) as further building blocks. Furthermore, for attributes of specific data types, e.g., currency or date, we could easily add fuzzy matching, e.g., prices around $ 20, with foreign exchange rates taken into account, or dates around Christmas. It is for this flexibility and easy extensibility at the level of basic comparisons that we have coined our language "flexible XML search language" (XXL). In this paper we restrict ourselves to a general similarity operator "~" for text data, which might also be called "semantic similarity" provided the underlying thesaurus is sufficiently rich.

The relevance-enabled semantics of a query then is to return a ranked list of approximately matching subgraphs each with a measure of its relevance (or "semantic similarity") to the query. These relevance measures are defined inductively as follows:

a) We interpret the similarity score for an elementary condition as a relevance probability. This is somewhat pragmatic, as we know that similarity scores are usually derived from various heuristics. However, virtually all text retrieval engines normalize their scores between zero and one, so that a probabilistic interpretation is at least not unreasonable.

b) Then we need to combine the relevance probabilities for elements with regard to elementary conditions into a relevance measure for a path or subgraph with regard to a composite query condition. In the absence of any better information, we simply postulate probabilistic independence between all elementary conditions, and derive the combined probabilities in the straightforward standard way (i.e., by simply multiplying probabilities for conjunctions and along the elements of a path, etc.)

For a more precise definition we define the *XML data graph* to be a directed, labeled graph $G=(V,E)$ where V denotes the set of nodes and E the set of edges. The set of nodes consists of the elements of the corresponding XML document (or document collection). The set E contains an edge from an element $e1$ to an element $e2$, if and only if $e2$ is a subelement of $e1$. Now we use the XXL notation also to describe concatenation and union of paths and subgraphs. For example, for a node $n1$

and its children n2 and n3 we write n1.n2 for path concatenation and n1.(n2|n3) for path union. The result of an XXL query is a set of subgraphs (often a path) of the XML data graph, called the *result graph*, with a relevance score for each subgraph. The actual output of a query is derived from the result graph according to the query's Select clause.

Relevance probabilities of elements of the XML data for given search conditions are inductively defined as follows:

- For an element e and an elementary condition (as previous defined) of the unary form like "~label" or of the binary form like "label ~ constant" (with label referring to an element or attribute name), the relevance probability π is obtained from a text search engine and its underlying ontology/thesaurus, i.e., assumed to be given as far as the global context of the query is concerned.
- For an element e and an exact-match condition (as defined in section 3.1) of the form like "label" or like "label op constant" (with op being any operator other than similarity), the relevance probability is either 1 or 0 depending on whether e satisfies the condition or not.

The relevance probabilities of paths of the XML data graph for given search conditions are then defined as follows:

- For paths p1 and p2 that have relevance probabilities $\pi1$ and $\pi2$ with regard to conditions c1 and c2, the relevance probability of the path p1.p2 with regard to conditions "c1.c2" is $\pi1*\pi2$.
- For a path p that has relevance probability π with regard to condition c, the relevance probability of p with regard to the condition "c?" is π.
- For paths p1, p2, ..., pm that have relevance probabilities $\pi1, \pi2, ..., \pim$ for condition c, the relevance probability of the concatenated path p1.p2. ... .pm with regard to conditions "c+", "c*", "cn", and "c-n", with an integer n, is $\pi1*\pi2*...*\pim$ in the first case, is $\pi1*\pi2*...*\pim$ if the concatenated path is not empty or 1 otherwise in the second case, $\pi1*\pi2*...*\pim$ if n=m or 0 otherwise in the third case, and $\pi1*\pi2*...*\pim$ if m≤n and 0 otherwise in the fourth case.
- For a path p and a condition of the form "%" (e.g., in "(%)*" as a shortcut for "#") the relevance probability is 1.

Finally the relevance probabilities of subgraphs of the XML data graph for given search conditions are evaluated as follows:

- For subgraphs g1 and g2 that have relevance probabilities $\pi1$ and $\pi2$ for conditions c1 and c2, the relevance probability of the disjunctive combined subgraph g with regard to condition "c1 | c2" is $\pi1 + \pi2 - \pi1*\pi2$.
- For subgraphs g1 and g2 that have relevance probabilities $\pi1$ and $\pi2$ for conditions c1 and c2, the relevance probability of the concatenated subgraph g with regard to condition "c1.c2" is $\pi1*\pi2$.
- For subgraphs g1 and g2 that have relevance probabilites $\pi1$ and $\pi2$ with regard to conditions c1 and c2 (each of them possibly being a conjunction of path expressions), the relevance probability of the conjunctive combined subgraph

with regard to condition "c1 And c2" is $\pi 1 * \pi 2$. (Remark that conjunctions only allowed at top level of the query.)

For illustration of this relevance estimation procedure reconsider example query Q4:

Select T
From http://my.cdcollection.edu/allcds.xml
Where ~cd.#.~track **As** T
  And T.# ~ "bass saxophone"

The result graph should include the paths to Roscoe Mitchell, Dewey Redman, and Keith Jarrett playing baritone sax, tenor sax, and soprano sax, respectively (and the actual result, the bindings of the element variable T would then be extracted from these result graph). Assume that "cd_title" has similarity 0.9 for condition "~cd" whereas the element name "cd" as a perfect match has similarity 1, and that condition "~track" is perfectly matched in all cases. Further assume as before that the two "instruments" elements of the first document and the "plays" element of the second document have similarities 0.4, 0.6, and 0.8 with regard to the condition "T.# ~ "bass saxophone"". Then the overall relevance scores would be 0.9*1*0.4=0.36, 0.9*1*0.6=0.54, and 1*1*0.8=0.8 for the paths with Keith Jarrett, Dewey Redman, and Roscoe Mitchell, respectively.

Relevance-enabled queries can be posed against XML data under a fixed root, as shown in the above examples, or by using a Web search engine (e.g., AltaVista, Google, etc.) to provide starting points. In the first case, the probability of the root being relevant is implicitly set to one. In the second case, the search engine already yields a ranked list of roots, and we initialize their relevance probabilities with the normalized scores computed by the search engine.

4 Prototype Implementation

Although our approach ultimately aims at more effective Web searching, we have initially restricted ourselves to a centralized experimental testbed as a first proof of concept. To this end, we have built a prototype search engine for XXL on top of Oracle8i interMedia [Ora8ia, Ora8ib] which is a full-fledged text retrieval system, including an extensible thesaurus, and provides us with elementary similarity comparisons for text data. So the search scope of our prototype is limited to the XML data in the underlying Oracle database; extending this scope to the Web is work in progress.

4.1 Storing XML Data

Oracle8i can directly store XML documents in its object-relational database through vendor-provided servlets without explicit user code for conversion. To have more control over how XML elements are accessed via SQL within our search algorithms, we nevertheless decided to explicitly map XML data onto relational tables, similarly to the mappings in [SGT+99, Kos99]. The schema that we are using essentially consists of four tables:

> Documents (<u>URL</u>, root_oid)
> Elements (<u>oid</u>, name, content)
> Attributes (<u>oid, name</u>, value)
> Edges (<u>oid, parent_oid</u>)

So we essentially represent each node and each edge of an *XML data graph* as a row in a table, with additional rows for document roots and element attributes, all identifiable through oids (object identifiers).

4.2 Similarity Search with Oracle interMedia

Oracle interMedia is a full-fledged text retrieval system [Ora8ia, Ora8ib], which supports a broad spectrum of text query operators including:

- keyword-based search, referred to as "fuzzy" search in interMedia, with similarity based on the classical tf*idf formula that considers term frequencies (tf) and inverse document frequencies (idf) [BR99],
- thesaurus lookup and thus support for thesaurus-based augmentation of fuzzy queries, using operators RT for related terms, SYN for synonyms, BT for broader terms, etc.
- linguistic or phonetic search, "stem" and "soundex" in interMedia terminology,
- textual proximity of words using the "near" operator.

These elementary similarity comparisons are embedded into SQL (using an additional keyword CONTAINS), and the similarity score of a comparison is returned via a special function SCORE (see below for examples). In our prototype we are using the keyword-based (fuzzy) search. A given keyword is dynamically extended in our prototype by making appropriate thesaurus lookups (using the RT operator) and generating a union query for all synonyms of the keyword in the original query.

For elementary search conditions that refer to element or attributes names, the tf*idf formula does not yield meaningful results (as an element or attribute name is typically only a single word). For this class of comparisons we use the Levenshtein text-editing distance to compute a similarity score. In future XXL versions we plan to incorporate also "semantic distance" functions derived from a hierarchical ontology for the similarity comparison of names (e.g., associating higher similarity between "reed instruments" and "saxophone" than between "brass instruments" and "saxophone").

4.3 Search Algorithm

Our prototype decomposes a query into elementary conditions and generates appropriate calls to interMedia. Each interMedia call yields a set of elements or attributes (i.e., rows of the Elements or Attributes tables) with associated relevance scores. These are inserted into a *result graph* that we maintain in memory to build the overall XXL result.

As defined in Section 3, an XXL query is a logical conjunction of regular path expressions over elementary conditions. Each of these path expressions can be represented by its finite state automaton. For a query Q = r1 AND ... AND rk with regular path expressions ri (i=1,...,k) we construct:

  a) the set of finite state automaton $FA_{r1},...,FA_{rk}$,
  b) the set of element variables that occur in Q, and
  c) the association of each element variable with the corresponding nodes of the finite state automata

as a *query representation* for the query Q.

Each state within these finite state automata is an elementary condition of the form "element name pattern" or "element content/name/attribute op constant" where "op" includes the similarity operator "~". The transitions between state correspond to the concatenation of elementary conditions in the path expressions of the XXL query. In addition, for the iteration of search patterns, i.e., the Kleene star and its bounded variations, an automaton is extended by adding transitions for all possible continuations of the pattern. So for a pattern c1.(c2)*.c3, the part of the automaton that represents c2 (which would be a single state if c2 were elementary) has c3 as a successor and also a transition back to the first state of c2 itself; furthermore, c1 is extended by a transition to the first state of c3 allowing us to skip c2. The latter construction is also applied to conditions of the form "(c)?", and finite iterations of the form "(c)n" or "(c)-n" (with integer n) are simply unfolded.

For example, the query pattern for Q4 of Section 3 is compiled into the following query representation:

Query Q4:   **Select** T
            From http://my.cdcollection.edu/allcds.xml
            Where ~cd.#.~track **As** T
            And T.# ~ "bass saxophone"

Query representation:

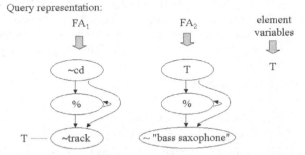

Our current implementation does not consider selectivity estimates and conceivable optimizations based on such estimates. Rather the path expressions in an XXL query are evaluated in the textual order in which they appear in the query. Elements that match the end node of a path expression (i.e., a final state in the corresponding automaton) are assigned to the corresponding element variable if there is an As clause for this path expression. These variable bindings are passed to the evaluation of the next automaton, according to the conjunctive combination of path expressions.

Matching an XML subgraph with a given finite state automaton amounts to finding a traversal of the automaton, connecting the root with all leaves, that is isomorphic to the data subgraph with all nodes approximately matching the corresponding elementary conditions. When traversing the XML data graph, our search engine maintains a list of "next-to-match" nodes of the automaton. If the automaton corresponds to a linear path without any recursion, then there is always exactly one next-to-match node. In the general case, either because of branching conditions or a Kleene star, the search engine needs to consider all next-to-match conditions when inspecting an element in the XML data graph. Once a condition is matched it is replaced by all its successors in the query graph, and the data-graph traversal proceeds on the outgoing edges of the previously inspected element. These matching tests are actually similarity comparisons, and a corresponding relevance probability is determined for the inspected element; in addition, the accumulated relevance probability is computed for the entire data subgraph visited so far. To summarize, the search algorithm traverses the XML data graph, initially in a breadth-first manner and starting from the roots of the documents, and attempts to match elementary conditions against the elements along its trajectory.

The similarity scores for elementary conditions are obtained by appropriate calls to Oracle8i interMedia of the form

> **Select** SCORE(1)
> **From** Elements e
> **Where** CONTAINS (e.content, "?string", 1)>0 And e.oid = ...

Here "?" is Oracle's metacharacter for keyword-based (fuzzy) similarity search, "1" is an arbitrary label to identify multiple occurrences of CONTAINS clauses in the same query, and "> 0" is merely a syntactic detail. The SCORE function , which uses the label "1" as a reference to the particular CONTAINS clause, returns a value between 0 and 100 for each of the retrieved records, which we normalize and interpret as probabilities between 0 and 1.

As an example consider again query Q4:

> **Select** T
> **From** http://my.cdcollection.edu/allcds.xml
> **Where** ~cd.#.~track **As** T **And** T.# ~ "bass saxophone"

The XXL search engine would generate the following calls to Oracle interMedia:

1) thesaurus lookup for terms used in similarity comparisons:

> **Select** ctx_thes.RT('term', 'ontology_name')
> **From** dual

repeated for "cd", "track", and "bass saxophone" in the place of "term".
For example, this could return the set {"bass saxophone", "baritone saxophone"} as terms related to "bass saxophone".

2) determine result graph roots:
   Select e, SCORE(1)
   From Elements e , Edges v
   Where CONTAINS (e.name, "?cd",1)>0
   And e.oid = v.oid
   And v.parent_oid = **Select** root_oid
                                   From Documents **Where** ...

3) iterate until approximate match found:
   append to result graph:
   Select e, SCORE(1)
   From Elements e, Edges v
   Where CONTAINS (e.name, "?track",1)>0
   And e.oid = v.oid
   And v.parent_oid = a current leaf in the result graph

4) append to result graph:
   Select e, SCORE(1)+SCORE(2)-SCORE(1)*SCORE(2)
   From Elements e, Edges v
   Where (CONTAINS (e.content, "?bass saxophone",1)>0
   Or (CONTAINS (e.content, "?baritone saxophone",2)>0
   And a.oid=e.oid)
   And e.oid = v.oid
   And v.parent_oid = a current leaf in the result graph

As mentioned before, our XXL search engine initially traverses the data graph in breadth-first order. It builds up a *result graph* whose nodes correspond to the visited data-graph nodes. The outgoing edges of the result graph's leaves are the data-graph nodes that are next to be visited. Now, because all subgraphs visited so far are annotated by their accumulated relevance, as computed up to this point in the query execution, we can actually maintain a *priority queue* for the next-to-visit data-graph nodes, and this priority queue is ordered by descending relevance. So the graph traversal can be viewed as a greedy search for the most relevant subgraphs with regard to the conditions of the query graph. This procedure, which resembles the well known A* search algorithm [RN95], is iterated until a subgraph of the data graph has been added to the result graph whose leaves have been compared against the leaves of the query graph and have resulted in a similarity score greater than zero. At this point we have the first complete result subgraph, and if the greedy traversal were optimal, then this first result would be the most relevant one. Typically, however, the greedy traversal is suboptimal and users are often interested in the top N (with integer N in the order of 10) results anyway. So the traversal is continued until the first N results are obtained (or we have exhausted the data graph).

5 Preliminary Experiments

We conducted preliminary experiments to study the retrieval quality of the XXL prototype. We focused on *precision* as the key metric that captures the capability of a search engine to provide relevant documents among the top N of a ranked result list. We use the following definition of precision:

$$precision = \frac{number\,of\,relevant\,results\,among\,top\,N}{\min(N,total\,number\,of\,results)}$$

where N is a parameter, often set to 10 (i.e., the first result page of a Web search engine).

5.1 Experimental Setup

We loaded the underlying Oracle database with four collections of XML documents, using the database schema given in Section 4.1:

- a collection of religious books (Bible, Koran, etc.) [Doc1]
- a collection of Shakespeare plays [Doc2]
- several issues of the German computer journal "CT" [Doc3]
- bibliographic data about ACM SIGMOD Record [Doc4]

Note that the diversity of this data posed a challenge for the search engine that would not be present with a homogeneous XML collection that follows a single DTD or XML schema.

Oracle interMedia also served as a competitor to our XXL protoype, using only its native IR capabilities. For this purpose we redundantly loaded all data into an additional table

EntireDocuments (url, doc_content)

where each XML document is captured in (a long text field "doc_content" of) a single row. Note that interMedia is unaware of the actual XML structure. The following table shows the resulting database size:

Number of rows for Oracle interMedia	Number of rows for XXL prototype
EntireDocuments: 98	Documents: 98 Elements: 240742 Attributes: 4357 Edges: 240644

In addition, we created a small user-specific thesaurus consisting of synonyms, e.g., a pair (headline, heading), and broader terms, e.g., for the element name hierarchy (title2, subtitle, playsubt), to reflect the specific test data. Finally, standard Oracle indexes were created for all primary and foreign keys, and interMedia text indexes were created for all text fields (i.e., "name", "content", and "doc_content").

5.2 Results

We specifically studied queries that combine search arguments for textual contents with search arguments for element names (i.e., XML tags). Three special instances that we discuss in the following are:

Q5: Find all (paths to) elements or documents that contain a title "testament"
   (with the expectation to retrieve the two top-level elements of the bible).
Q6: Find all (paths to) elements or documents that contain an author "King"
   (with the expectation to retrieve bibliographic data from ACM SIGMOD Record).
Q7: Find all (paths to) elements or documents that contain a character "King"
   (with the expectation to retrieve data on key figures in Shakespeare dramas such
as
   Henry VIII or King Lear).

Results for Q5:

In native interMedia the query was phrased as follows:
   Q5i: Select URL, score(1) From EntireDocuments x
            Where contains (x.doc_content, '(title)&(testament)', 1)>0
Additionally we ran the variation:
   Q5ii: Select URL, score(1) From EntireDocuments x
            Where contains (x.doc_content, 'near (title,testament)', 1)>0
The corresponding XXL query looked as follows:
   Q5xxl: Select T From Documents
            Where #.~title AS T and T ~ 'testament'

The following table shows the precision for the top 10 results for each of these
variants, along with some example results from the top 10. Results that are
(intellectually assessed to be) relevant to the query are typed in boldface.

	Q5i	Q5ii	Q5xxl
# results	12	4	16
Precision	0.2	0.5	0.8
Results: 1) 2) 3) 4) 5)	*nt.xml* *ot.xml* bom.xml as_you.xml j_caesar.xml	*nt.xml* *ot.xml* bom.xml quran.xml	*tstmt.titlepg.title="The Old Testament"* *tstmt.coverpg.title="The Old Testament"* *tstmt.titlepg.title="The New Testament"* *tstmt.coverpg.title="The New Testament"* play.title="The Tempest"

Here interMedia yields a noticeable fraction of irrelevant documents among its
results; using the "near" operator in the query fixes this problem to a large extent, but
does not completely eliminate it. XXL, on the other hand, finds more or less exactly
the title elements for the bible's old and new testament, with only very few spurious
extra results.

Results for Q6:

In native interMedia the query was phrased as follows:
   Q6i: Select URL, score(1) From EntireDocuments x
            Where contains (x.doc_content, '(author)&(king)', 1)>0

The variation that uses the "near" operator instead of the conjunction of search terms is denoted as Q6ii. Finally, the corresponding XXL query looked as follows:

Q6xxl: Select A From Documents
          Where #.~author AS A and A ~ 'king'

The search results were the following:

	Q6i	Q6ii	Q6xxl
# results	15	5	51
Precision	0.1	0.2	0.6
Results: 1) 2) 3) 4) 5)	*SigmodRecord.xml* bom.xml nt.xml troilus.xml ot.xml	*SigmodRecord.xml* Hen_v.xml ot.xml hamlet.xml hen_vi_3.xml	*Sigmod. ... .author="King-Ip Lin"* *Sigmod. ... .author="Roger King"* *Sigmod. ... .author="Won Kim"* *Sigmod. ... .author="Tim King"* *Sigmod. ... .author="Roger King"*

Again, we observed the phenomenon that interMedia yields an irritating fraction of irrelevant documents. A typical problem was that some documents contain the terms "king" and "authorities" in close proximity, so that some of the Shakespeare plays were erroneously provided as search results.

Results for Q7:

The last query for this paper was phrased in native interMedia as follows:

Q7i: Select URL, score(1) From EntireDocuments x
        Where contains (x.doc_content, '((figure)|(character)|(person))&(king)', 1)>0

The variation with the "near" operator is referred to as Q7ii, and the corresponding XXL query looked as follows:

Q7xxl: Select F From Documents
          Where #.~figure AS F and F ~ 'king'

The search results were the following:

	Q7i	Q7ii	Q7xxl
# results	39	21	63
Precision	0.7	0.9	1.0
Results: 1) 2) 3) 4) 5)	ot.xml *hen_viii.xml* nt.xml *rich_iii.xml* *hen_iv_2.xml*	*hen_viii.xml* rich_ii.xml ot.xml *hen_v.xml* hen_iv_1.xml	*play.personae.persona="King Lewis ... "* *play.personae.persona="Polixenes, King ... "* *play.personae.persona="Leontes, King of ... "* *play.personae.persona="Priam, King of Troy"* *play.personae.persona="Ferdinand,...King ... "*

For this query, XXL exploited its ontology by augmenting the search term "figure" with its synonyms "character" and "person". Of course, interMedia did internally make use of its thesaurus, too, but even drew wrong conclusions in some instances.

For example, a document with the following text fragment was considered as an approximative match:

> ...
> <LINE>for a day of <u>kings</u>' entreaties a mother should not</LINE>
> <LINE>sell him an hour from her beholding, I, considering</LINE>
> <LINE>how honour would become such a <u>person</u>. that it was</LINE>
> ...

This shows an inherent disadvantage of a pure text retrieval engine that has no awareness of the XML structure; it has no way of inferring that the speaking figure himself is not a king.

Discussion:

The experiments show that, in contrast to a pure text search engine, knowledge about document structure and corresponding search operators that combine structural pattern matching with semantic similarity significantly increase the precision of search. Obviously, the interMedia queries could be further refined to provide better results, but this would require intellectual work, the most precious resource today (and usually not exactly amply invested by users of Web or Intranet search engines). Also note that interMedia yields only documents URLs as results; it does not point out the elements within a document that led to a document being considered as relevant. On the other hand, the same queries performed on the Elements table would often fail to find any useful results as they would myopically consider only single elements disregarding the surrounding context.

As far as runtimes are concerned, XXL is orders of magnitude slower than native interMedia. The simple explanation is that XXL makes several thousand calls to Oracle for each of the above queries, whereas the queries correspond to single SQL statements with native interMedia. This is an issue where our XXL prototype still needs substantial optimization.

6 Ongoing and Future Work

The message of this paper is to advocate the integration of XML query languages with IR-style similarity comparisons for ranked retrieval of XML data on the Web. The presented XXL search language along with is prototype implementation on top of Oracle8i interMedia, albeit simple and fairly limited, already indicates the benefits of the presented approach. Currently, we are working on the robustness and efficiency of our prototype, and also on a more easy-to-use graphical interface. As for efficiency, we are confident that the centralized version will eventually perform well even for larger data volumes. In this regard we plan to devise appropriate index structures, and we may leverage the underlying Oracle technology by issuing more compound SQL statements. In addition, we plan to address the problem of query optimization, for example, choosing the evaluation order of regular path expressions in a query based on selectivity estimation.

The biggest challenge in our future work lies in making the approach scalable and perform well on distributed Web data. In this broader context, Oracle8i interMedia as a thesaurus-backed text search engine would have to be replaced by a Web search engine, which is relatively easy with our modular architecture. In addition and more importantly, the presented traversal procedure has to be extended for this purpose. For more efficient traversal we consider prefetching techniques, and we are looking into approximative index structures as a search accelerator. Both techniques may exploit the fact that we are heuristically computing a relevance ranking, so that a faster but less complete result is usually tolerable.

References

[ABS00] S. Abiteboul, P. Buneman, D. Siciu: Data on the Web – From Relations to Semistructured Data and XML. San Francisco: Morgan Kaufmann Publishers, 2000.

[AQM+97] S. Abiteboul, D. Quass, J. McHugh, J. Widom, J. L. Wiener: The Lorel Query Language for Semistructured Data. International Journal of Digital Libraries 1(1): 68-88 (1997).

[BR99] R. Baeza-Yates, B. Ribeiro-Neto: Modern Information Retrieval, Addison Wesley, 1999.

[BAN+97] K. Böhm, K. Aberer, E.J. Neuhold, X. Yang: Structured Document Storage and Refined Declarative and Navigational Access Mechanisms in HyperStorM, VLDB Journal 6(4), 1997.

[CCD+99] S. Ceri, S. Comai, E. Damiani, P. Fraternali, S. Paraboschi, L. Tanca: XML-GL: A Graphical Language for Querying and Restructuring XML Documents. WWW8/Computer Networks 31(11-16): 1171-1187 (1999).

[CSM97] M. Cutler, Y. Shih, W. Meng: Using the Structure of HTML Documents to Improve Retrieval, USENIX Symposium on Internet Technologies and Systems, Monterey, California, 1997.

[Coh98] W.W. Cohen: Integration of Heterogeneous Databases Without Common Domains Using Queries Based on Textual Similarity, ACM SIGMOD Conference, 1998.

[Coh99] W. W. Cohen: Recognizing Structure in Web Pages using Similarity Queries. 16. Nat. Conf. on Artif. Intelligence (AAAI) / 11. Conf. on Innovative Appl. on Artif. Intelligence (IAAI), pp. 59-66, 1999.

[DFF+99] A. Deutsch, M. F. Fernandez, D. Florescu, A. Y. Levy, D. Suciu: A Query Language for XML. WWW8/Computer Networks 31 (11-16): 1155-1169 (1999).

[Doc1] http://metalab.unc.edu/bosak/xml/eg/rel200.zip

[Doc2] http://metalab.unc.edu/bosak/xml/eg/shaks200.zip

[Doc3] http://www.heise.de/ct/inhverz/

[Doc4] http://www.acm.org/sigmod/record/xml/index.html

[FR98] N. Fuhr, T. Rölleke: HySpirit – a Probabilistic Inference Engine for Hypermedia Retrieval in Large Databases, 6th International Conference on Extending Database Technology (EDBT), Valencia, Spain, 1998.

[Kos99] D. Kossmann (Editor), Special Issue on XML, IEEE Data Engineering Bulletin Vol.22 No.3, 1999.

[MJK+98] S.-H. Myaeng, D.-H. Jang, M.-S. Kim, Z.-C. Zhoo: A Flexible Model for Retrieval of SGML Documents, ACM SIGIR Conference on Research and Development in Information Retrieval, Melbourne, Australia, 1998.

[NDM+00] J. Naughton, D. DeWitt, D. Maier, et al.: The Niagara Internet Query System. http://www.cs.wisc.edu/niagara/Publications.html

[Ora8ia] Oracle 8i interMedia: Platform Service for Internet Media and Document Content, http://technet.oracle.com/products/intermedia/

[Ora8ib] Oracle 8i interMedia Text Reference Release 8.1.5

[RN95] S. Russell, P. Norvig: Artificial Intelligence - A Modern Approach, Prentice-Hall, 1995.

[SGT+99] J. Shanmugasundaram, G. He, K. Tufte, C. Zhang, D. DeWitt, J. Naughton: Relational Databases for Querying XML Documents: Limitations and Opportunities. Proc. of the Very Large Databases (VLDB) Conference, September 1999.

[XMLQL] XML-QL: A Query Language for XML, User's Guide, Version 0.6, http://www.research.att.com/~mff/xmlql/doc

Appendix A: Syntax of the Where Clause of XXL

Let Σ a finite alphabet that does not contain the special symbols #, %, and _, which are reserved for wildcards. The where clauses of XXL queries are words of the following context free grammar CF = (N, T, P, S), where N and T are alphabets (N $\cap$ T=$\emptyset$), N is the set of non-terminal symbols, T the set of terminal symbols, P $\subseteq$ N $\times$ (N $\cup$ T)* the set of production rules, and S $\in$ N the start symbol. The terminal symbols are defined as T = LABELEXPR $\cup$ VAR $\cup$ CONST $\cup$ OP, where LABELEXPR $\subseteq$ (Σ $\cup$ {%, _})+ is the set of expressions for element or attribute names, VAR is the set of element variable names, and CONST is the set of (string) constants. The production rules, with keywords in boldface, are as follows:

P = {

S	$\rightarrow$ path | path bop condition | path **AS** variable | S **AND** path | S **AND** path bop condition | S **AND** path **AS** variable
path	$\rightarrow$ element | variable | path.path | (path)**?** | (path)**+** | (path)* | (path)**n** | (path)**-n** | # | #**n** | #**-n** | (pathend ' | ' pathend)
pathend	$\rightarrow$ path | path bop condition
condition	$\rightarrow$ variable | constant
element	$\rightarrow$ object$_{LABELEXPR}$ | uop object$_{LABELEXPR}$
object$_{LABELEXPR}$	$\rightarrow$ l | l.**NAME** | l.**CONTENT**
l	$\rightarrow$ LABELEXPR

variable	$\rightarrow$ v | v.**NAME** | v.**CONTENT**
v	$\rightarrow$ VAR
constant	$\rightarrow$ c | constant **and** c | constant **or** c
c	$\rightarrow$ CONST
uop	$\rightarrow \sim$
bop	$\rightarrow \sim$ | $=$ | $\neq$ | LIKE | ...

}

where uop stands for unary operator and bop for binary operator.

Evaluating Queries on Structure with eXtended Access Support Relations

Thorsten Fiebig and Guido Moerkotte

Fakultät für Mathematik und Informatik
University of Mannheim
68131 Mannheim
{fiebig moerkotte}@informatik.uni-mannheim.de

Abstract. There are three common design decisions taken by today's search engines. First, they do not replicate the data found on the Web. Second, they rely on full-text indexes instead. Third, they do not support the querying of document structure. The main reason for the latter is that HTML's ability to express semantics with syntactic structure is very limited. This is different for XML since it allows for self-describing data. Due to its flexibility by inventing arbitrary new element and attribute names, XML allows to encode semantics within syntax. The consequence is that search engines for XML should support the querying of structure. In our current work on search engines for XML data on the Web, we want to keep the first two design decisions of traditional search engines but modify the last one according to the new requirements implied by the necessity to query structure. Since our search engine accepts queries with structural information, a full-text index does not suffice any longer. What is needed is a scalable index structure that allows to answer queries over the structure of XML documents.

One possible index structure called *eXtended Access Support Relation* (XASR) is introduced. Further, we report on a search engine for XML data called *Mumpits*. Due to its prototypical character, we intentionally kept the design and implementation of Mumpits very simple. Its design is centered around a single XASR and its implementation heavily builds on a commercial relational database management system.

1 Introduction

The World-Wide Web (Web for short) currently consists of more than one billion documents. A consequence of this enormous size of the Web is that finding documents that meet a user's current information need becomes impossible without further tools. The most widely used tools are search engines that crawl the Web, index the documents found, and process Boolean queries often enhanced with a sophisticated ranking. Most of today's search engines have three underlying design decisions in common:

1. They do not replicate the documents found on the Web.
2. They rely on full-text indexes instead.

D. Suciu and G. Vossen (Eds.): WebDB 2000, LNCS 1997, pp. 125–136, 2001.

3. They do not allow to query the structure of the indexed documents.

The main reason for the latter is that HTML's ability to express semantics with syntactic structure is very limited and, hence, querying the structure of HTML documents is not very useful.

This limitation of HTML has driven the development of XML [4]. XML's biggest strength is its flexibility to invent arbitrary new element and attribute names accompanied by a mechanism to specify the structure of documents according to the application's need. These features allow to encode semantics into structure. Given that, querying the structure of a document which now may encode valuable data becomes a necessity.

It is our hypothesis that sufficient XML data will be available on the Web to justify a search engine specialized for these XML data. Such a search engine must depart from at least the third design decision and support queries incorporating structural information. In our current work on search engines for XML data on the Web, we further want to keep the first two design decisions of traditional search engines, i.e. we do not want to replicate the documents found on the Web but rely on indexes instead. Obviously, since we must allow our search engine to process queries which include structural information, a full-text index no longer suffices. What is needed is a scalable index capturing the structure of documents.

Therefore we introduce an index structure called *eXtended Access Support Relation* (XASR). Further, we report on a search engine for XML data called *Mumpits*. Its design is centered around a single XASR and its implementation heavily builds on a commercial relational database management system.

The design decisions for Mumpits are:

1. Mumpits does not replicate the XML documents found on the Web.
2. Mumpits contains three index structures: a full-text index, a full-number index (comparable to the VIndex of Lore [14]), and the XASR.
3. Mumpits supports queries over the structure of documents.

Due to its prototypical character, we intentionally keep the design and implementation of Mumpits very simple. Only after having gained some more experience, we will take further steps to refine its design and implementation.

The differences between Mumpits and traditional search engines should be obvious. Lately, some search engines appeared with both commercial and research background. Commercial search engines are *GoXML*[1] and IBM's *XML Central*[2]. GoXML's only support for structure is that a user may specify an element's name together with a word contained in an element of the given name. There is no information available about the internal implementation of GoXML. IBM's XML Central does not support any queries over the structure. In that it is identical to traditional search engines except that it is specialized to XML. In the research community there is the Niagara search engine [5]. Niagara is a very ambitious project which not only allows to query documents but also supports continuous queries. This necessitates caching of all the documents found

---

[1] www.goxml.com

[2] www.ibm.com/xml

on the Web. Unfortunately, there is no further information available whether Niagara has index structures to support queries against the structure of documents. Xyleme[3] is the second major research project whose goal is to implement a search engine for XML data. Again it is very ambitious in its functionality. Delta-queries will be supported and it will replicate the XML documents found on the Web. Several other research projects have been concerned with the problem to store XML documents in relational database management systems [8,9, 15,17]. All these projects store the whole documents in such a way that they can be reconstructed. In contrast to that, the XASR only stores an abstraction of the document structure without any contents. There is no way a document can be reconstructed from the information contained in all of Mumpits' relations.

Access support relations are an index structure to accelerate the evaluation of path queries. For every heavily traversed path an access support relation materializes all possible matches found in the object base [11]. The XASR generalizes access support relations in several ways. First, access support relations are based on paths found in the schema. This is not possible for XML documents. For documents without a DTD it is impossible to predict the set of potentially paths. Even if a DTD is specified, disjunction and recursion within an element specification lead to a potential infinite set of possible paths. Further, access support relations were not designed to cover generalized path expressions, i.e. those containing wild cards. This is also true for other path indexes [3,12,13,16].

The rest of the paper is organized as follows. Section 2 introduces the Mumpits query language. Section 3 discusses the design and implementation of Mumpits. Section 4 demonstrates how Mumpits queries can be translated into SQL queries. Some preliminary performance results are presented in section 5. Section 6 concludes the paper.

2 Query Language

Mumpits is a search engine for querying XML data found on the web. As such, its query language must be sufficiently simple in order to allow ordinary users to understand and use it efficiently. Hence, we kept Mumpits' query language intentionally very simple. The base of the query is the set of documents available in Mumpits. Further, a query returns a set of URIs to qualifying documents. A document qualifies if a user specified predicate evaluates to true when evaluated on the document. As we can see, the query language is similar in conception to a query language for information retrieval systems and much simpler than a query language for semistructured data or XML [2].

The predicates a user can formulate must follow the grammar shown in Table 1.

A Mumpits query is a Boolean expression in **and**, **or**, and **not** built from base predicates which returns a set of URIs of qualifying documents. A base predicate can be a predicate on the document structure or on the document contents. A

---

[3] Xyleme is a joint project between INRIA Rocquencourt and the University of Mannheim.

Table 1. The Mumpits query syntax.

Definition
predicate   ::= predicate 'and' predicate
| predicate 'or' predicate
| 'not' predicate
| '(' predicate ')'
| base_predicate
base_predicate ::= 'exists' '(' path ')' |
| path op const
const   ::= any string or number constant
possibly enclosed in two quotation marks ('"')
path   ::= ('/'| '//') relative_path
relative_path ::= node_specifier (path_connector node_specifier) *
node_specifier ::= node_name | *
path_connector ::= '/' | '//'
op   ::= '=' | '!=' | '<' | '>' | '<=' | '>='

predicate on the structure is formed by **exists** and a path expression. The semantics is that the path expression exists in the retrieved document. A predicate on the contents is formed by a path expression followed by a comparison operator and a constant. The semantics is that the path exists in the document and the element it leads to contains a word or number that fulfills the comparison predicate. If the constant is a word, we further convert it to lower case. Only if the constant is enclosed by quotation marks, we search for literal occurrences.

The element can either be an XML attribute or an XML element. For user convenience, Mumpits does not distinguish between XML attributes and XML elements. We strongly believe that the additional selectivity gained by allowing to differentiate between attributes and elements does not justify the additional burden (knowing the DTDs or document structures). The hypothesis that the distinction between attributes and elements is most of the time of no importance in query languages is also expressed in [10].

To lower the threshold for users even further, we abbreviate the base predicate **//* = const** by **const**. This abbreviation then checks for occurrences of **const** within documents.

Let us consider some example queries:

– **Anton**
  retrieves documents containing the word "Anton" somewhere.
– **//car/price >= 100,000**
  retrieves documents containing an element **price** directly underneath an element **car**. Further, there is a number in the element **price** larger than **100,000**.
  In general, the path connector '/' requires that the following element is a child and the path connector '//' requires that the following element is a descendant. Herein, Mumpits follows the X-Path [6] specification.

The semantics of Mumpits' query language is specified by its translation into SQL (see Section 4).

3   Mumpits: Implementation

This section gives a high-level overview of the implementation of Mumpits. The first subsection gives the conceptual view of the managed data while the second subsection briefly provides an architectural overview.

3.1   Mumpits: Conceptual View

Figure 1 provides the conceptual view of Mumpits. It describes the different kinds of data kept persistent in Mumpits as well as the index supported access possibilities to the data.

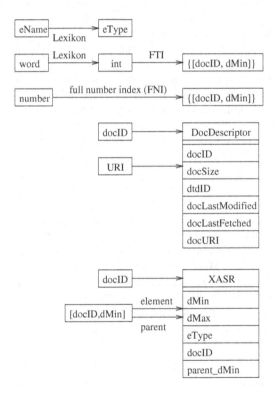

Fig. 1. Mumpits: Conceptual View.

The DocumentDescriptor contains base data of every document including a document identifier, the document size, the identifier of the DTD the document adheres to (if existent), the date of the document's last modification as well as the last date it was fetched, and the URI of the document. There exist indexes on *docID* and *URI*.

A lexicon maps each word to a number which then is the key into the full-text index containing occurrences of the word in indexed documents. Additionally, we number the nodes of a document with a depth-first traversal. Every node gets two numbers: the entry number when the node is first visited (*dMin*) and an exit number when the node is left by the depth-first traversal (*dMax*) [7]. Any of these two numbers uniquely identifies a node in a document. A full-number index keeps track of all numbers contained in a document. It is essentially the same as the VIndex in Lore [14].

The XASR is the main index to support queries over the structure of a document. It contains the XML element type of the document and the *dMin* number of the parent node (*parent_dMin*) for every node of a document (identified by *docID* and *dMin*). This number is NULL for root nodes. Additionally, it contains the *dMax* number of the node. This way, we can check whether a node is a descendant of another node. For two nodes x and y of the same document, y is a descendant of x if and only if $x.dMin < y.dMin$ and $x.dMax > y.dMax$ [7]. For more information concerning query processing see Section 4. Let us illustrate the XASR by an example. Figure 2(a) shows a simplified document tree of a document that adheres to the BIOpolymer Markup Language (BIOML) DTD. A DTD that was designed for the annotation of biopolymer sequence information [1]. The nodes that represent XML elements or attributes are labeled with the XML element or XML attribute name and additionally with the *dmin* and *dmax* value that result from a depth-first traversal. Figure 2(b) shows the according XASR.

3.2   Mumpits: Architecture

Figure 3 gives an overview of Mumpits' architecture. At the bottom, a relational database management system (RDBMS) stores the data represented in Fig. 1. The left path shows the modules involved in finding and indexing documents from the Web. The Trawler[4] crawls the Web and fishes for XML documents. All documents found are inspected by the Extractor which extracts the data. The Loader fills the according relations. The right path shows the query processing. The Web-Interface accepts queries and represents results. The Transformer translates Mumpits queries into SQL queries which are evaluated by the Evaluator.

3.3   Mumpits: Relational Schema

The relational schema Mumpits uses to represent the data of Fig. 1 consists of the following relations:

---

[4] Encyclopedia Britannica: fishing vessel that uses a trawl, a conical net that snares fish by being dragged through the water or along the bottom.

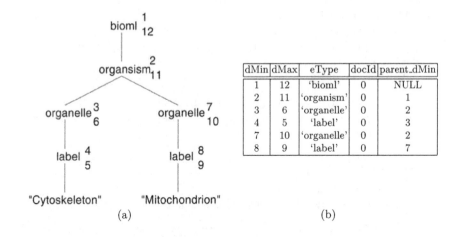

dMin	dMax	eType	docId	parent_dMin
1	12	'bioml'	0	NULL
2	11	'organism'	0	1
3	6	'organelle'	0	2
4	5	'label'	0	3
7	10	'organelle'	0	2
8	9	'label'	0	7

(a)   (b)

Fig. 2. (a) Example document tree. The nodes that represent XML elements or XML attributes are labeled with the element or attribute name and with the *dmin* and *dmax* value that result from a depth-first traversal. (b) The XASR of the document tree. It stores a tuple for each XML element or XML attribute representing node.

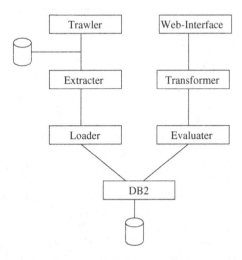

Fig. 3. Mumpits: Architecture.

- LexikonName2Number(<u>eName</u>,eType)
- LexikonWord2Number(<u>word</u>,wordNo)
- FTI(number, docID, dMin)
- FNI(number, docID, dMin)
- DocDesc(<u>docID</u>, docSize, dtdID, docLastModified, docLastFetched, docURI)
- XASR(<u>docID</u>, <u>dMin</u>, dMax, eType, parent_dMin)

where the key attributes are underlined. In order to improve the query performance we define an index for each relation on its key attributes. Additionally there is an index on

- DocDesc with key (docURI),
- FTI with key (number),
- FNI with key (number) and
- XASR with key (docID, parent_dMin),

Note that the treatment of the full-text index and the full-number index within DB2 is suboptimal. But we felt that for rapid prototyping it was very convenient to implement it this way. Further, we hope that we can gain sufficient experience with our Mumpits prototype so that later a more sophisticated version can be designed.

4   SQL Query Generation

Mumpits queries are directly translated into SQL queries. Since the result of a Mumpits query is always a set of URIs, the outer SQL block always reads like this:

```
SELECT DISTINCT dd.uri
FROM            DocDesc DD
WHERE           ...
```

After pushing the NOTs down just in front of base predicates, every base predicate is translated into an EXISTS or NOT EXISTS subquery. These translated base predicates are connected the same way via AND and OR as in the original Mumpits query. We now concentrate on the translation of base predicates into subqueries. More specifically, we discuss subqueries of the form exists(<path>) and <path> <op> <const>.

A path is always translated into the equivalent of a sequence of joins of XASRs. For every node in the path, there is one occurrence of the XASR in the FROM clause of the subquery. If the node specifier is an element (or attribute) name, we generate a join predicate between the XASR and the lexicon on the eType attribute of the XASR and the number attribute of the lexicon. We further add a selection on the word attribute of the lexicon. If the node specifier is '*', no predicate is generated in this step. Let x_i and x_{i+1} be two nodes in the path. Depending on the path connector ('/' or '//'), the join predicate is

- x_i.docID = x_{i+1}.docID AND x_1.dMin = x_{i+1}.parentID, or
- x_i.docID = x_{i+1}.docID AND x_i.dMin < x_{i+1}.dMin AND x_i.dMax > x_{i+1}.dMax.

Last but not least, we add the correlation predicate to connect the subquery to the outer block. If the query contains a comparison with a constant, either the full-text index and the lexicon are joined with the XASR of the final element or the full-number index is joined with the XASR of the final element. We further introduce some optimizations for simple base predicates like testing the occurrence of a word.

Consider the very simple query //person/name = ''Anton'' This query translates into

```
SELECT DISTINCT dd.uri
FROM            DocDesc dd
WHERE           EXISTS( SELECT *
                FROM    XASR p, XASR n,
                        Lexicon lp, Lexicon ln
                        FTI fti, Lexicon lf
                WHERE   p.docID = n.docID
                AND     p.dMin = n.parent_dMin
                AND     p.eTYPE = lp.number
                AND     lp.word = "person"
                AND     n.eTYPE = ln.number
                AND     ln.word = "name"
                AND     fti.docID = p.docID
                AND     fti.dMin = n.dMin
                AND     fti.number = lf.number
                AND     lf.word = "Anton"
                AND     dd.docID = p.docID)
```

As a second example we use the query //car//price < 1000 which involves a different path connector and the full-number index. This query translates into

```
SELECT DISTINCT dd.uri
FROM            DocDesc dd
WHERE           EXISTS( SELECT *
                FROM    XASR c, XASR p,
                        Lexicon lc, Lexicon lp
                        FNI fni
                WHERE   c.docID = p.docID
                AND     c.dMin < p.dMin
                AND     c.dMax > p.dMax
                AND     p.eTYPE = lp.number
                AND     lc.word = "car"
                AND     p.eTYPE = lp.number
                AND     lp.word = "price"
```

AND	fni.docID = c.docID
AND	fni.dMin = p.dMin
AND	fni.number < 1000
AND	dd.docID = c.docID)

5   Evaluation

To get some preliminary Mumpits performance results we ran a loading and a querying experiment. For the underlying RDBMS we choose IBM DB2 Universal Database V6.1. We performed the experiments on a Sun Enterprise 450 workgroup server with Solaris 2.5.6 and 512 Mb main memory. For the loading experiment we loaded several XML documents adhering to the BIOML DTD. The documents were transformed by a loader written in C++ that filled the relational tables via the DB2 call level interface. Table 2 summarizes the results of the loading process.

Table 2. Mumpits load performance.

Number of XML Documents	XML Data Size	Relational Database Size	Running Time
4772	50.1 MB	5.8 MB	19,402 s

Since Mumpits stores only the first 30 bytes of each text value and the XML files contain textual representations of long peptide sequences, the size of the relational database exhibits a significant reduction in comparison to the size of the loaded XML data. Unfortunately the loader has a low loading performance. We hope that the bottleneck is not the DB2 call level interface and that we are able to increase the loading performance by improving the Loader implementation.

Because the performance of Mumpits queries depends on the performance of the evaluation of path expression we measured the running times of the following test queries.

Query 1 ``mitochondrion''
Query 2 //label = ``mitochondrion''
Query 3 //organelle/label = ``mitochondrion''
Query 4 //organelle//label = ``mitochondrion''
Query 5 //organism/organelle/label = ``mitochondrion''
Query 6 //organism/organelle//label = ``mitochondrion''
Query 7 //organism//organelle//label = ``mitochondrion''

The running times of the test queries are shown in Table 3.

The query benchmarks results illustrate how the evaluation of a Mumpits path expression depends on the number of path connectors and on their type. The running times increase with the number of path connectors. Especially the occurance of a '//' path connector gives a burst to them.

Table 3. Mumpits query performance.

Query	Number of Result Tuples	Running Time
1	76	0.047 s
2	75	0.024 s
3	75	0.029 s
4	75	1.166 s
5	18	0.059 s
6	18	1.206 s
7	75	2.040 s

In order to improve the evaluation of path expressions with a '//' path connector we introduced an additional index on the XASR with the key (docID, dMin, dMax). The effect of the additional index is shown in table 4. The running times of the test queries containing a '//' path connector exhibit a significant reduction in comparison to those listed in Table 3.

Table 4. Improved Mumpits query performance.

Query	Number of Result Tuples	Running Time
1	76	0.046 s
2	75	0.024 s
3	75	0.028 s
4	75	0.349 s
5	18	0.059 s
6	18	0.359 s
7	75	0.420 s

6   Conclusion

In this paper we described Mumpits, which is a search engine for XML data found on the Web. In order to get a prototype without tremendous implementation efforts, we built Mumpits on top of a commercial RDBMS. The implementation is based on the following design decisions:

1. Mumpits does not replicate data found on the Web.
2. Mumpits relies on a full-text index, a full-number index, and XASRs.
3. Mumpits allows to query the structure of documents.

The XASR was introduced to evaluate queries over document structure efficiently without replicating XML documents. To express Mumpits queries we proposed a simple query language using base predicates with existential semantics. The Mumpits schema allows to translate these queries easily into SQL. As a result most of the query evaluation work can be done by the underlying RDBMS.

Benchmark results showed us that albeit its prototypical character, Mumpits exhibits a good query performance. However, the Mumpits loading performance needs to be improved.

References

1. The BIOpolymer Markup Language (BIOML) Home Page. http://www.bioml.com/BIOML/index.html.
2. S. Abiteboul, P. Buneman, and D. Suciu. *Data on the Web: From Relations to Semistructured Data and XML*. Morgan Kaufman, 1999.
3. E. Bertino and W. Kim. Indexing techniques for queries on nested objects. *IEEE Trans. on Knowledge and Data Engineering*, 1(2):196–214, Jun 1989.
4. T. Bray, J. Paoli, and C. M. Sperberg-McQueen. Extensible markup language (xml) 1.0. Technical report, World Wide Web Consortium, 1998. W3C Recommendation 10-Feb-98.
5. J. Chen, D. DeWitt, F. Tian, and Y. Wang. NiagaraCQ: A scalable continuous query system for internet databases. In *Proc. of the ACM SIGMOD Conf. on Management of Data*, 2000. to appear.
6. J. Clark and S. DeRose. XML path language (XPath) version 1.0. Technical report, World Wide Web Consortium, 1999. W3C Recommendation 16 Nov. 1999.
7. T. Cormen, C. Leiserson, and R. Rivest. *Introduction to Algorithms*. MIT Press, 1989.
8. A. Deutsch, M. Fernandez, and D. Suciu. Storing semistructured data with STORED. In *Proc. of the ACM SIGMOD Conf. on Management of Data*, 1999.
9. D. Florescu and D. Kossmann. Storing and querying XML data using and RDBMS. *IEEE Data Engineering Bulletin*, 22(3):27–34, 1999.
10. R. Goldman, J. McHugh, and J. Widom. From semistructured data to XML: Migrating the Lore data model and query language. In *ACM SIGMOD Workshop on the Web and Databases (WebDB)*, 1999.
11. A. Kemper and G. Moerkotte. Access support in object bases. In *Proc. of the ACM SIGMOD Conf. on Management of Data*, pages 364–374, 1990.
12. A. Kemper and G. Moerkotte. Advanced query processing in object bases using access support relations. In *Proc. Int. Conf. on Very Large Data Bases (VLDB)*, pages 294–305, 1990.
13. D. Maier and J. Stein. Indexing in an object-oriented DBMS. In *Proc. IEEE Intl. Workshop on Object-Oriented Database Systems, Asilomar, Pacific Grove, CA*, pages 171–182. IEEE Computer Society Press, 1986.
14. J. McHugh, S. Abiteboul, R. Goldman, D. Quass, and J. Widom. Lore: A database management system for semistructured data. *ACM SIGMOD Record*, 26(3):54–66, 1997.
15. J. Shanmugasundaram, H. Gang, K. Tufte, C. Yhang, D. J. DeWitt, and J. Naughton. Relational databases for querying xml documents: Limitations and opportunities. In *Proc. Int. Conf. on Very Large Data Bases (VLDB)*, pages 302–314, 1999.
16. B. Shidlowsky and E. Bertino. A graph-theoretic approach to indexing in object-oriented databases. In *Proc. IEEE Conference on Data Engineering*, pages 230–237, 1996.
17. R. Van Zwol, P. Apers, and A. Wilschut. Modeling and querying semistructured data with MOA. In *ICDT'99 Workshop on Query Processing for semistructured data*, 1999.

Efficient Relational Storage and Retrieval of XML Documents

Albrecht Schmidt, Martin Kersten, Menzo Windhouwer, and Florian Waas

Centre for Mathematics and Computer Science (CWI)
Kruislaan 413, 1098 SJ Amsterdam
The Netherlands
firstname.lastname@cwi.nl

Abstract. In this paper, we present a data and an execution model that allow for efficient storage and retrieval of XML documents in a relational database. The data model is strictly based on the notion of binary associations: by decomposing XML documents into small, flexible and semantically homogeneous units we are able to exploit the performance potential of vertical fragmentation. Moreover, our approach provides clear and intuitive semantics, which facilitates the definition of a declarative query algebra. Our experimental results with large collections of XML documents demonstrate the effectiveness of the techniques proposed.

1 Introduction

XML increasingly assumes the role of the *de facto* standard data exchange format in Web database environments. Modeling issues that arise from the discrepancy between semi-structured data on the one hand side and fully structured database schemas on the other have received special attention. Database researchers provided valuable insights to bring these two areas together. The solutions proposed include not only XML domain specific developments but also techniques that build on object-oriented and relational database technology (*e.g.*, see [1,6,7,9, 10,11,14,15,16]).

To make XML the language of Web databases, performance issues are the upcoming challenge that has to be met. Database support for XML processing can only find the widespread use that researchers anticipate if storage and retrieval of documents satisfy the demands of impatient surfers.

In this paper, we are concerned with providing effective tools for the management of XML documents. This includes tight interaction between established standards on the declarative conceptual level like the DOM [18] and efficient physical query execution. Starting from the syntax tree representation of a document, we propose a data model that is based on a complete binary fragmentation of the document tree. This way, all relevant associations within a document like parent-child relationships, attributes, or topological orders can be intuitively described, stored and queried. In contrast to general graph databases like Lore [1], we draw benefit from the basic tree structure of the document and incorporate

D. Suciu and G. Vossen (Eds.): WebDB 2000, LNCS 1997, pp. 137–150, 2001.

```
<bibliography>
  <article key="BB88">
    <author>Ben Bit</author>
    <title>How To Hack</title>
  </article>
  <article key="BK99">
    <editor>Ed Itor</editor>
    <author>Bob Byte</author>
    <author>Ken Key</author>
    <title>Hacking & RSI</title>
  </article>
</bibliography>
```

Fig. 1. XML document and corresponding syntax tree

information about the association's position within the syntax tree relative to the root into our data model. References such as IDREFs that escape the tree structure are taken care of by views on the tree structure. Associations that provide semantically related information are stored together in the binary relations of the database repository. Along with the decomposition schema we also present a method to translate queries formulated on paths of the syntax tree into expressions of an algebra for vertically fragmented schemas [3].

Our approach is distinguished by two features. Firstly, the decomposition method is independent of the presence of DTDs, but rather explores the structure of the document at parse time. Information on the schema is automatically available after the decomposition. Secondly, it reduces the volume of data irrelevant to a query that has to be processed during querying. Storing associations according to their context in the syntax tree provides tables that contain semantically closely related information. As a result, data relevant for a given query can be accessed directly in form of a separate table avoiding large and expensive scans over irrelevant data making associative queries with path expressions rather inexpensive. Especially the need for hierarchical projections and semijoins vanishes completely.

Reservations exist that a high degree of fragmentation might incur increased efforts to reconstruct the original document, or parts of it. However, as our quantitative assessment shows, the number of additional joins is fully made up for as they involve only little data volume. Our approach displays distinctly superior performance compared to previous work.

2   Data Model and Algebra

XML documents are commonly represented as syntax trees. With **string** and **int** denoting sets of character strings and integers and **oid** being the set of unique object identifiers, we can define an XML document formally (*e.g.*, see [19]):

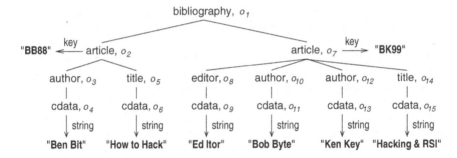

Fig. 2. Syntax tree of example document

Definition 1. *An XML document $d = (V, E, r, label_E, label_A, rank)$ is a rooted tree with nodes V and edges $E \subseteq V \times V$ and a distinguished node $r \in V$, the root node. The function $label_E : V \to$ **string** assigns labels to nodes, i.e., elements; $label_A : V \to$ **string** $\to$ **string** assigns pairs of strings, attributes and their values, to nodes. Character Data (CDATA) are modeled as a special 'string' attribute of cdata nodes, $rank : V \to$ **int** establishes a ranking between sibling nodes. For elements without any attributes $label_A$ maps to the empty set.*

Figure 1 shows an XML document which describes a fragment of a bibliography; the corresponding syntax tree is displayed in Figure 2. The representation is largely self-explanatory, o_i denote object identifiers (OIDs) whose assignment is arbitrary, e.g., depth-first traversal order. We apply the common simplification not to differentiate between PCDATA and CDATA nor do we take rich datatypes into account. Note that OID assigned nodes represent only elements and not attributes.

2.1   Preliminaries

Before we discuss techniques how to store a syntax graph as a database instance, we introduce the concepts of *associations* and *path summaries*. They identify spots of interest and constitute the basis for the Monet XML Model.[1]

Definition 2. *A pair $(o, \cdot) \in$ **oid** $\times$ (**oid** $\cup$ **int** $\cup$ **string**) is called an* association.

The different types of associations describe different parts of the tree: associations of type **oid** $\times$ **oid** represent edges, i.e., parent-child relationships. Attribute values (including character data, represented by vertices with label *'string'*, that start from *'cdata'* labelled nodes) are modeled by associations of type **oid** $\times$ **string**, while associations of type **oid** $\times$ **int** are used to preserve the topology of a document.

---

[1] We chose the name Monet XML Model because the home-grown database engine Monet [3] serves as implementation platform.

Definition 3. *For a node o in the syntax tree, we denote the sequence of labels along the path (vertex and edge labels) from the root to o with* path(o).

As an example, consider the node with OID o_3 in Figure 2; its path is *bibliography* $\xrightarrow{e}$ *article* $\xrightarrow{e}$ *author*. The corresponding character data string "Ben Bit" has path *bibliography* $\xrightarrow{e}$ *article* $\xrightarrow{e}$ *author* $\xrightarrow{e}$ *cdata* $\xrightarrow{a}$ *string*, where $\xrightarrow{e}$ denotes edges to elements and $\xrightarrow{a}$ to attributes.

Paths describe the schematic position of the element in the graph relative to the root node, and we use *path(o)* to denote the *type* of the association $(\cdot, o)$. The set of all paths in a document is called the document's *path summary*.

2.2   The Monet XML Model

As we pointed out at the beginning, the question central to querying XML documents is how to store the syntax tree as a database instance that provides efficient retrieval capabilities. Given Definition 1 the tree could be stored using a single database table for the parent-child relations (similar to [17]), another one for the elements labels and so on. Though space effective, such a decomposition makes querying expensive by enforcing scans over large amounts of data irrelevant to a query instance, since structurally unrelated data are possibly stored in the same tables. Even if the query consist of a few joins only, large data volumes may have to be processed (see [9] for a discussion of storage schemes of this kind).

We pursue a rather different approach using the structures defined above, *i.e.*, storing all associations of the same type in the same *binary relation*. A relation that contains the tuple $(\cdot, o)$ is named *path(o)*, and, conversely, a tuple is stored in exactly one relation. This idea results in the following definition:

Definition 4. *Given an XML document d, the* Monet transform *is a quadruple* $M_t(d) = (r, \mathbf{R}, \mathbf{A}, \mathbf{T})$ *where*

R *is the set of binary relations that contain* all *associations between nodes;*

A *is the set of binary relations that contain* all *associations between nodes and their attribute values, including character data;*

T *is the set of binary relations that contain* all *pairs of nodes and their rank;*

r remains the root of the document.

Encoding the *path* to a component into the name of the relation often achieves a significantly higher degree of semantic fragmentation than implied by plain data guides [10]. In other words, we use *path* to group semantically related associations into the same relation. As a direct consequence of the decomposition schema, we do not need to introduce novel features on the storage level to cope with irregularities induced by the semi-structured nature of XML, which are typically taken care of by NULLs or overflow tables [7]. Moreover, it should be noted, that the complete decomposition is linear in the size of the document with respect to running time. Concerning memory requirements, it is in $O(h)$, h being

$$bibliography \xrightarrow{e} article = \{\langle o_1, o_2 \rangle, \langle o_1, o_7 \rangle\},$$

$$bibliography \xrightarrow{e} article \xrightarrow{e} author = \{\langle o_2, o_3 \rangle, \langle o_7, o_{10} \rangle, \langle o_7, o_{12} \rangle\},$$

$$bibliography \xrightarrow{e} article \xrightarrow{e} author \xrightarrow{e} cdata = \{\langle o_3, o_4 \rangle, \langle o_{10}, o_{11} \rangle, \langle o_{12}, o_{13} \rangle\},$$

$$bibliography \xrightarrow{e} article \xrightarrow{e} author \xrightarrow{e} cdata \xrightarrow{a} string = \{\langle o_4, \text{``Ben Bit''} \rangle, \langle o_{11}, \text{``Bob Byte''} \rangle, \langle o_{13}, \text{``Ken Key''} \rangle\},$$

$$bibliography \xrightarrow{e} article \xrightarrow{e} title = \{\langle o_2, o_5 \rangle, \langle o_7, o_{14} \rangle\},$$

$$bibliography \xrightarrow{e} article \xrightarrow{e} title \xrightarrow{e} cdata = \{\langle o_5, o_6 \rangle, \langle o_{14}, o_{15} \rangle\},$$

$$bibliography \xrightarrow{e} article \xrightarrow{e} title \xrightarrow{e} cdata \xrightarrow{a} string = \{\langle o_6, \text{``How to Hack''} \rangle, \langle o_{15}, \text{``Hacking \& RSI''} \rangle\},$$

$$bibliography \xrightarrow{e} article \xrightarrow{e} editor = \{\langle o_7, o_8 \rangle\},$$

$$bibliography \xrightarrow{e} article \xrightarrow{e} editor \xrightarrow{e} cdata = \{\langle o_8, o_9 \rangle\},$$

$$bibliography \xrightarrow{e} article \xrightarrow{e} editor \xrightarrow{e} cdata \xrightarrow{a} string = \{\langle o_9, \text{``Ed Itor''} \rangle\},$$

$$bibliography \xrightarrow{e} article \xrightarrow{a} key = \{\langle o_2, \text{``BB88''} \rangle, \langle o_7, \text{``BK99''} \rangle\}\}$$

Table 1. Monet transform M_t of the example document

the height of the syntax tree, in addition to the space the binary relations in the database engine occupy, *i.e.*, it is not necessary to materialize the complete syntax tree.

Proposition 1. *The above mapping is lossless, i.e., for an XML document d there exists an inverse mapping M_t^{-1} such that d and $M_t^{-1}(M_t(d))$ are isomorphic.*

A sketch of the proof of Proposition 1 is given in the appendix. Table 1 shows the Monet transform of the example document.

In addition to the relational perspective we adhered to so far, the Monet transform also enables an object-oriented perspective, *i.e.*, object being interpreted as node in the syntax tree, which is often more intuitive to the user and is adopted by standards like the DOM [18]. Particularly in querying, approaches that bear strong similarities with object-oriented techniques have emerged. Given the Monet transform, we have the necessary tools at hand to reconcile the relational perspective with the object-oriented view.

It is natural to re-assemble an object with OID o from those associations whose first component is o: *e.g.*, the node with OID o_2 is easily converted into $object(o_2) = \{key\langle o_2, \text{``BB88''}\rangle, author\langle o_2, o_3\rangle, title\langle o_2, o_5\rangle\}$, an instance of a suitably defined class *article* with members *key*, *author* and *title*. However, XML is regarded as an incarnation of the semi-structured paradigm. One consequence of this is that we cannot expect all instances of one type to share the same structure. In the example, the second publication does have an *editor* element whereas the first does not. We therefore distinguish between two kinds of associations: (strong) associations and weak associations. Strong associations constitute the structured part of XML – they are present in every instance of a type; weak associations account for the *semi*-structured part: they may or may not appear in a given instance. Objects o_2 and o_7 reflect this: o_7 has a *editor* member whereas o_2 has not. Therefore, we define the following:

Definition 5. *An object corresponding to a node o in the syntax tree is a set of strong and weak associations $\{A_1\langle o, o_1\rangle, A_2\langle o, o_2\rangle, \dots\}$.*

The next question we address directly arises from the modeling of objects: How can we re-formulate queries from an object-oriented setting to queries in relational Monet XML?

2.3   Execution Model and Algebra

The unified view provided by the Monet XML model extends directly to querying. For the relational layer, a multitude of operators implementing the relational algebra, including specialties intrinsic to vertical fragmented schemas, have been proposed. Hence, we omit a discussion of technical issues concerning bare, relational query processing in the context of vertical fragmentation and refer the interested reader to [3] for a comprehensive overview.

More interesting is the actual translation of an OQL-like query to match the facilities of the underlying query execution engine. We only outline the translation by an example query. The process bears strong resemblance to mapping techniques developed to implement object-oriented query interfaces on relational databases; thus, we can resort to the wealth of techniques developed in that field. See [4] for a comparative analysis of different query languages for XML.

Consider the following query which selects those of Ben Bit's publications whose titles contain the word 'Hack'; the semantics of the statements are similar to [2]:

select p

from $bibliography \xrightarrow{e} article \ p,$

$\qquad p \xrightarrow{e} author \xrightarrow{e} cdata \ \ a,$

$\qquad p \xrightarrow{e} title \xrightarrow{e} cdata \ \ t$

where $a =$ "Ben Bit" **and** t **like** "Hack";

The query consists of two blocks, a *specification* of the elements involved, which translates to computing the proper binary relations, and *constraints* that define the actual processing. For resolving path expressions, we need to distinguish two types of variables in the **from** clause: variables that specify sets, p in the example, and variables, which specify associations, a and t.

We collapse each path expression that is not available in the database by joining the binary relations along the path specification. This establishes an association between the first and last element of the path. Finally, we take the intersection of the specified elements. Matching the variables against the running example, the **from** clause specifies the following elements:

$$p = \{o_2, o_7\},$$
$$assoc(p \rightarrow a) = \{(o_2, \text{"Ben Bit"}), (o_7, \text{"Bob Byte"}),$$
$$(o_7, \text{"Ken Key"})\},$$
$$assoc(p \rightarrow t) = \{(o_2, \text{"How To Hack"}),$$
$$(o_7, \text{"Hacking \& RSI"})\}$$

Queries containing regular expressions over paths directly benefit from the availability of the path summary. Standard methods for the evaluation of regular expressions can be applied to the textual representation of the paths and enable the immediate selection of the candidate relations.

The evaluation of the **where** clause is not of particular interest in this context. Though processing of binary tables differs from the conventional relational model in several aspects, these differences have no direct impact on our method.

2.4 Optimization with DTDs

As XML documents are not required to conform to DTDs we do not assume that they do. However, in this section we show that our data model is flexible enough to take advantage of additional domain-knowledge in the form of DTDs or XML Schema specifications. Again, the first-class paths in Monet XML are

```
<!ELEMENT bibliography (article*)>
<!ELEMENT article (editor?, author*, title)>
<!ATTLIST article key CDATA #REQUIRED>
<!ELEMENT editor (#PCDATA)>
<!ELEMENT author (#PCDATA)>
<!ELEMENT title (#PCDATA)>
```

Fig. 3. DTD for example document

the focal feature necessary for a seamless integration. We present an approach that is similar in spirit to [14].

For motivation, consider again the example document in Figure 1 and 2 suppose we are given the DTD in Figure 3. The DTD says that each publication may only have a single title element. Given this rule, we can collapse each path from the publication nodes to the character data of title elements without losing information; thus,

$$\{ \ bibliography \xrightarrow{e} article \xrightarrow{e} title\{\langle o_2, o_5\rangle, \langle o_7, o_{14}\rangle\},$$
$$bibliography \xrightarrow{e} article \xrightarrow{e} title \xrightarrow{e} cdata\{\langle o_5, o_6\rangle, \langle o_{14}, o_{15}\rangle\},$$
$$bibliography \xrightarrow{e} article \xrightarrow{e} title \xrightarrow{e} cdata \xrightarrow{a} string\{\langle o_6, \text{``How to Hack''}\rangle,$$
$$\langle o_{15}, \text{``Hacking \& RSI''}\rangle\} \ \}$$

may be reduced to

$$\{ \ bibliography \xrightarrow{e} article \xrightarrow{e} title\{\langle o_2, o_5\rangle, \langle o_7, o_{14}\rangle\},$$
$$bibliography \xrightarrow{e} article \xrightarrow{e} title \xrightarrow{a} string\{\langle o_5, \text{``How to Hack''}\rangle,$$
$$\langle o_{14}, \text{``Hacking \& RSI''}\rangle \ \}\}.$$

That is we take advantage of DTDs by identifying and subsequently collapsing 1 : 1 relationships to reduce storage requirements and the number of joins in query processing. The result of hierarchically joining the associations takes the place of the original data. Some of these 1 : 1 relationships can be inferred from a DTD, others require domain-specific knowledge: our common sense knowledge of bibliographies tells us that in bibliographies the only elements whose order is important are author and editor elements. Thus, we may, on the one hand, drop all rank relations that do not belong to author or editor tags and furthermore reduce the before mentioned path to:

$$\{ \ bibliography \xrightarrow{e} article \xrightarrow{a} title\{\langle o_2, \text{``How to Hack''}\rangle, \langle o_7, \text{``Hacking \& RSI''}\rangle \ \}.$$

Note that we apply this technique not to the DTDs themselves to derive a storage schema but rather simplify the paths present in the actual document instance.

Table 2. Sizes of document collections in XML and Monet XML format

Documents	size in XML	size in Monet XML	#Tables	Loading
ACM Anthology	46.6 MB	44.2 MB	187	30.4 s
Shakespeare's Plays	7.9 MB	8.2 MB	95	4.5 s
Webster's Dictionary	56.1 MB	95.6 MB	2587	56.6 s

Table 3. Comparison of response times for query set of SYU

		Q1	Q2	Q3	Q4	Q5	Q6	Q7	Q8	Q9	Q10
1A	Monet XML	1.2	5.6	6.8	8.0	4.4	4.9	5.0	5.0	8.8	12.7
2A	SYU / Postgres	150	180	160	180	190	340	350	370	1300	1040
1B	Monet XML	–	4.4	5.6	6.8	3.2	3.7	3.8	3.8	7.6	11.5
2B	SYU / Postgres	–	30	10	30	40	190	200	220	1150	890

3   Quantitative Assessment

We assess the techniques proposed with respect to size of the resulting database, as well as querying and browsing the database. As application domains we chose readily available XML document collections: the ACM SIGMOD Anthology [12], Webster's Dictionary [8], and Shakespeare's Plays [5].

We implemented Monet XML within the Monet database server [3]. The measurements were carried out on an Silicon Graphics 1400 Server with 1 GB main memory, running at 550 MHz. For comparisons with related work, we used a Sun UltraSPARC-IIi with 360 MHz clock speed and 256 MB main memory.

Database Size. The resulting sizes of the decomposition scheme are a critical issue. Theoretically, the size of the path summary can be linear in the size of the document as the worst case – if the document is completely *un*-structured. However, in practical applications, we typically find large structured portions within each document so that the size of the path summary and therefore the number of relations remains small. Table 2 shows the database sizes for our examples in comparison with the size of the original XML code. The third column contains the number of tables, *i.e.*, the size of the path summary. The last column shows the complete time needed to parse, decompose and store the documents.

It leaps out that the Monet XML version of the ACM Anthology is of smaller size than the original document. This reduction is due to the 'automatic' compression inherent in the Monet transform (tag names are stored only once as meta information) and the removal of redundantly occurring character data. For example there are only few different publishers compared to the number of entries in general. In the decomposition, full entries of these fields can be replaced with references; this is done automatically by the DBMS. We can expect similar effects to occur with other decomposition schemas, like object-oriented mappings.

Scaling. In order to inspect the scaling behavior of our technique we varied the size of the underlying document. In doing so, we took care to maintain the ratio of different elements and attributes of the original document. We scaled

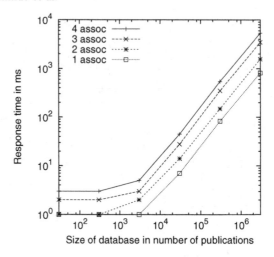

Fig. 4. Scaling of document

the ACM Anthology from 30 to $3 \cdot 10^6$ publications which corresponds to XML source sizes between 10KB and 1GB. The database sizes and the insertion times scaled linear in the size of the XML document.

Querying. To test for query performance under scaling we ran 4 queries consisting of path expressions of length 1 through 4 for various sizes of the Anthology. As Figure 4 shows, the response times for each query, given as a function of the size of the document, is linear in the size of the database. Only for small sizes of the database, the response time is dominated by the overhead of the database system. Notice, both axes are logarithmic.

Only few of the performance analyses published so far offer the possibility to reproduce and compare results, which makes meaningful comparison difficult at this time. The results we use to compare Monet XML against were reported in [15] who implemented their algorithms as a front-end to Postgres. In [15], the authors propose a set of 10 queries using Shakespeare's plays [5] as an application domain. We refer to their approach as SYU in the following. In Table 3 we contrasted response times of Monet XML with SYU obtained from experiments on the abovementioned Sun Workstation.

The figures display a substantial difference in response time showing that Monet XML outruns the competitor by up to two orders of magnitude (rows 1A,2A). The times for SYU include a translation of XQL to SQL that is handled outside the database server. To allow for this difference, we additionally computed the response times relative to query 1 for both systems separately, assuming that preprocessing costs have a constant contribution. These figures exhibit actual query processing time only (rows 1B,2B). Monet XML shows an increase of processing time by less than 12 ms whereas SYU is up to 1150 ms slower than its fastest response time.

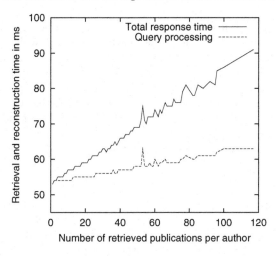

Fig. 5. Response time vs. result size

An analysis of the figures exhibits the advantages of the Monet model. While SYU store basically all data on a single heap and have to scan these data repeatedly, the Monet transform yields substantially smaller data volumes. In some extreme cases, the query result is directly available in Monet XML without any processing and only needs to be traversed and output. Another noticeable difference concerns the complexity of queries: the straight-forward semantics of the Monet XML model result in relatively simple queries; conversely, the compiled SQL statements that SYU present are quite complex.

The comparison with Lore [13] exhibited essentially the same trends on small document instances. However, we were not able to bulkload and query larger documents like the ACM anthology as Lore requested more than the available 1 GB main memory. In contrast, using Monet XML we engineered a system functionally equivalent to the online DBLP server [12] that operated in less than 130 MB.

Browsing a database. Our last experiments aim at assessing the systems capabilities with respect to browsing. As an example consider a typical query as it is run on the Anthology server several thousand times a day: Retrieve all conference publications for a given author. Clearly, the size of the output may vary drastically and it is of particular interest for a browsing session that response times are kept low independent of the size of the answer.

Figure 5 shows both the total response time including textual rendering and response time of the repository. As expected, the time for rendering the output increases significantly yet linear in the result size. However, the response time of the repository increases at significantly lower rate. This is due to the reconstruction of the associations in form of joins rather than chasing individual chains of pointers. Even for authors with a large number of publications the overall response time is well under one tenth of a second, which makes interactive browsing affordable. Also note that the lower line in Figure 5 could also be interpreted as the cost of constructing a view while the upper line additionally includes rendering the view to textual XML.

The results presented demonstrate the performance potential of our approach deploying fully vertical fragmentation. As the low response times show, reducing the data volume involved in single database operations on the expense of additional joins pays very well not only in terms of overall performance but also when scaling is an issue.

4   Conclusions

We presented a data model for efficient processing of XML documents. Our experiences show that it is worth taking the plunge and fully decompose XML documents into binary associations. The experimental results obtained with a prototype implementation based on Monet underline the viability of our approach: the effort to reduce data volume quickly pays off as gains in efficiency. Overall, our approach combines the elegance of clear semantics with a highly efficient execution model by means of a simple and effective mapping between XML documents and a relational schema.

Concerning future work, we will concentrate on exploring possibilities of parallel processing and efficient handling of multi-query workloads as found in typical interactive Web-based information systems. As we have seen with own experiments, there is also the need for a general, standardized methodology that allows conclusive performance analyses and facilitates comparisons of different approaches.

References

1. S. Abiteboul, D. Quass, J. McHugh, J. Widom, and J. L. Wiener. The Lorel Query Language for Semistructured Data. *International Journal on Digital Libraries*, 1(1):68–88, 1997.
2. C. Beeri and Y. Tzaban. SAL: An Algebra for Semistructured Data and XML. In *International Workshop on the Web and Databases*, pages 37–42, Pennsylvania, USA, 1999.
3. P. A. Boncz and M. L. Kersten. MIL Primitives for Querying a Fragmented World. *The VLDB Journal*, 8(2):101–119, 1999.
4. A. Bonifati and S. Ceri. Comparative Analysis of Five XML Query Languages. *ACM SIGMOD Record*, 1(29):68–79, 2000.
5. J. Bosak. Sample XML documents. `shakespeare.1.01.xml.zip`, available at `ftp://sunsite.unc.edu/pub/sun-info/standards/xml/eg/`.
6. P. Buneman, S. B. Davidson, G. G. Hillebrand, and D. Suciu. A Query Language and Optimization Techniques for Unstructured Data. In *Proc. of the ACM SIGMOD Int'l. Conf. on Management of Data*, pages 505–516, Montreal, Canada, 1996.

7. A. Deutsch, M. F. Fernandez, and D. Suciu. Storing Semistructured Data with STORED. In *Proc. of the ACM SIGMOD Int'l. Conf. on Management of Data*, pages 431–442, Philadephia, PA, USA, 1999.
8. M. Dyck. The GNU version of The Collaborative International Dictionary of English, presented in the Extensible Markup Language. Available at http://metalab.unc.edu/webster/.
9. D. Florescu and D. Kossmann. Storing and Querying XML Data Using an RDBMS. *Data Engineering Bulletin*, 22(3), 1999.
10. R. Goldman and J. Widom. Dataguides: Enabling Query Formulation and Optimization in Semistructured Databases. In *Proc. of the Int'l. Conf. on Very Large Data Bases*, pages 436–445, Athens, Greece, 1997.
11. C. Kanne and G. Moerkotte. Efficient Storage of XML Data. In *Proceedings of the 16th International Conference on Data Engineering*, page 198, 2000.
12. M. Ley. DBLP Bibliography. http://www.informatik.uni-trier.de:8000/~ley/db/.
13. J. McHugh, S. Abiteboul, R. Goldman, D. Quass, and J. Widom. Lore: A Database Management System for Semistructured Data. *ACM SIGMOD Record*, 3(26), 1997.
14. J. Shanmugasundaram, K. Tufte, G. He, C. Zhang, D. DeWitt, and J. Naughton. Relational Databases for Querying XML Documents: Limitations and Opportunities. In *Proc. of the Int'l. Conf. on Very Large Data Bases*, pages 302–314, Edinburgh, UK, 1999.
15. T. Shimura, M. Yoshikawa, and S. Uemura. Storage and Retrieval of XML Documents Using Object-Relational Databases. In *Database and Expert Systems Applications*, pages 206–217. Springer, 1999.
16. Software AG. *Tamino – Technical Description*. Available at http://www.softwareag.com/tamino/technical/description.htm.
17. R. van Zwol, P. Apers, and A. Wilschutz. Implementing semi-structured data with MOA. In *Workshop on Query Processing for Semistructured data and Non-Standard Data Formats (in conjunction with ICDT)*, 1999.
18. W3C. Document Object Model (DOM). Available at http://www.w3.org/DOM/.
19. W3C. Extensible Markup Language (XML) 1.0. Available at http://www.w3.org/TR/1998/REC-xml-19980210.

A   Appendix

Proof of Proposition 1.   Definition 4 introduces the Monet transform $M_t(d) = (r, \mathbf{R}, \mathbf{A}, \mathbf{T})$ of a document d. For a document d the sets $\mathbf{R}, \mathbf{A}$ and $\mathbf{T}$ are computed as follows:

for elements:
$$\mathbf{R} = \bigcup_{(o_i, o_j, s) \in \tilde{E}} [path(o_i) \xrightarrow{e} s]\langle o_i, o_j\rangle,$$

for attributes including CDATA:
$$\mathbf{A} = \bigcup_{(o_i, s_1, s_2) \in label_A} [path(o_i) \xrightarrow{a} s_1]\langle o_i, s_2\rangle,$$

for ranking integers:
$$\mathbf{T} = \bigcup_{(o_i, i) \in rank} [path(o_i) \rightarrow rank]\langle o_i, i\rangle),$$

where E and $label_E$ are combined into one set

$$\tilde{E} = \{(o_1, o_2, s) | (o_1, o_2) \in E, s = label_E(o_2)\},$$

$label_A$ is interpreted as a set $\subseteq \mathbf{oid} \times \mathbf{string} \times \mathbf{string}$ as well as $rank \subseteq \mathbf{oid} \times \mathbf{int}$, and $[expr]$ means that the value of $expr$ is a relation name. To see that the mapping given in definition 4 is lossless we give the inverse mapping. Given an instance of the Monet XML model $M_t(d)$ we can reconstruct the original rooted tree $d = (V, E, r, label_E, label_A, rank)$ in the following way ($second\text{-}last(p)$ returns the second-last component of path p).

1. $V = \{o_i | (\exists R \in \mathbf{R})(\exists o_j \in \mathbf{oid}) : R\langle o_i, o_j\rangle\}$,
2. $E = \{(o_i, o_j) | (\exists R \in \mathbf{R}) : R\langle o_i, o_j\rangle\}$,
3. r remains,
4. $label_E = \{(o_i, s) | (\exists R \in \mathbf{R})(\exists o_j \in \mathbf{oid})(\exists s \in \mathbf{string}) : R\langle o_i, o_j\rangle \wedge$
$$second\text{-}last(R) = s\},$$
5. $label_A = \{(o_i, s_1, s_2) | (\exists A \in \mathbf{A}) : A\langle o_i, s_2\rangle \wedge last(A) = s_1\}$,
6. $rank = \{(o, i) | (\exists T \in \mathbf{T}) : T\langle o, i\rangle\}$.

XML and Object-Relational Database Systems
Enhancing Structural Mappings Based on Statistics

Meike Klettke and Holger Meyer

Database Research Group
University of Rostock
Germany
`meike,hme@informatik.uni-rostock.de`

Abstract. XML becomes the standard for the representation of structured and semi-structured data on the Web. Relational and object-relational database systems are a well understood technique for managing and querying such large sets of structured data.

Using an object-relational data model and an XML datatype, we show how a relevant subset of XML documents and their implied structure can be mapped onto database structures.

Besides straight-forward mappings, there are some XML structures that cannot be easily mapped onto database structures. These structures would sometimes result in large database schemas and sparsely populated databases. As a consequence, such XML document fragments should be mapped onto database attributes of type XML and kept as is. The XML datatype implementation should support evaluating path expressions and fulltext operations.

We present an algorithm that finds a type of optimal mapping based on the XML Document Type Definition (DTD) and statistics. The statistics are derived from sample XML document sets and some knowledge about queries on XML document collections.

Keywords: XML, DTD, Mapping, Object-relational Databases, Partitioned Normal Form (PNF)

1 Motivation

At present, many applications on the Web use, or intend to use, XML as an intermediate format for representing large amounts of structured or semi-structured data. XML [15] can be seen as a popular subset of the SGML markup language customized for the Web age. It is better suited for automatic processing and not as complex as SGML. If necessary, there are techniques for transforming SGML to XML [3].

XML documents have a well-formed structure, e.g., they have a properly nested element structure. DTDs are used to describe the structure of several similarly structured XML documents. Documents satisfying such a document type definition are called valid XML documents.

D. Suciu and G. Vossen (Eds.): WebDB 2000, LNCS 1997, pp. 151–170, 2001.

```
<!ELEMENT publications (book | article | conference)*>
<!-- book -->
<!ELEMENT book (front, body, references)>
<!ELEMENT front (title, author+, edition, publisher)>
<!ELEMENT title (#PCDATA)>
<!ELEMENT author (first, second, email?)>
<!ELEMENT first (#PCDATA)>
<!ELEMENT second (#PCDATA)>
<!ELEMENT email (#PCDATA)>
<!ELEMENT edition (#PCDATA)>
<!ELEMENT publisher (#PCDATA)>
<!ELEMENT body (part+ | chapter+)>
<!ELEMENT part (ptitle, chapter+)>
<!ATTLIST part id ID #REQUIRED>
<!ELEMENT ptitle (#PCDATA)>
<!ELEMENT chapter (ctitle, section+)>
<!ATTLIST chapter id ID #REQUIRED>
<!ELEMENT ctitle (#PCDATA)>
<!ELEMENT section (stitle, paragraph+)>
<!ATTLIST section id ID #REQUIRED>
<!ELEMENT stitle (#PCDATA)>
<!ELEMENT paragraph (#PCDATA)>
<!ELEMENT references (publications*)>
<!ATTLIST references reftype (book | article | conferences | wwwaddress)
          "article">
<!-- article -->
<!ELEMENT article (meta, body, references)>
<!ELEMENT meta (author+, title, conference)>
<!-- conference -->
<!ELEMENT conference (conftitle, editor+, city, year)>
<!ELEMENT editor (first, second, email?)>
<!ELEMENT conftitle (#PCDATA)>
<!ELEMENT city (#PCDATA)>
<!ELEMENT year (#PCDATA)>
```

Fig. 1. Book-DTD Example

Alternatively, the structure of an XML document can be extrapolated from the individual document. Using only the implied structures leads to several problems: e.g., discovering schema similarities between several XML documents, finding an optimal common schema, and handling schema evolution are more difficult without a DTD. So, we assume the existence of such a document description in the sequel.

An application field of XML, where many subsequent XML standards are defined, is in the management of multi-media documents in large scale, distributed digital libraries. Even if the management of documents and their describing and supplementing information in a typical digital library results in similar DTDs, the contents and the usage of these document collections could vary. To illustrate this, consider the following examples of popular digital libraries, even if XML is not used:

- DBLP [1], Michael Ley, maintains about 150,000 XML documents resembling BibTeX-style references which describe his bibliographic network of database and logic programming publications, conferences, research groups, projects, and authors.
- Springer LINK-Service[2] offers fulltexts of journal publications, e.g., as articles from the VLDB journal, on a subscription basis.
- Amazon Bookstore[3], a big e-commerce Web site selling CDs, DVDs, and books.

A simplified DTD for the examples above would look like our DTD shown in Figure 1. But the DTD is only one aspect influencing the mapping of XML structures onto databases. Other important aspects are the frequency of element and attribute occurrences in document collections and the most-often queried elements and attributes.

For example, the DBLP system contains documents in which nearly all elements occur with the same frequency. Users mainly ask for author names, or conference, journal, or article titles, and they browse through references, sections of articles, or table of contents of conference proceedings. Since DBLP does not store fulltexts, there are no chapters, sections, paragraphs etc., except for the extracted references.

In contrast, articles from the VLDB journal at Springer contain many sections, paragraphs, and ordinary text, #PCDATA in XML jargon. Nevertheless, querying these articles is based on author names, titles, volumes, or journal numbers.

At Amazon we not only have information on books, but also on movies, DVDs, etc. The search is based on book titles, keywords, "what's related" classifications, author names, or small ISBNs. You can additionally browse through reviews and annotations by other customers or journalists.

These examples illustrate how different the document collections are on an instance level and how wide the range of query profiles is. This article outlines how this kind of information can improve the mapping of XML onto object-relational structures. However, we begin with a seemingly straight forward transformation of XML structures onto object-relational ones.

2   XML and "Hybrid" Databases

In the next two sections, we demonstrate a method for translating XML documents into object-relational databases supporting an XML datatype.

---

[1] http://dblp.uni-trier.de/

[2] http://link.springer.de/

[3] http://www.amazon.com/

First, in Section 3, we describe straight forward mappings of XML documents based on DTDs. The element hierarchy and attributes are represented using object-relational structures. There are some DTD constructs that can be mapped in several ways onto database structures or not mapped at all.

These mappings work well for applications using XML to represent structured data but not for characteristics of semi-structured data. The translation often results in large database schemas and the resulting databases are sparsely populated. Since standard databases do not support content based retrieval, the semi-structured part of the data can not be sufficiently queried.

Second, we add an abstract datatype XML to the object-relational database, and exploit statistics on element and attribute frequencies in XML document collections and queries to improve the design and resolve ambiguities.

In Section 5, we present an algorithm that decides which elements and/or attributes are translated into attributes of an object-relational database and which are combined into attributes of type XML.

The advantage of this two-step approach is that in many applications, formal and informal information belong closely together. For example, in libraries, structured data (e.g., title, author, publisher, year, etc.) exist in addition to the documents. With hybrid databases, regular and irregular information can be represented in one database. We can use database functionality for the most important and often queried terms and use content-based retrieval for the semi-structured parts.

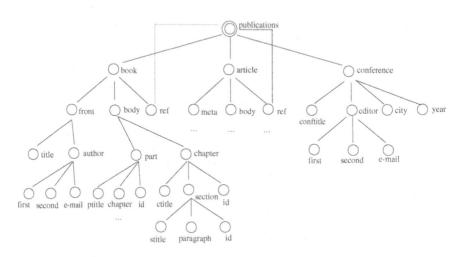

Fig. 2. DTD graph for the sample DTD

3   Object-Relational Mappings

Object-relational databases allow the use of structured or nested attributes in NF^2-relations [11]. These characteristics can be used to map XML documents onto databases in a more natural way. The element hierarchy of a DTD can be directly mapped onto nested attributes of a database. Furthermore, we have the possibility of using set-valued attributes to represent elements with the '*' and '+' quantifiers.

Because there are quite different object-relational models, we use a simple data model that can be mapped onto existing systems, like IBM DB2 UDB or Informix Universal Server. In addition to the set of basic datatypes, such as string, numeric, etc., we assume the following type constructors: set-of, tuple-of, which lead to an NF^2 database model. Moreover, we restrict this model to a subset, the partitioned normal form (PNF). In situations where element ordering matters, a third type constructor, list-of, is used.

Relations in partitioned normal form (PNF), introduced in [11], are an important subclass of nested relations. The atomic or elementary attributes of a relation in PNF are a superkey of the relation. Any non-atomic or composed attribute of the relation has to be in PNF too. A flat key on each nesting level is required for relations to be in PNF.

As it relates to the basic datatypes, we assume the existence of an XML datatype, which adds the following functionality to the object-relational database:

- it stores XML fragments [16],
- it supports the evaluation of path expressions [17], and
- it has fulltext operations on the embedded #PCDATA, as proposed in SQL-MM [8].

There is a prototypical implementation ([10]), that supports fulltext retrieval functionality sensitive to the implicit XML structure.

Table 1 gives a summary of the rules for mapping DTD components onto object-relational structures. A detailed description of these mapping rules can be found in [9].

The following notations are used: ⟨⟩ describes a tuple constructor; {} represents a set constructor or the list constructor, if order matters; xml() , str(), and ref() represent the datatypes of interest; i.e., the XML, a string, and a reference datatype.

A function $\mu(e)$ maps an element to a database schema. This is done by applying the mapping rules to the element and all its sub-elements *depth-first*, e.g. $\mu(e) = \{\mu(e_1)\}$ means that the mapping of e is defined as a set-of of an attribute with a schema resulting from the mapping of the sub-element e_1.

∪ represents a union on the schema level, e.g., $\mu(e) \cup str(a_1)$ adds attribute a_1 of type string to the schema that results from the mapping of e.

There is no easy translation of *alternatives*, but we can identify some basic cases. If all elements are simple elements (of type #PCDATA, EMPTY), the mapping could be done by an attribute with element names as values or with a tuple-of

Table 1. Mapping DTD components to object-relational structures

DTD structure	ORDB structure	Remark
Elements		
e (#PCDATA)	$\mu(e) = \mathtt{xml}(e)$	may be NULL
$e\ (e_1, \ldots, e_n)$	$\mu(e) = \langle \mu(e_1), \ldots, \mu(e_n) \rangle$	
$e\ (e_1?)$	$\mu(e) = \langle \mu(e_1) \rangle$	e_1 may has NULL value
$e\ (e_1+)$	$\mu(e) = \{\mu(e_1)\}$	
$e\ (e_1*)$	$\mu(e) = \{\mu(e_1)\}$	may be NULL
mixed-content type	$\mu(e) = \mathtt{xml}(e)$	store as XML fragment
$e\ (e_1 | \ldots | e_n)$	$\mu(e) = \mathtt{xml}(e)$	alternative as XML type
	or $\mu(e) = \mu(e_1) \cup \ldots \cup \mu(e_n)$	may contain lots of NULL
	or *split into separate relations*	
recursion, simple	$\mu(e) = \mu(e) \cup \mathtt{ref}(e)$	involuted relationship
recursion, complex	*split into separate relations*	needs query support
Attributes		
$e\ a_1\ \ldots$	$\mu(e) = \mu(e) \cup \mathtt{str}(a_1), \ldots$	may be NULL
#REQUIRED	$\mu(e) = \mu(e) \cup \mathtt{str}(a_1), \ldots$	NOT NULL
#IMPLIED	$\mu(e) = \mu(e) \cup \mathtt{str}(a_1), \ldots$	DEFAULT value
name group	$\mu(e) = \mu(e) \cup \mathtt{str}(a_1), \ldots$	CREATE DOMAIN, CHECK clause
#NMTOKENS	$\mu(e) = \mu(e) \cup \{\mathtt{str}(a_1)\}, \ldots$	
IDREF	$\langle a_1\,\mathrm{value}, a_1\,\mathrm{where}\rangle$	store value and path of referenced element
IDREFS	$\{\langle a_1\,\mathrm{value}, a_1\,\mathrm{where}\rangle\}$	

the element name and the corresponding #PCDATA. It's almost the same as the mapping of *name groups*. If the elements of the alternative are complex in structure, we can either store each element in one separate relation or combine the alternative into one attribute of type XML. The decision to divide or to combine elements should take the following into account: the ratio of the structural depths of each branch and the usage in documents and queries.

The *mixed-content type* model is used to allow text spanning several elements, to mix fulltext with element structures, or to embed element structures within a fulltext. As done previously, we map such elements to a single attribute of type XML. A more structured solution should take advantage of a list-of type constructor and allow for separately querying the concatenated #PCDATA or the embedded elements.

There is no recursion on the (XML document) instance level, but it may exist in the document type definition. Each element definition, that references an element of which it is a descendent, should be marked. Marked elements are not combined into a tuple-of but are mapped onto a separate PNF relation.

Within the scope of XML, there are at least three different standards concerning hyperlinks: the basic ID, IDREF mechanism and the complementary XLink and XPointer standards. The first type of hyperlinks (ID, IDREF) is part of the XML standard. These links can only be used within a single, logical document.

IDREFs are stored as a tuple of the key value and a reference to the "linked" element.

Entity references are some kind of indirect containment and similar to the macro mechanism in programming languages. The question arises, when to perform the macro expansion: when the document is inserted into the database or when it is extracted? For now, we store the unresolved entity reference.

For example, the `conference` and `editor` elements of the given DTD can be translated into PNF as follows.

$$\text{conference} \ = \ \langle \text{str}(\text{conftitle}), \{\text{editor}\}, \text{str}(\text{city}), \text{str}(\text{year}) \rangle$$

with

$$\text{editor} \ = \ \langle \text{str}(\text{first}), \text{str}(\text{second}), \text{str}(\text{email}) \rangle$$

could be combined into

$$\text{conference} = \langle \textbf{conftitle}, \{ \langle \textbf{first}, \textbf{second}, \textbf{email} \rangle \}, \textbf{city}, \textbf{year} \rangle$$

A more natural representation of this database would be a nested table structure (see Table 2).

Table 2. PNF relation as nested table

conference	conftitle	editors			city	year
		first	second	email		
	VLDB '99	Malcom	Atkinson	...	...	'99
		Maria E.	Orlowska	...		
		Patrick	Valduriez	...		
		Stan	Zdonik	sbz@cs.brown.edu		
		Michael	Brodie	...		
	ADL '98	...	...	...	...	'98
		...				
	WebDB '00	Dan	Suciu	...	Dallas	'00
		Gottfried	Vossen	...		

3.1 Straight-Forward Mappings

In the following sections we provide mapping rules for several DTD structures which can easily be transformed.

Simple elements: Though simple elements and attributes can be used interchangeably to model several real-world aspects, there are some differences. Attributes of an element are unordered but the ordering of elements matters most times. Attributes usually have atomic values but elements can be repeated and have a complex structure, i.e. can contain other elements.

Nevertheless, simple elements just containing `#PCDATA`, or `EMPTY` elements without attributes can be mapped directly into database attributes.

Sequences of elements: As with elements containing attributes, sequences of elements are translated into a `tuple-of` database attributes representing the components of the sequence.

Optional elements '?': XML elements which are optional result in database attributes which can have NULL values.

```
<!ELEMENT author (first, second, email?)>
<!ELEMENT first (#PCDATA)>
<!ELEMENT second (#PCDATA)>
<!ELEMENT email (#PCDATA)>
```

is translated into

$$author = \langle \mathbf{first}, \mathbf{second}, \mathbf{email} \rangle$$

Attributes: Elements with attributes are mapped into a database attribute of type `tuple-of`. The attributes become components/database attributes of that tuple. All atomic attributes together form the key of that tuple (this is a property of the PNF).

```
<!ELEMENT part (ptitle, chapter+)>
<!ATTLIST part id ID #REQUIRED>
```

can be mapped onto

$$part = \langle \mathbf{id}, \mathbf{ptitle}, \{chapter\} \rangle$$

If XML attributes are `#REQUIRED`, `#IMPLIED`, have *default values*, or are *name groups* (a finite set of values), they can be transformed into corresponding database concepts, e.g. concepts of SQL-99 like `NOT NULL`, `DEFAULT VALUES`, `CREATE DOMAIN`, `CHECK`.

```
<!ATTLIST references reftype (book | article | conferences |
         wwwaddress) "article">
```

is equivalent to

```
create domain reftype varchar(12) default 'article'
  check (
    value in ('book', 'article', 'conference', 'wwwaddress')
  )
```

Set-valued attributes: However, some XML attributes not only contain atomic values but are set-valued, such as `IDREFS` and `NMTOKENS`. These attributes are transformed into a `set-of`, set-valued attribute.

Missing identifying elements or attributes: If there is no element or attribute with a key property (e.g. attribute of type `ID`), we add artificial keys for the PNF and the pure relational mapping.

Repeatable elements: XML elements which can occur zero, one, or several times are marked with '`*`', elements which occur one or several times are marked with '`+`'. Both elements are transformed into a set-valued database attribute, where '*' elements are allowed to have NULL values, but '+' are not (NOT NULL constraint in SQL).

Complex combinations of elements: Given the example definition of the `chapter` element, we can perform the following more complex transformations by combining the simple ones.

```
<!ELEMENT chapter (ctitle, section+)>
<!ATTLIST chapter id ID #REQUIRED>
<!ELEMENT ctitle (#PCDATA)>
```

The attribute `id` is translated into a database attribute. The same is done with the element `ctitle`, which is of type #PCDATA. The element `section` which occurs one or more times within a `chapter` element is transformed into a set-valued database attribute.

$$chapter = \langle \mathbf{id}, \mathbf{ctitle}, \{section\} \rangle$$

A similar translation can be done for the `section` element:

```
<!ELEMENT section (stitle, paragraph+)>
<!ATTLIST section id ID #REQUIRED>
<!ELEMENT stitle (#PCDATA)>
```

This DTD fragment would result in:

$$section = \langle \mathbf{id}, \mathbf{stitle}, \{paragraph\} \rangle$$

Both translations for the `chapter` and the `section` element can be combined into one definition:

$$chapter = \langle \mathbf{id}, \mathbf{ctitle}, \{ \langle \mathbf{id}, \mathbf{stitle}, \{paragraph\} \rangle \} \rangle$$

3.2   Mapping Problems

The following XML structures are especially difficult to express in structured databases, because there are often no obvious transformations. If no further decomposition of an element is possible, we use a database attribute of type XML to store the element with its whole structure as an XML fragment. The decision whether to use the XML type or not is based on the algorithm presented in Section 5.

Alternatives: There is no easy translation of alternatives, but we can identify some basic cases. If all elements are simple elements (of type #PCDATA, EMPTY), the mapping could be done by an attribute with the element names as values, or a **tuple-of** the element name and the corresponding #PCDATA. It's almost the same as the mapping of *name groups*.

If the elements of the alternative have a more complex structure, we can either store each element in one separate relation or combine the alternative into one attribute of type XML. The decision should be reached based on heuristics, which will be discussed later. Whether to divide or to combine should at least take the ratio of the structural depths of each branch, and the usage in documents and queries into account.

For instance, the following alternative on a very high structural level is a candidate for dividing into separate PNF relations.

```
<!ELEMENT publications (book | article | conference)*>
<!ELEMENT book (front, body, references)>
<!ELEMENT article (meta, body, references)>
<!ELEMENT conference (conftitle, editor+, city, year)>
```

is translated into

$$\text{publication} = \text{book} \cup \text{article} \cup \text{conference}$$
$$\text{book} = \{\langle \mathbf{front}, \mathbf{body}, \mathbf{references} \rangle\}$$
$$\text{article} = \{\langle \mathbf{meta}, \mathbf{body}, \mathbf{references} \rangle\}$$
$$\text{conference} = \{\langle \mathbf{conftitle}, \{\text{editor}\}, \mathbf{city}, \mathbf{year} \rangle\}$$

Recursive structures: There is no recursion on the instance level but it may exist in the document type definition. Each element definition which references an element of which it is a descendent should be marked. Elements marked are not combined into a `tuple-of` but are mapped onto a separate PNF relation.

```
<!ELEMENT publications (book | article | conference)*>
<!-- book -->
<!ELEMENT book (front, body, references)>
...
<!ELEMENT references (publications*)>
```

Another problem related somewhat to recursion is common sub-expression (CSE). In the following example `chapter` can be a direct member of `body` or sub-element of `part`. Such elements are marked during the DTD analysis and duplicated afterwards.

```
<!ELEMENT body (part+ | chapter+)>
<!ELEMENT part (ptitle, chapter+)>
<!ATTLIST part id ID #REQUIRED>
<!ELEMENT ptitle (#PCDATA)>
<!ELEMENT chapter (ctitle, section+)>
<!ATTLIST chapter id ID #REQUIRED>
<!ELEMENT ctitle (#PCDATA)>
```

Although, Shanmugasundaram et. al. [13] map DTDs onto relational databases and our technique maps onto object-relation databases, recursion in the DTDs causes the same problems. Therefore, the handling of recursive structures is similar. Both approaches use a basic technique for handling common sub-expressions as known from compiler construction [1].

Mixed-content type model: The so-called mixed-content type model is used to allow text spanning several elements, to mix fulltext with element structure, or to embed element structures within a fulltext. As up to now, we map such elements to a single attribute of type XML. A more structured solution should take advantage of a `list-of` type constructor and allow separately querying the concatenated `#PCDATA` or the embedded elements.

Hyperlinks: Within the scope of XML, there are at least three different standards concerning hyperlinks: the basic `ID`, `IDREF` mechanism and the complementary XLink and XPointer standards. The first type of hyperlinks (`ID`, `IDREF`) is part of the XML standard. These links can only be used within a single, logical document.

Even the mapping of the basic `ID`/`IDREF` mechanism is non-trivial since there is no restriction on `IDREF`s pointing to different element types. So `IDREF`s are mapped to a two-tuple of the `IDREF` value and the target element name.

Entity references: This kind of indirect containment is similar to the macro mechanism in programming languages. The question arises, when to perform the macro expansion; when the document is inserted into the database or when it is extracted? For now, we store the unresolved entity reference.

Document ordering: In applications where the document ordering matters, we have to extend our mapping using a type constructors for ordered sets, i.e. `list-of` for sorted lists. Alternatively, we can introduce redundancies by storing the whole XML document as it is in addition to the structured part.

4   XML and Relational Databases

Up to this point, we enumerated the mapping of a DTD onto an object-relational database. Even if object-relational databases are powerful tools for handling XML data, it is desirable to have the same functionality with existing relational systems.

Our translation using PNF can be easily mapped to relations in 1NF. Hulin [7] presents a bijective transformation with special nest and unnest operations without information loss. Applying the unnest operation to the result of our transformation would decompose the PNF relations into 1NF relations.

Nested relations are divided into separate relations in the following way: the key of the nesting level becomes the primary key of the 1NF relation, and the key of the upper or surrounding relation becomes a foreign key of this relation.

The above example of the composed attribute `conference` results in two 1NF relations `conferences` and `editors` assuming `conftitle` is the primary key for `conferences`:

conferences

conftitle	city	year
VLDB '99	Edinburgh	1999
ADL '98	Santa Barbara	1998
...		

editors	conftitle	first	second	email
	VLDB '99	Malcom	Atkinson	...
	VLDB '99	Maria E.	Orlowska	...
	VLDB '99	Patrick	Valduriez	...
	VLDB '99	Stan	Zdonik	sbz@cs.brown.edu
	VLDB '99	Michael	Brodie	...
	...			

5   Design of Hybrid Databases

The following algorithm is used to design an optimal hybrid database.

Step 1 We build a graph representing the hierarchy of the elements and the attributes of the DTD.

Step 2 For every element/attribute of the graph, we determine a measure of significance, w.

Step 3 We derive the resulting hybrid database design from the graph.

5.1   Step 1 — Determining a Graph for a DTD

For a given DTD, we can create a corresponding graph representing the structure of the DTD (similar to the DTD graph suggested in [13]). We want to show an example of the graph representation. Therefore, we sort the elements and attributes into the graph according to their hierarchical order.

Our sample DTD is represented by the graph in Figure 4 and recursions are represented by marked nodes. We visualize marked nodes by an additional border (**publications** in the example). Furthermore, common sub-expressions of the DTD are duplicated.

5.2   Step 2 — Calculation of Weights

The next step is determining weights which specify the degree of relevance for every node of the graph (or the corresponding elements or attributes of the DTD). Thereby, three kinds of information are included.

The first kind is the *DTD structure*, but it can't deliver all the information we need to suggest an optimal database schema. In our motivation, we showed that same or similar DTDs can be used in various applications in different ways. For this reason, we also use the *available data* in our approach. However, the available information in XML documents often doesn't coincide with the information the users search for. Therefore, we also include information about *queries* into the estimation of the weights. In Figure 3, we show a visualization of these three characteristics for one node.

All characteristics use a value between 0 and 1 for the degree of relevance. The following estimation specifies the calculation of the degree of relevance for every node based on these characteristics.

$$w = \frac{1}{2} * w_S + \frac{1}{4} * w_D + \frac{1}{4} * w_Q$$

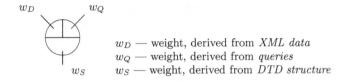

w_D — weight, derived from *XML data*
w_Q — weight, derived from *queries*
w_S — weight, derived from *DTD structure*

Fig. 3. Node weightings

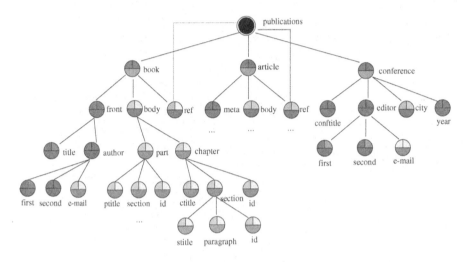

Fig. 4. Visualization of the weights — DBLP

For simplicity, we map the weights onto a grey-scale between *white* (0.0) and *black* (1.0) in our visualization. Using three input parameters, we subsequently show how to estimate w_S. Thereby, three characteristics are examined.

S_H — position in the hierarchy
   This parameter can be calculated in the following way:

$$S_H = 1 - \frac{N_P}{N_D}$$

N_P — number of predecessors (ancestors)
N_D — maximal depth of the graph

S_A — exploitation of alternatives

DTD characteristic	S_A
mixed content	0
alternative on the same level exists	0.5
otherwise	1

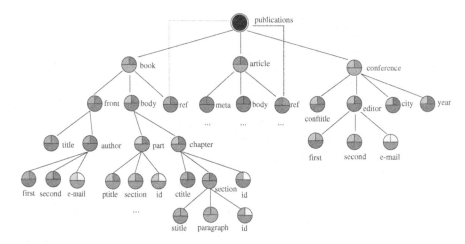

Fig. 5. Weights for Springer LINK

S_Q — exploitation of quantifiers

DTD characteristic		S_Q
ELEMENT	no quantifier	1
	?	0.5
	+	0.75
	*	0.25
ATTRIBUTE	REQUIRED	1
	IMPLIED	0.5

Using these three structural characteristics, we can estimate the parameter w_S for every element and attribute of the DTD in the following way:

$$w_S = \frac{S_Q + S_A + S_H}{3}$$

Some information cannot be derived from a DTD. For instance, we do not know how often an element with the quantifier '?' or '*' is available in the documents. This is also true in cases where the attributes are IMPLIED. Therefore, the weight w_D is calculated:

$$w_D = \frac{D_A}{D_T}$$

D_A — number of documents containing the element/attribute
D_T — total number of XML documents

We determine D_A for every element/attribute on every place in the DTD tree. Thereby, we identify the elements and attributes by the complete path. Optionally, a numbering is used if the same element is sub-element of another element multiple times.

In the following table, we show the occurrence of data derived from the Michael Ley DBLP-Server, which contains about 150,000 references at present.

Element	abs. Frequency	D_A	w_D
article	65353	65353	1.0
article.author	124061	65353	1.0
article.title	65353	65353	1.0
article.title.sub	106	106	0.0
article.title.sup	135	135	0.0
article.title.a	5	5	0.0
article.title.b	6	6	0.0
article.journal	65352	65352	1.0
article.year	65353	65353	1.0
article.references	19529	6509	0.1

This statistic on the occurrence of data distinguishes the regular and irregular portions of the DTD very clearly.

Furthermore, we cannot derive from DTDs which information is often requested and which information is of lower interest. But, a-priori knowledge about queries is very valuable for optimizing the mapping process. Sometimes, this information can be derived from already existing systems processing the same or similar data. It is also possible to ask the user for typical queries. Thereby, we can derive information on how often an element or attribute is requested within queries in contrast to how often it occurs in documents.

The weight w_Q representing this information is calculated in the following way:

$$w_Q = \frac{Q_A}{Q_T}$$

Q_A — number of queries containing the element/attribute
Q_T — total number of queries

We calculate Q_A and distinguish elements and attributes which occur multiple in the DTD by unique path information. Summarizing these estimations, we get the following result:

$$w = \frac{1}{6}(S_Q + S_A + S_H) + \frac{1}{4}\frac{D_A}{D_T} + \frac{1}{4}\frac{Q_A}{Q_T}$$

Typical weights for the sample DTD with a bibliography application as the DBLP server are represented in Figure 4. Figure 5 shows different weightings for the Springer LINK service.

5.3   Step 3 — Deriving Hybrid Databases from the Graph

First, we determine a limit specifying which attributes and/or elements are represented as attributes of the databases and which attributes and/or elements

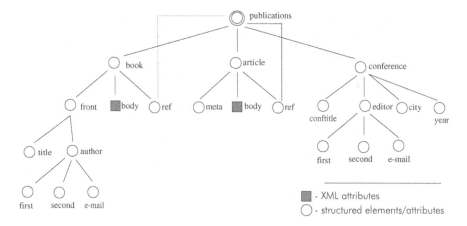

Fig. 6. Resulting XML attributes — DBLP

are represented as XML attributes. The limit can influence the level of detail of the resulting databases. The limit depends, among other things, on the response times of the query language for databases and XML.

Next, we search for all nodes of the graph which fulfill the conditions that:

- The node is not a leaf of the graph.
- The node and all its descendents are below the limit given.
- There exists no predecessor of the node which fulfills the same conditions.

All subgraphs consisting of these nodes and their descendents are replaced by an XML attribute. If we apply this method onto the graph in Figure 4, we get the graph in Figure 6 as a result. Thereby, we used the DTD graph for only one reason, to distinguish the regular and irregular portions of the DTDs. Figure 6 shows the determined XML attributes. All other elements and attributes of the graph are represented in the database according to the description in Section 3.

Besides a combination of structured and semi-structured parts, our method can result into totally different mappings:

- All elements/attributes of the DTD belong to structured document parts and are mapped onto structured attributes in the database.
- All elements/attributes of the DTD belong to the irregular portions of a document and are summarized to one XML attribute.

Both cases are found in applications, the first one is suited for structured data interchange, the second one can be found in document-centric software solutions.

6   Application of the Mapping Algorithm

In this paper, we described an algorithm that determines a database design for storing large documents collections. It is possible to do this automatically. But there are two reasons that let us prefer a semi-automatic approach whereby an user can influence the design process.

– *The quality of DTDs is often not sufficient.* There are many document collections with ad-hoc defined DTDs. In [12] some examples are given and typical errors are analyzed. By integrating statistics on data and queries, we can improve the results of our algorithm but we cannot compensate all design errors of the DTDs.
– *A database is quite static and long-living.* Therefore, it is important that the design meets all requirements of the application. We think that a human designer can improve the design because he/she understands the semantics of the elements and attributes and therefore can detect errors or pitfalls in the database design.

The idea is that we suggest a database design, then the database designer can make the following decisions:

– Modify structured attributes to XML attributes,
– Alter XML attributes to structured attributes, or
– Explicitly map sub-elements of a more semi-structured document fragment to structured attributes.

We integrate these design decisions by changing the corresponding weights and afterwards creating a new database design. In that case, we extent the automatic process to an iterative semi-automatic approach.

7   Related Work

In [6], the authors suggest storing the graph structure of XML documents in relational databases. All elements are stored as pairs consisting of the full path to each element and the element content itself in one relation. One advantage of this method is that the approach works for every document and is easy to implement. It even works for documents without a DTD. The drawback is that queries are difficult to realize. All queries containing elements related to each other can only be realized by joins.

Another approach for storing XML documents in relational databases is suggested in [13]. In contrast to [6], this method maps the element structure of the documents onto database structure. This approach results in large database schemas but provides better query performance. Additionally, optimization of elements results in separate relations.

In [4], the authors describe mappings of semistructured data onto relational databases. The focus of this article is on the development of a mapping language (named STORED) for this task. So, the user has to specify the mapping or an automatic method can be applied. This automatic method derives the mapping from a document collection by using text mining algorithms. The results of the mapping are in both cases relational database. The portion that cannot be mapped onto the database structure are represented as graphs.

This approach is in some aspects similar to our method. Both approaches employ statistical methods to distinguish regular portion (structured data) from irregular portions (semi-structured data). In our approach, we use an XML data type for the irregular portions in contrast to the graph structure employed in STORED. The regular portions are mapped onto an object-relational database and nested table structures, whereas STORED maps to flat relations. In our approach the DTD drives the the mapping. In STORED only statistics influence the automatic mapping.

In [2], an approach is suggested for storing SGML documents inside of an object-oriented database. For performance reasons, it is impossible to transform all elements of the SGML structure into a one-to-one-relation of the object-oriented database. Only the "large elements" are mapped; the others are combined as "flat objects" which contain SGML. Thereby, the number of objects in the database is minimal. There are some similarities to our algorithm, but the approach doesn't automate the decision regarding which element structures remain as SGML fragments. The decision regarding how to represent elements is left to a DTD and database designer.

One application of [2] is described in [5]. Thereby, a used-car market application is realized with a hybrid database. A relational database is employed for the structured parts of XML documents and an XML attribute is used for all "irregular" portions. The design of the database is determined by the programmer. Queries are realized as a combination of SQL and XQL on the application level.

There are many other approaches, dealing with mapping SGML or XML onto database structures, but none of the approaches takes statistics on the document collections and query profiles into account. Most approaches which are based on a DTD accept only subsets of document type definitions for their database design.

8   Conclusion and Future Work

This paper suggests mapping DTDs onto object-relational databases schemas. To overcome the typical problems (sparsely populated database, large schemas), we suggested an algorithm for determining an optimal hybrid database schema.

Database systems like DB2 with XML Extender support two methods for storing XML data. The first one maps the data onto relational databases, whereby the user must specify how this should be done. The second one stores the data as XML data without changes. The database designer decides which representation is used. Thereby, the method suggested in this paper can support the designer.

Initial practical experiences exist within the context of the GETESS project (German Text Exploitation and Search System) in the tourism domain. Here we use object-relational databases (DB2) with XML attributes to store and query semi-structured information [14].

Future work will include experiments with large document collections and associated DTDs. Thereby, the enumerated heuristics and their weightings have to be checked and validated.

Aspects not focused on in depth in this article are how to preserve document ordering, support update operations, and allow restructuring of the document. Other important points for future investigation are query evaluation, optimization aspects, and automatic view definitions for better querying support.

Acknowledgment. The work was partially funded by the BMB+F under contract 01IN802. We would like to thank all people (colleagues and students) contributed to this work, namely Andreas Heuer, Beate Porst, Denny Priebe, Jens Timm and Franka Reuter.

Implementation

Besides the implementation of an XML extender as described in [10], there is an set of tools available, which implements the proposed mapping algorithm. The Python[4] implementation is available at our web site[5].

The tool needs resource locators for the DTD, an XML document collection, and an (optional) file with sample queries as input. The output of the program is a database design and metadata that describe the mapping. Data definition and manipulation statements can be generated for a generic PNF model, IBM DB2 UDB, and Informix Universal Server.

References

1. A. V. Aho, R. Sethi, and J. D. Ullman. *COMPILERS Principles, Techniques and Tools.* Bell Telephone Laboratories, Inc., 1987.
2. K. Boehm. *Verwendung objektorientierter Datenbanktechnologie zur Verwaltung str ukturierter Dokumente.* PhD thesis, Technische Hochschule Darmstadt, 1997. (in German).
3. J. Clark. Comparison of SGML and XML, December 1997. http://www.w3.org/TR/NOTE-sgml-xml-971215.
4. A. Deutsch, M. F. Fernandez, and D. Suciu. Storing Semistructured Data with STORED. In A. Delis, C. Faloutsos, and S. Ghandeharizadeh, editors, *SIGMOD 1999, Proceedings ACM SIGMOD International Conference on Management of Data, June 1-3, 1999, Philadephia, Pennsylvania, USA,* pages 431–442. ACM Press, 1999.
5. L. Dittmann, P. Fankhauser, and A. Maric. AMetaCar – a mediated eCommerce-Solution for the Used-Car-Market. In R.-D. Kutsche, U. Leser, and J. C. Freytag, editors, *4. Workshop "Federated Databases", November 1999, Berlin, Germany, Proceedings,* pages 18–33. Technical University of Berlin, 1999.
6. D. Florescu and D. Kossmann. Storing and Querying XML Data Using an RDBMS. *Bulletin of the Technical Committee on Data Engineering,* 22(3):27–34, September 1999.

---

[4] http://www.python.org
[5] http://wwwdb.informatik.uni-rostock.de/xml/

7. G. Hulin. On restructuring nested relations in partitioned normal form. In D. McLeod, R. Sacks-Davis, and H.-J. Schek, editors, *16th International Conference on Very Large Data Bases, August 13-16, 1990, Brisbane, Queensland, Australia, Proceedings*, pages 626–637. Morgan Kaufmann, 1990.

8. Joint Technical Committee ISO/IEC JTC 1, Information Technology, Subcommittee SC32, Data Management and interchange, Working group 4. *SQL Multimedia and Application Packages — Part 2: Full-Text, FDIS 13249-2*, February 2000.

9. M. Klettke and H. Meyer. Managing XML documents in object-relational databases. *Rostocker Informatik Fachberichte*, 24, 1999.

10. B. Porst. Untersuchungen zu Datentyperweiterungen für XML-Dokumente und ihre Anfragemethoden am Beispiel von DB2 und Informix. Master's thesis, Universität Rostock, 1999. (in German).

11. M. A. Roth, H. F. Korth, and A. Silberschatz. Extended algebra and calculus for nested relational databases. *TODS*, 13(4):389–417, 1988.

12. A. Sahuguet. Everything You Ever Wanted to Know About DTDs, But Were Afraid to Ask. In *WebDB (Informal Proceedings)*, pages 69–74, 2000.

13. J. Shanmugasundaram, K. Tufte, G. He, C. Zhang, D. DeWitt, and J. Naughton. Relational Databases for Querying XML Documents: Limitations and Opportunities. In *Proceedings of the 25th VLDB Conference, Edinburgh, Scotland*, pages 302–314, 1999.

14. S. Staab, C. Braun, I. Bruder, A. Düsterhöft, A. Heuer, M. Klettke, G. Neumann, B. Prager, J. Pretzel, H.-P. Schnurr, R. Studer, H. Uszkoreit, and B. Wrenger. GETESS — Searching the Web Exploiting German Texts. In M. Klusch, O. Shehory, and G. Weiss, editors, *Cooperative Information Agents III, Proceedings 3rd International Workshop CIA-99*, volume 1652. Springer Verlag, July 1999.

15. World-Wide Web Consortium. *Extensible Markup Language (XML) 1.0*, 1998. http://www.w3.org/TR/1998/REC-xml-19980210.

16. World-Wide Web Consortium. *XML Fragment Interchange (Working Draft)*, June 1999. http://www.w3.org/TR/WD-xml-fragment.

17. World-Wide Web Consortium. *XML Path Language (XPath) Version 1.0*, November 1999. http://www.w3.org/TR/1999/REC-xml-19991116.

Everything You Ever Wanted to Know About DTDs, But Were Afraid to Ask

(Extended Abstract)

Arnaud Sahuguet

Penn Database Research Group,
University of Pennsylvania.
`sahuguet@gradient.cis.upenn.edu`

Abstract. For the last two years, XML has become an increasingly popular data-format unanimously accepted by a lot of different communities. In this paper, we present some preliminary results that explore how XML DTDs are actually being used. By studying some publicly available DTDs, we look at how people are actually (mis)using DTDs, show some shortcomings, list some requirements and discuss possible replacements.

1   Introduction

For the last two years, XML has become an increasingly popular data-format embraced by a lot of different communities. XML is extremely attractive because it offers a simple, intuitive and uniform text-based syntax and is extensible. One can find today XML proposals for messages, text content delivery and presentation, data content, documents, software components, scientific data, real-estate ads, financial products, cooking recipes, etc.

Unfortunately this also means that XML is far too general and if people plan to use it in serious applications (mainly for Electronic Document Interchange, in a broad sense), they will need to provide a specification (i.e. structure, constraints, etc.) for *their* XML, which XML itself cannot offer. In order to specify and enforce this structure, people have been using Document Type Definitions (DTDs), inherited from SGML.

In this paper, we present some preliminary results that explore how DTDs are being used for specifying the structure of XML documents. By studying some publicly available DTDs, we look at how people are actually (mis)using DTDs, show some shortcomings, list some requirements and discuss possible replacements.

But before getting further, let us ask the following legitimate question: *why bother?*. And to answer it, let us review what DTDs should be good for.

Historically, DTDs have been invented for SGML. The purpose of a DTD is to permit "*to determine whether the mark-up for an individual document is correct and also to supply the mark-up that is missing because it can be inferred unambiguously from other mark-up present*" [ISO 8879].

D. Suciu and G. Vossen (Eds.): WebDB 2000, LNCS 1997, pp. 171–183, 2001.

The two historical functions of DTDs have been parsing and validation. The parsing function is less relevant with XML (since XML does not permit to omit tags). The validation still plays – and will play – an important role: once an XML document has been validated it can be directly processed by the application. This is a way to offer runtime guarantees. It is crucial to keep in mind that XML documents exist without DTDs: an XML document is *well-formed* if its tag structure is correct, and valid (against a DTD) if moreover it complies with this DTD. However, with the advent of XML as the data-format for both text and data content, DTDs are promised to be used in a broader scope.

From a database perspective [ABS99], DTDs can be useful to trigger optimizations for XML query languages. For instance some structural knowledge about an XML document permits to resolve path-expressions with wild-cards and perform both horizontal and vertical optimization ([Lie99,FS98,MW99]). This role of DTDs is similar to *dataguides* [GW97].

More recently, some research about efficient storage [DFS99] and compression [LS00] of XML showed that some information about the structure of the document can dramatically improve performance. For instance, knowing that an attribute can have a finite number of values permits to encode it more efficiently using a dictionary.

DTD information can be used to create a language binding from XML to a programming language such as C++, Java, etc. Such a binding [Jav00,Jav99] can offer better performance and some static (i.e. compile-time) guarantees for XML processing.

Finally, DTDs can also be extremely useful as meta-information about the document they describe, for query formulation, clustering or documentation purposes.

The rest of this paper is organized as follows. We first give a brief overview of XML DTDs (Section 2). In Section 3, we explain the methodology of our survey and present some preliminary results about how DTDs are being misused to specify the structure of XML documents. In Section 4 we explain what we think is wrong with the current DTDs and what they should offer. In Section 5, we look at some replacements that have been proposed. In Section 6, we present some future directions of research before we offer some conclusions.

2   DTDs in a Nutshell

We briefly describe the structure of a DTD, which can consists of the following items listed below.

Elements represent the tag names that can be used in the document. Element declarations are introduced using `<!ELEMENT >`. Elements can contain sub-elements or be empty. Elements can have some attributes. The structure of sub-elements is defined via a *content-model* built out of operators applied to sub-elements. Elements can be grouped as sequences (a,b) or as choices (a|b). For every element or group of elements, the content-model can specify its occurrence by using regular expression operators (?,*,+). There are also some special case of the content-model: EMPTY for an element with no sub-elements; ANY for an element that can contain any sub-element; #PCDATA for an element that can contain only text. When the element can contain sub-elements mixed with text, the content-model is called *mixed-content*.

Attribute definitions are introduced using <!ATTLIST >. Attributes can be of various types such as ID for a unique identifier, CDATA for text or NMTOKEN for tokens. They can be optional (#IMPLIED) or mandatory (#REQUIRED). Attributes can also be of an arbitrary type defined by a notation, introduced using <!NOTATION >. Optionally, attributes can have a default or a constant value (#FIXED).

Entity references are constants that can be used inside XML documents[1]. Entity references are introduced using <!ENTITY name> and referred to using &*name* ;. Entity references can be used inside the DTD itself – to define other entities – and inside documents.

Entity parameters can be seen as text macros that can be used internally inside the DTD: they have no meaning outside of the DTD. They are introduced using <!ENTITY % name > and are referred to inside the DTD using %*name* ;.

A given XML document can refer to its DTD in 4 different ways, defined by the required mark-up declaration (RMD) <?XML version="1.0" RMD=""?>. First it can point to no DTD[2] and corresponds to RMD="NONE". Second, it can point to an external DTD, as a remote resource. Third, it can include an internal DTD, in-lined inside the document (RMD="INTERNAL"). Fourth, it can use a combination of both (RMD="ALL").

In the previous description, we have omitted on purpose some details that are not relevant for the results of the survey.

3   The DTD Survey

We present the details of the survey we have conducted on DTDs and we first describe the methodology. The first step is the **harvesting** of DTDs. Fortunately, repositories are emerging such as Microsoft BizTalk. For this paper, we have been using http://www.xml.org. Harvesting is done by hand since the repository points to the web page of the corresponding project and not the DTD itself. In some cases, access requires a registration. We have selected DTDs from different domains (see Figure 4) in order to get a representative sample of XML applications. Unexpectedly, the second step is the **cleansing** of the DTDs. Our experience proved that most of the DTDs are incorrect, with some missing declarations or some typos. This is a paradoxical discovery since DTDs are made to validate XML documents: *Quis custodiet custodes ipsos!* The third step is to **normalize,** by expanding parameter entities and translating the DTD structure into a convenient data-structure. The next step is the **mining** of the DTDs. The term *mining* is actually misleading since in most cases we know what we are looking for. The final step is **reporting and visualization** of the results.

---

[1] Like < and > that represent < and > in HTML.
[2] In this case, only well-formedness matters

The experiments were done using **sgrep**[3], Perl, shell scripts, and Java programs based of the IBM XML API. The entity expansion was performed using a modified version of **xmlproc**[4], by Lars M. Garshol. We used Graphviz[5] from AT&T to generate DTD graphs.

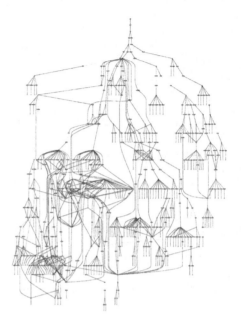

Fig. 1. View of a DTD for financial transactions

3.1 What We Have Been Looking At

We are interested in various properties of a DTD.

First we look at its structure in terms of size: number of elements, attributes, entity references, etc. The size is a very important piece of information since it potentially influences the size of the corresponding XML document. Moreover, a "big" DTD will make validation more expensive and will yield a more complex corresponding data-type.

Second, we look at its structure, in terms of complexity: number of root elements, complexity of the the content-model. In Figure 4, CM represents the maximum depth of the content model: 0 for EMPTY; 1 for a single element, a sequence or a choice; ...; n for an alternation[6] of sequences and choices of depth

---

[3] http://www.cs.helsinki.fi/~jjaakkol/sgrep.html

[4] http://www.stud.ifi.uio.no/~lmariusg/download/python/xml/xmlproc.html

[5] http://www.research.att.com/sw/tools/graphviz

[6] (a,(b|(c,d))) has depth 3.

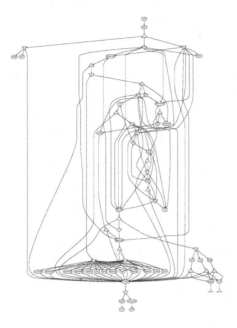

Fig. 2. View of the XML-Schema DTD

n. We also introduce two notions: *redundancy* and *CM redundancy*[7]. Two DTD elements are *CM redundant* is they have the same content-model; two elements are *redundant* if they are *CM redundant* and have the same attributes.

Third, we look at some specific aspects such as the use of mixed-content (MX), **ANY, IDREFs**, and the kind of attribute decorations used (I,R,F for implied, required and fixed).

Finally, we draw graphs (Figures 1 and 2) to get some insights about DTD patterns. Graphs only display elements; $\triangle$ corresponds to sequences; ∇ to choices.

3.2   Results

Some quantitative results from the survey are presented in Figure 4. The detailed results will be available in the full version of this paper.

As mentioned previously, the first striking and unexpected observation is that most published DTDs are not correct, with missing elements, wrong syntax or incompatible attribute declarations. This might prove that such DTDs are being used for documentation purposes only and are not meant to be used for validation at all. The reason might be that because of the ad-hoc syntax of DTDs (inherited from SGML), there are no standard tools to validate them. This issue

---

[7] CM stands for content model.

will be addressed by proposals that use XML as the syntax to describe DTDs themselves (see Section 5).

DTDs vary a lot in terms of their size. The main reason is that XML is used to represent anything one can imagine. From a sample of around 60 DTDs from xml.org, the size fluctuations are presented in Figure 3.

	min	max	average	median
nb. of elements	5	590	74	36
nb. of attributes	0	5,700	390	82
nb. of entities	0	190	15	2

Fig. 3. DTD sizes

The second remark is that a DTD is not always a connected graph. This is not an issue for validation since the XML document will mention the root that needs to be used for validation. But it is not clear why in such cases the DTD is not split into multiple DTDs.

DTD name	Domain	Elem/Attr	MX	CM	ID/IDREF	I/R/F	ANY	Ent. Ref/Para
Adex	classifieds	365/5194	7	2	366 / 4	4550 / 13 / 4	0	0/17
BSML	DNA sequencing	111 / 2595	0	3	88 / 105	2490 / 58 / 6	0	5/36
EcoknowMics	economics	105 / 264	0	2	89 / 0	0 / 93 / 171	0	0/0
HL7	medical informatics	109 / 252	69	2	102 / 7	115 / 14 / 119	0	1/24
ICE	content syndication	48 / 157	0	3	0 / 0	82 / 63 / 1	1	0/10
MusicML	music	12 / 17	0	2	0 / 0	6 / 5 / 0	0	0/12
OSD	software description	15 / 15	0	1	0 / 0	3 / 11 / 0	0	0/0
PML	web portals	46 / 293	1	2	0 / 0	90 / 203 / 0	0	0/3
XMI	UML data modeling	398 / 1636	23	1	119 / 122	1587 / 46 / 1	22	0/2
XHTML	HTML	77 / 1373	44	5	70 / 3	1344 / 12 / 4	0	252/59
XML-Schema		37 / 91	0	4	12 / 0	43 / 23 / 2	2	0/46
Xbel	bookmarks	9 / 13	0	2	3 / 1	8 / 3 / 2	0	0/6

Fig. 4. Some quantitative results for DTDs from http://www.xml.org.

A third really interesting observation – that we got from visual representations of DTDs (see Figure 5) concerns the encoding tuples. Unlike SGML that offer the & operator to create unordered sequences, XML only offer sequences (",") or choices ("|"). In order to encode a tuple <a,b,c>, where SGML would use (a & b & c), XML requires (a,b,c)|(a,c,b)| (b,c,a)|(b,a,c)|(c,a,b)|(c,b,a). The *official workaround* [8] seems to be (a|b|c)*, which will validate the tuple but has a totally different meaning!

We also notice that DTD authors try to mimic inheritance and capture modularity via entity references. Unfortunately, this inheritance is purely syntactic and sometimes leads to some cascading mistakes. This observation is confirmed by looking at the redundancy of element declarations as presented in Figure 6.

---

[8] This way to model tuples is actually recommended by some people and is being used for the description of the XML-Schema DTD.

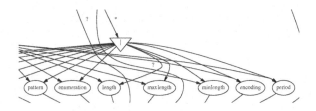

Fig. 5. The tuple encoding issue

	CM Redundancy	Redundancy
minimum	0%	0%
maximum	95%	95%
average	55%	34%
median	57%	37%

Fig. 6. Redundancy

The use of mixed-content is a good indication of the kind of application intended for the DTD. No mixed-content implies pure data processing (BSML, OSD) while the presence of mixed content suggests more textual content (XHTML, XMI/UML, Adex).

An intriguing fact is the presence of very complex and *deep* content models (up to depth 5 !). Some DTDs contain some really strange patterns where for instance empty elements are systematically used instead of attributes.

Finally, it is clear that most of the features (from the SGML legacy) of DTDs are not being used, such as notations and fancy attribute types. More surprisingly, ID and especially IDREFs are very infrequently considered (see Figure 4): since ID and IDREFs are not typed (an IDREF can point to any ID, people prefer not to use them. These mechanism can always be implemented at the application level.

Some conclusions from this preliminary survey are that: (1) DTD have all sort of shapes and sizes and are used for many diverse purposes; (2) DTD features are not properly understood (some features are never used, and some are misused); (3) there are many ways to do the same things and it is not clear why people are using one solution rather than another; (4) people use *hacks* to solve DTD shortcomings, sometimes for better, sometimes for worse.

A more practical conclusion from our database perspective is that relying on DTDs for storage, compression and optimization seems foolish since DTDs are often a misleading approximation of the intended structure (e.g. tuple encoding example). Moreover, a DTD offers only fuzzy guarantees about the structure of the XML document: a* might mean 0, 1 or 20 repetitions. We would therefore recommend to use the actual structure of documents like in [DFS99,LS00] rather to bet[9] on the DTD [STZ+99].

4   Shortcomings & Requirements

The conclusions of the survey show that DTDs – as they are – are not suitable for what we want to do with them. DTDs are suffering from the heavy SGML ancestry. Even though some complex features have been removed, XML DTDs are still too complex, with text processing rather than data processing in mind. DTDs are also suffering from a big lack of understanding. For instance, people are still confused about element vs attributes. But more critically, DTDs seem to suffer from the same shortcomings as the first programming languages. In Figure 7, we "compare" DTD with the C programming language.

XML DTD	Programming language
validation	type-checking
entity references	constants
entity parameters	macros
ANY	void
IDREF	void*
DTD	header file
|	variant
,	tuple (with order)
?	nil
+/*	list

Fig. 7. DTDs vs programming languages

All these analogies are good news because it means we can get some inspiration from modern programming languages. We briefly list some features that DTDs could benefit from.

From an engineering point of view, DTDs would strongly benefit from a convenient system for modularity. The actual system of entities and catalogue is clumsy and does not really scale. The use of namespaces[10] and packages would be a big improvement.

XML DTDs would also benefit from a more expressive content-model that is suitable for both text and data processing.

As clearly shown by the survey, in the absence of typed references, people are reluctant to use of them. Being able to specify keys and foreign keys is crucial.

Finally, we think that DTDs will soon face the critical problem of versioning, including backward and forward compatibility. To the best of our knowledge, this

---

[9] The author has to acknowledge that before conducting the survey, he was heavily betting on DTDs too.

[10] Not part pf the XML 1.0 specification

issue has not been elegantly resolved in the SGML world. Database schemas are well known for evolving and DTDs should be expected to do exactly the same.

5   Replacement for DTDs

After denigrating DTDs and writing down the *wish list* for the *New Document Type Descriptors*, let us look at the current proposals. XML users have realized very early the shortcomings of DTDs and have come up with some extensions such as SOX, DCD, XML-Data, etc. In the rest of this section, we present various approaches to replace DTDs and some recent corresponding proposals. It is worth noting that most of these proposals use XML itself as the syntax, which permits to use the XML tools to check them.

Grammar-based, parsing based approaches: These approaches define the structure of an XML document in terms of production rules, starting from the root of the document, just like DTDs.

XML-Schemas[11] is the official W3C replacement for DTDs. Their goal is to *"constrain and document the meaning, usage and relationships of their* [XML documents] *constituent parts"*. The proposal is split into two specifications: one for data-types [W3Cd] (parsing oriented) and one for structures [W3Ce].
Even though the proposal does not address all the issues pointed out by the survey, it is interesting to note that it brings back a tuple construct (SGML &, but with some syntactic restrictions) and offers a replacement for ANY. It also addresses the issue of modeling by offering grouping, modularity and restriction/extension mechanisms for data-structures. The proposal also permits to define *identity constraints*, where keys (including composite keys) can be defined using elements and/or attributes.

Another proposal is the *Document Structure Definition* (DSD) [KMS99] which among other things offer context dependent descriptions, constraints and typed references. It also supports evolution via *document inclusion and redefinition*.

RELAX (REgular LAnguage description for XML)[Mur00] offers modularity, typed references, datatypes, annotations and context-sensitive content-model.

Constraints: A different approach exemplified by the Schematron [Jel99], is to describe the structure of an XML document using only constraints and pattern-matching. Such constraints are defined by a *context* where they apply and a *predicate* they must satisfy. Both are expressed as XPath expressions[12]. An interesting aspect is that constraints can be used to describe the structure with different granularities. Schematron constraints are much more expressive than the ones offered by XML-Schema's. For instance, it is possible to type references by using a constraint that states that the node reached by following an IDREF is

---

[11] See [W3Cc] for a tutorial.
[12] The Schematron is similar to an XSL-T transform that would output validation messages instead of content.

of a given type. It is not clear though if all constraints expressed in the language are decidable.

Type systems: Another proposed approach is to use type systems borrowed from programming languages in order to enforce some structure on XML documents. A type-system for semi-structured data has been proposed in [BP99]. Embedding XML into functional languages has also been looked at in [HP99, WR99]: in this case the emphasis has been to offer a framework to validate programs written against a given DTD rather than validate documents. Various toolkits also offer some ad-hoc mappings from XML into Java classes.

Other data-models: Finally, there are some proposals to use other representation to describe DTDs such as description logics or UML [Kim99]. For the latter, a mapping from DTDs to UML has been defined and – not surprisingly – the main glitches occur at the level of the content-model.

In most cases, these approaches are complementary and do not address the same kind of issues. It is already interesting to remark that constraint-based and grammar-based approaches are being put together by the XML-Schemas proposals.

6   Future Work

We present some future work that has arisen, sometimes unexpectedly, from this survey.

Systematic mining: As we mentioned above, the term mining is misleading because we somehow knew what we were looking for. The advent of XML gives us the unique opportunity to analyze and compare data modeling strategies[13]. This would hopefully lead to the discovery of XML patterns ([GHJV94,XML]) and the creation of XML modeling *recipes* ([Ext]).

DTD complexity: For a given domain are there some DTDs better than others? In the object-oriented community, metrics [CK94] have been defined and applied to define the structural complexity of programs. Can these be adapted to DTDs? In the database community, database design relies on normal forms, which are based on dependencies (functional dependencies, integrity constraints). Can such dependencies and normal forms be adapted to XML ([FS00])?

The meaning of DTDs: XML is claimed to be a self-describing format. By using NLP techniques and ontologies, it would be interesting to see if DTDs (element and attributes names) are useful to characterize the domain of a given document. This exercise is not as trivial as it appears: elements and attributes are not always words but acronyms, abbreviations including namespaces that will require smart tokenization programs.

---

[13] This is to be contrasted with database schema that remain the secret property of organizations.

7 Conclusion

By its extensible nature, the XML language imperatively needs a constraint structure that is represented today by DTDs. Unfortunately, DTDs have been designed for a specific domain (text processing applications) which represents a small part of the scope of XML. As a specification tool for XML, DTDs are simply inadequate.

In this paper we have presented the preliminary results of a survey we have started in Fall 1999. Its primary motivation was to better understand DTDs by looking at *how they are actually being used* to describe the structure of XML documents. Surprisingly, not unlike living organisms, XML DTDs have mutated from SGML DTDs into something that tries to fit the requirements of XML (both text and data processing). Because of their inherited shortcomings, XML DTDs have been *hacked* by users, in order to resolve serious issues such as tuple encoding and modularity. Other issues such as reference typing and versioning have simply been postponed, for lack of immediate workarounds.

However, in this survey we have only scratched the surface of the problem: we not only need a better way to capture the structures of XML documents, but also tools and methodologies to define them properly.

It is encouraging though to note that the current proposals to replace DTDs are taking some of these issues into account and offer cleaner constructs to capture what is needed by XML applications.

Finally, even though DTDs are flourishing, the corresponding XML documents are still nowhere to be found. The next interesting question will be to see how XML documents are being instantiated for a given DTD. This will be of special interest to the database community who will be "responsible" for efficiently storing, indexing, querying, mediating and transforming such documents. But this is another story...

Acknowledgements. The author would like to thank Byron Choi, Val Tannen, the members of the *Database Research Group* and the *Programming Languages Club* for stimulating discussions about XML, constraints and types.

References

ABS99.   Serge Abiteboul, Peter Buneman, and Dan Suciu. *Data on the Web : From Relations to Semistructured Data and XML* . Morgan Kaufmann, 1999.

BP99.   Peter Buneman and Benjamin Pierce. Union Types for Semistructured Data. Technical Report MS-CIS-99-09, University of Pennsylvania, Apr 1999.

CK94.   S. R. Chidamber and C. F. Kemerer. A Metrics suite for Object-Oriented Design. *IEEE Transaction on Software Engineering*, 20(6):476–493, 1994.

DFS99.   Alin Deutsch, Mary F. Fernandez, and Dan Suciu. Storing Semistructured Data with STORED. In *SIGMOD*. ACM Press, 1999.

Ext.   Extensibilty. XML Resources – Best Practices.
`http://www.extensibility.com/xml_resources/best_practices/`.

FS98.   Mary F. Fernandez and Dan Suciu. Optimizing regular path expressions using graph schemas. In *ICDE*. IEEE Computer Society, 1998.

FS00.   Wenfei Fan and Jérôme Siméon. Integrity constraints for xml. In *ACM-SIGMOD, May 15-17, 2000, Dallas, Texas, USA*, pages 23–34. ACM, 2000.

GHJV94.   Erich Gamma, Richard Helm, Ralph Johnson, and John Vlissides. *Design Patterns: Elements of Reusable Object-Oriented Software*. Addison-Wesley, 1994.

GW97.   Roy Goldman and Jennifer Widom. Dataguides: Enabling query formulation and optimization in semistructured databases. In *VLDB'97*. Morgan Kaufmann, 1997.

HP99.   Haruo Hosoya and Benjamin C. Pierce. XDuce: An XML Processing Language. Available from
           `http://www.cis.upenn.edu/~hahosoya/papers/xduce-prelim.ps`,   Dec 1999.

Jav99.   JavaSoft. An XML Data-Binding Facility for the Java Platform, July 1999. http://java.sun.com/xml/docs/bind.pdf.

Jav00.   JavaSoft. Code Fast, Run Fast with XML Data Binding, May 2000. http://java.sun.com/xml/docs/binding/DataBinding.html.

Jel99.   Rick Jelliffe. The Schematron. Available from
           `http://www.ascc.net/xml/resource/schematron`, 1999.

Kim99.   W. Eliot Kimber. Using UML To Define XML Document Types. Available from `http://www.drmacro.com/hyprlink/uml-dtds.pdf`, Dec 1999.

KMS99.   N. Klarlund, A. Moller, and M. Schwartzbach. DSD: A Schema Language for XML. Available at `http://www.brics.dk/DSD/`, Nov 1999.

Lie99.   Hartmut Liefke. Horizontal Query Optimization on Ordered Semistructured Data. In *WebDB*, 1999.

LS00.   Hartmut Liefke and Dan Suciu. XMill: an Efficient Compressor for XML Data. In *SIGMOD*. ACM Press, 2000.

Mur00.   Makoto Murata. RELAX (REgular LAnguage description for XML), July 2000. `http://www.xml.gr.jp/relax`.

MW99.   Jason McHugh and Jennifer Widom. Query Optimization for XML. In *VLDB*. Morgan Kaufmann, 1999.

STZ+99.   Jayavel Shanmugasundaram, Kristin Tufte, Chun Zhang, Gang He, David J. DeWitt, and Jeffrey F. Naughton. Relational Databases for Querying XML Documents: Limitations and Opportunities. In *VLDB*. Morgan Kaufmann, 1999.

W3Ca.   W3C. Extensible Markup Language (XML) 1.0. W3C Recommendation 10-February-1998. Available from
           `http://www.w3.org/TR/1998/REC-xml-19980210`.

W3Cb.   W3C. XML Path Language (XPath) 1.0. W3C Recommendation 16 November 1999. Available from `http://www.w3.org/TR/xpath`.

W3Cc.   W3C. XML Schema Part 0: Primer. Working Draft 25 February 2000. Available from `http://www.w3.org/TR/xmlschema-0`.

W3Cd.   W3C. XML Schema Part 1: Structures. Working Draft 25 February 2000. Available from `http://www.w3.org/TR/xmlschema-1`.

W3Ce.   W3C. XML Schema Part 2: Datatypes. Working Draft 25 February 2000. Available from `http://www.w3.org/TR/xmlschema-2`.

W3Cf.   W3C. XSL Transformations (XSL-T) 1.0. W3C Recommendation 16 November 1999. Available from `http://www.w3.org/TR/xslt`.

WR99.   Malcolm Wallace and Colin Runciman. Haskell and XML: Generic Combina-
          tors or Type-Based Translation? In *International Conference on Functional
          Programming*, Paris, France, Sept 1999.
XML.   XML Patterns. `http://www.xmlpatterns.com/`.

Version Management of XML Documents

Shu-Yao Chien[1], Vassilis J. Tsotras[2]*, and Carlo Zaniolo[3]

[1] Computer Science Department, UCLA.
csy@cs.ucla.edu.
[2] Department of Computer Science and Engineering,
UC Riverside.
tsotras@cs.ucr.edu.
[3] Computer Science Department, UCLA.
zaniolo@cs.ucla.edu.

Abstract. The problem of ensuring efficient storage and fast retrieval for multi-version structured documents is important because of the recent popularity of XML documents and semistructured information on the web. Traditional document version control systems, e.g. RCS, which model documents as a sequence of lines of text and use the shortest edit script to represent version differences, can be inefficient and they do not preserve the logical structure of the original document. Therefore, we propose a new approach where the structure of the documents is preserved intact, and their sub-objects are timestamped hierarchically for efficient reconstruction of current and past versions. Our technique, called the Usefulness Based Copy Control (UBCC), is geared towards efficient version reconstruction while using small storage overhead. Our analysis and experiments illustrate the effectiveness of the overall approach to version control for structured documents. Moreover UBCC can easily support multiple concurrent versions as well as partial document retrieval.

1 Introduction

The problem of managing multiple versions for XML and semistructured documents is of significant interest for content providers and cooperative work. The XML standard is considering this problem at the transport level. The WEB-DAV working group [14] is developing a standard extension to HTTP to support version control, meta data and name space management, and overwrite protection. In this paper, we take a database-oriented view of the problem of storing, processing, and querying efficiently multiple versions of documents, by adapting techniques used for temporal databases and persistent object managers. In fact, the flat structure of traditional file systems, currently used for the storage of these documents, is not best suited to support the raising demand for more powerful, complex computations on XML-based information, such as querying

* This research was partially supported by NSF (IIS-9907477) and by the Department of Defense.

D. Suciu and G. Vossen (Eds.): WebDB 2000, LNCS 1997, pp. 184–200, 2001.

on content and document restructuring. Our interest focuses on managing structured documents where tagged objects are timestamped with either their version number or their lifespan.

The rest of the paper is organized as follows: in the next section, we review the state of the art in version management and the limitations of current methods in dealing with XML documents. Then, the UBCC method is proposed in Section 3 to overcome these limitations, and its performance is evaluated in Section 4. In Section 5, we discuss two generalizations. One is the management of multiple concurrent versions as required, e.g., to support cooperative authoring. The other is efficient retrieval of document segments, instead of whole documents, which, e.g., occurs when particular sections of interest are identified through a table of contents or a keyword index.

2   Previous Work

Traditional line-based methods for version management, such as RCS [11] and SCCS [8], are not efficient for object-oriented structured documents. In fact, since these methods store versions using editing differences, information from many such differences are often required to reconstruct a single version. This results in more I/O cost and computation complexity in reconstructing the document's objects.

In particular, RCS [11] stores the most current version intact while all other revisions are stored as reverse editing scripts. These scripts describe how to go backward in the document's development history. For any version except the current one, extra processing is needed to apply the reverse editing script to generate the old version. Another popular text version management tool is SCCS [8]. Instead of appending version differences at the end like RCS, SCCS interleaves editing operations among original document/source code and associates a pair of timestamps with each text segment specifying the lifespan of that segment. Versions are retrieved from an SCCS file via scanning through the file and retrieving valid segments based on their timestamps. Both RCS and SCCS may read extra text segments which are invalid for the retrieved (target) version, resulting in additional processing cost. For RCS, the total I/O cost is proportional to the size of the current version plus the size of changes from the retrieved version to the current version. For SCCS, the situation is even worse: the whole version file needs to be read for any version retrieval. RCS further reduces version retrieval cost by maintaining an index for valid segments of each version; but it still has the problem that valid document segments may be stored sparsely among pages generated in different versions thus creating many page I/Os. Another missing feature of RCS and SCCS for XML documents is that they do not preserve the logical structure of the original document; this makes structure-related computation on the documents difficult and expensive to support.

3   Usefulness-Based Copy Control (UBCC)

To control version retrieval efficiency, we propose a new technique, the *Usefulness-Based Copy Control*, for storing versioned document objects. This strategy guarantees that the total I/O cost is linear in the size of the target version, instead of the size of the total number of changes between the most current (latest) and the target versions. UBCC clusters document objects using the notion of *page usefulness*, which is described below.

3.1   Page Usefulness

For simplicity assume that the document's evolution creates versions with a linear order: V_1, V_2, ..., where version V_i is before version V_{i+1}. This implies that a new version is established by applying a number of changes (object insertions, deletions or updates) to the latest version. Each document object is represented in the database by a record that contains the object id (oid), the object attributes (data, text) and a *lifespan* interval of the form: (insertion_version, deletion_version). The insertion_version is filled with the version when the object was added in the document. An object deletion at version V_i is not physical but *logical*: the deletion_version of the object's record is updated with the version when the deletion took place. This formulation concentrates on object insertions/deletions. An update of object O at version V_j is represented by an "artificial" deletion of the object followed by an "artificial" insertion of the updated object O at the same version V_j. The artificial insertion creates a new database record that shares the same oid O but has a subsequent non-overlapping lifespan interval.

Initially we may assume that objects in the document's very first version are physically stored in pages according to their logical order. After a number of changes, objects of a specific version may be physically scattered around different disk pages. Moreover, a page may store objects from different versions. Hence, when retrieving a specific version, a page access (read) may not be completely "useful". That is, some objects in an accessed page may be invalid for the target version. For example, assume that at version V_1, a document consists of five objects O_1, O_2, O_3, O_4 and O_5 whose records are stored in data page P. Let the size of these objects be 30%, 10%, 20% 25% and 15% of the page size, respectively. Consider the following evolving history for this document: At version V_2, object O_2 is deleted; at V_3, object O_3 is updated; at V_4, object O_5 is deleted, and at version V_5, object O_1 is deleted.

We define the *usefulness* of a full page P, for a given version V, as the percentage of the page that corresponds to valid objects for V. Hence page P is 100% useful for version V_1. Its usefulness falls to 90% for version V_2, since object O_2 is deleted at V_2. Similarly, P is 70% useful during version V_3. The update of O_3 invalidates its corresponding record in P (a new record for O_3 will be stored in another page since P is full of records). Finally page P falls to 25% usefulness after V_5.

Usefulness influences how well objects of a given version are clustered into pages. High usefulness implies that the objects of a given version are stored in fewer pages, i.e., this version will be reconstructed by accessing fewer pages. Clearly, a page maybe more useful for some versions and less for others. We would like to maintain a minimum page usefulness over all versions (setting this minimum is a performance parameter of our schemes). When a page's usefulness falls below the minimum the currently valid records in this page are copied to another page. This is similar to the "time-split" operation in temporal indexing [12] [7] [10]. Reconstructing a given version is then reduced to accessing only the useful pages for this version; this is very fast since each useful page contains a good part of the requested version. Moreover, the overall space used by the database remains linear in the number of changes in the document's version history.

The usefulness as defined above refers to full pages. If we assume that data records are written in pages sequentially, there can be a single page (the last one) that may not be full of records. We can extend the usefulness definition to include such non-full pages as useful by default. This will not affect performance since for each version there will be at most one such page.

3.2   UBCC Scheme

The RCS scheme performs the best when the changes from a version to the next are minimal. For instance, consider a first case, where only 0.1% of the document is changed between versions. Then, reconstructing the 100th version only requires 10% retrieval overhead. But RCS performs poorly when the changes grow larger. For instance, consider a second case, where each new version changes 70% of the document; retrieving the 100th version could cost 70 times retrieving the first one. In this second case, storing complete time-stamped versions is a much better strategy, costing zero overhead in retrieving each version and only a limited (43%) storage overhead. Most real-life situations range between these two cases— with minor revisions and major revisions often mixed in the history of a document. Thus, we need adaptable self-adjusting methods that, in the first case, operate as RCS, while in the second case tend to store complete time-stamped copies. The UBCC scheme achieves this desirable behavior by merging the old RCS scheme with an usefulness-based copy control scheme.

Another RCS' problem solved by UBCC is that RCS stores the editing script together with the new value of the revised objects. This increases the size of the script and the reconstruction time. A better approach is to separate the document objects from the editing script. Moreover, UBCC clusters both the document objects and editing script using the page usefulness clustering, thus reducing overhead for very long version histories. We will now summarize the UBCC scheme.

Example. Figure 1 shows three versions of a document. These versions are stored as shown in Figure 2. The first version is stored in pages P1, P2 and P3. We have assumed that the sizes of document objects, Root, CH A, SEC D, SEC E, CH B, SEC F, SEC G, SEC H, CH C, SEC I, SEC J are 50%, 25%, 10%, 15%,

```
         VERSION 1                      VERSION 2                      VERSION 3
------------------------      ---------------------------      ---------------------------

<Root>                        <Root>                           <Root>
  <CH A>                        <CH A>                           <CH A>
    <SEC D> ... </SEC>            <SEC E> ... </SEC>               <SEC E'> ... </SEC>
    <SEC E> ... </SEC>         </CH>                            </CH>
  </CH>                         <CH B>                           <CH B>
  <CH B>                          <SEC F> ... </SEC>               <SEC G'> ... </SEC>
    <SEC F> ... </SEC>            <SEC G'> ... </SEC>              <SEC N> ... </SEC>
    <SEC G> ... </SEC>         </CH>                            </CH>
    <SEC H> ... </SEC>          <CH K>                           <CH K>
  </CH>                           <SEC L> ... </SEC>               <SEC L> ...</SEC>
  <CH C>                        </CH>                              <SEC P> ...</SEC>
    <SEC I> ... </SEC>          <CH C>                           </CH>
    <SEC J> ... </SEC>            <SEC I> ... </SEC>             <CH C>
  </CH>                           <SEC J> ... </SEC>               <SEC J> ... </SEC>
</Root>                           <SEC M> ... </SEC>               <SEC M'> ...</SEC>
                              </CH>                                <SEC Q> ...</SEC>
                            </Root>                             </CH>
                                                              </Root>
```

Fig. 1. Sample XML document versions.

5%, 30%, 35%, 30%, 5%, 10%, and 5% of a data page size, respectively. Assume that we want to maintain a minimum page usefulness of 70%. Then pages P1 and P2 are well above the threshold for version V_1 (P3 is useful by default for version V_1).

Version V_2 is created by the following changes: *((delete SEC D) , (update SEC G with SEC G') , (delete SEC H) , (insert CH K after CH B) , (insert SEC L after CH K) , (insert SEC M after SEC J))* . The sizes of SEC G', CH K, SEC L and SEC M are 20%, 20%, 25% and 50% of a data page size, respectively. Hence, the logical order of objects in version 2 are: Root, CH A, SEC E, CH B, SEC F, SEC G', CH K, SEC L, CH C, SEC I, SEC J, SEC M. After applying these changes, Page P1 becomes 90% useful (SEC D is not part of version V_2), page P2 becomes 35% useful (since the original SEC G and SEC H are not part of V_2) and page P3 remains 20% useful (no change affected it). Then, pages P2 and P3 are *useless* for the second version and, thus, valid objects in P2 and P3 are copied into a new data page. Copied objects include CH B, SEC F , CH C , SEC I, and SEC J.

After determining which objects need copying, the copied objects are inserted into new pages in their logical order as shown in Figure 2. All new objects and copied objects are stored in page P4 and P5 based on the linear order they appear in Version 2.

UBCC Edit Script. To be able to reconstruct any version, we need to record an *UBCC edit script* for each version. The script for version V_2, E_2, is shown in Figure 2. E_2 is derived from the original edit script as follows:

– Each copied object is treated as a delete operation followed by an insert operation. For example, a delete operation is added for CH B and followed by an insert operation.

```
                        VERSION 1
-------------------------------------------------------------------------
  DATA PAGES :                        UBCC Script, E1 :

     +---------------------------+    ins(Root,1,P1), ins(CH A,2,P1),
  P1 | Root, CH A, SEC D, SEC E  |    ins(SEC D,3,P1), ins(SEC E,4,P1),
     +---------------------------+    ins(CH B,5,P2), ins(SEC F,6,P2),
  P2 | CH B, SEC F, SEC G, SEC H |    ins(SEC G,7,P2), ins(SEC H,8,P2),
     +---------------------------+    ins(CH C,9,P3), ins(SEC I,10,P3),
  P3 | CH C, SEC I, SEC J        |    ins(SEC J,11,P3)
     +---------------------------+


                        VERSION 2
-------------------------------------------------------------------------
  DATA PAGES :                        UBCC Script, E2 :

     +---------------------------+    del(SEC D,3),
  P4 | CH B, SEC F, SEC G', CH K |    del(CH B,4), ins(CH B,4,P4),
     | SEC L                     |    del(SEC F,5), ins(SEC F,5,P4),
     +---------------------------+    del(SEC G,6), ins(SEC G',6,P4),
  P5 | CH C, SEC I, SEC J, SEC M |    del(SEC H,7), ins(CH K,7,P4),
     +---------------------------+    ins(SEC L,8,P4),
                                      del(CH C,9), ins(CH C,9,P5),
                                      del(SEC I,10), ins(SEC I,10,P5),
                                      del(SEC J,11), ins(SEC J,11,P5),
                                      ins(SEC M,12,P5)


                        VERSION 3
-------------------------------------------------------------------------
  DATA PAGES :                        UBCC Script, E3 :

     +---------------------------+    del(SEC E,3), ins(SEC E',3,P6),
  P6 | SEC E', SEC N, SEC P      |    del(SEC F,5), ins(SEC N,6,P6),
     +---------------------------+    ins(SEC P,9,P6), del(CH C,10),
  P7 | CH C, SEC J, SEC M',      |    ins(CH C,10,P7), del(SEC I,11),
     | SEC Q                     |    del(SEC J,11), ins(SEC J,11,P7),
     +---------------------------+    del(SEC M,12), ins(SEC M',12,P7),
                                      ins(SEC Q,13,P7)
```

Fig. 2. UBCC version file.

– Attach to each operation the position of its target object in the new version. For example, the position of SEC F in the new version is 5.

Notice that, the position for a deleted object is its position in the new version as if it was not deleted. For example, the position of SEC D is 2 in the new version if it was not deleted, so, the delete operation *del(SEC D)* has a position value of 2. These position values are useful for recovering the total order of these objects. Their meaning will be discussed in more detail later.

Version V_3, is generated by the following changes: *((update SEC E with SEC E'),(delete SEC F),(insert SEC N after SEC G'), (insert SEC P after SEC L),(delete SEC I),(update SEC M with SEC M'), (insert SEC Q after SEC M'))*. Here the sizes of SEC E', SEC N, SEC P, SEC M', and SEC Q are 35%,15%,45%, 30% and 29% of the page size, respectively. As a result, pages P1, P4, and P5 become 75%, 70%, and 10% useful, respectively. Thus, valid objects in P5, *CH C, and SEC J,*

must be copied. New objects and copied objects are stored into new data pages
P6 and P7 in their logical order in Version 3. The *UBCC script*, E_3, for version
V_3 is shown in Figure 2. The insertion algorithm is illustrated in Figure 3.

```
INSERT() {
    Compute page usefulness based on the version editing script, Diff, and find pages need
        copying;

    Insert new objects and copied objects into new data pages based on their appearing
        order in the new version;

    Generate the UBCC script :
    For each (update Obj with New-Value)
        in DIFF replace the update operation, to two consecutive operations - (delete Obj),
        (insert New-Value);

    For each copied object insert an insert operation - ins(new_copy) - and a delete
        operation - del(old_copy) - into Diff by their logical position;

    Associate a position value for each operation in Diff. If the object is new or copied,
        its position value is its position in the new version. If the object is deleted, its
        position value is the same as that of the object right in front of it in the new
        version;

    Associate each insert operation with the page number of the page which contains its
        target object;

    Store UBCC script.
    Update hash tables.
}
```

Fig. 3. Version Insert Algorithm

Two auxiliary hash tables are used to improve the version insertion process.
The first hash table stores for each valid object of the current version the data
page which contains the object. The second hash table keeps the usefulness of
each page in the current version.

Version Reconstruction. Now, let us discuss how to retrieve a version, say
V_i. Since the objects of V_i may be stored in data pages generated in versions
V_1, V_2, ..., V_{i-1} and V_i, these objects may not be stored in their logical order.
Therefore, the first step is to reconstruct the logical order of V_i objects. The
logical order is recovered in a *gap-filling* fashion based on the UBCC script.
Let's take the sample version in Figure 1 as an example. We will explain the
algorithm by describing how to reconstruct Version 3.

The reconstruction starts by retrieving the first object of Version 3 from its
UBCC script, E3. We try to find the first object in the first edit operation. However, we get a *gap* from the operation. The position value of the first operation,
del(SEC E,3), is 3. That means, we miss the first two objects and need to *fill
the gap* from the previous version, Version 2. Recursively, we start to retrieve
the first two objects of Version 2. This retrieval starts from the first operation,
del(SEC D,3), of E2. We get a gap again and need to retrieve two objects from
the previous version, Version 1. From E1, we find the first two objects of Version

```
RECOVER(UBCC_SCRIPT S, INT request) {
    count = 0;
    while (count < request) {
        if (s is out of edit operation)
        {
            gap = request - counter;
            RECOVER(UBCC script of previous version of S, gap);
            Append returned object list.
            count = count + gap;
        }
        else if (target position < the position of current operation)
        {
            gap = position of current operation - target position;
            RECOVER(UBCC script of previous version of S, gap);
            Append returned object list.
            count = count + gap;
        }
        else if (current operation is delete)
        {
            RECOVER(UBCC script of previous version of S, 1);
            Nullify the retrieved object.
        }
        else if (target position = the position of current operation) {
            Append the object of current operation to return_object_list.
            count++;
        }
    }
    return return_object_list;
}
```

Fig. 4. Version Retrieval Algorithm

1 and return them to Version 2. Recursively, these two objects are sent back to Version 3. When Version 3 receives these two records, it reads the data page P1 which contains these two objects, Root and CH A, and output them. Page P1 is kept in main memory because it still contains one valid object, SEC E, for Version 3. The reconstruction of Version 3 continues from the previous stop point, *del(SEC D,3)* and the next object is the third object. Since the current operation is a delete, that means its target object is deleted from the previous version. Therefore, Version 3 requests the next object of Version 2 and it is expected to be SEC E. To answer the request for next object, Version 2 needs to retrieve its third object, because its first two objects have been retrieved in the previous run. In a similar manner, Version 2 needs to request one next object from Version 1 because of its *del(SEC D,3)* operation. As expected, the returned record is *ins(SEC D,3,P1)* and it is nullified by the delete operation. However, at this point, the third object of Version 2 has not been retrieved yet. So another next-object request is issued from Version 2 to Version 1 and Version 2 gets back SEC E which is the third object of Version 2. Version 2 sends the *ins(SEC E,4,P1)* record back to Version 3 to reply its next-object request as expected. And this insert record is nullified with the *del(SEC E,3)* record of E3. The search for the third object of Version 3 continues with checking the next edit operation in E3 which is *ins(SEC E',3,P6)*. Then we find the third object

because its position value is 3. This gap-filling procedure continues through the script E3 until all objects of Version 3 are retrieved.

Edit Script Snapshots. The above recursive gap-filling algorithm is used to reconstruct any version in the UBCC version file. Reconstructing version V_i may need to involve UBCC script E_1, E_2, ..., E_i, but only useful data pages for each version are read. As a result, the requested version is reconstructed with few page I/Os. However, as the total number of versions grows, the size of total edit scripts will accumulate and, sooner or later, will affect the version retrieval efficiency. To control the overhead of reading edit scripts, whenever the size of the edit scripts needed for reconstructing a particular version gets over a threshold (e.g. 10% of the size of the version) an *edit script snapshot* is built for this version. The *edit script snapshot* contains one insert record for each object in this version. The edit script $E1$ in Figure 2 is an example of an edit script snapshot. Generating an edit script snapshot will prevent the following versions from back-tracking to edit scripts of earlier versions.

3.3 Complexity Analysis

To reconstruct a version, only data pages which are useful for that version need to be read. Take Version 3 as an example. The total order of Version 3 objects is first recovered from edit scripts E3, E2 and E1. The resultant edit operation list is : *ins(Root , 1 , P1), ins(CH A , 2 , P1), ins(SEC E' , 3 , P6), ins(CH B , 4 , P4), ins(SEC G' , 6 , P4), ins(SEC N , 6 , P6), ins(CH K , 7 , P4), ins(SEC L , 8 , P4), ins(SEC P , 9 , P7), ins(CH C , 10 , P7), ins(SEC J , 11 , P7), ins(SEC M' , 12 , P7), ins(SEC Q , 13 , P7)*. Pages pointed by the pointers in these records are read sequentially and objects are retrieved from those pages. Useless pages, such as pages P2, P3, and P5, need not be read because valid objects in those pages have been copied into useful pages. However, consider the way in which the objects of Version 3 are stored. These objects are stored in useful pages generated for Version 3 (page P6 and page P7), Version 2 (page P4) and Version 1 (page P1). Objects generated in the same version are stored in the order in which they appear in the version. Therefore, the retrieving process is actually a merge of these 3 ordered object lists. Merging 3 object lists will involve at most 3 pages at any instance during the process. That means that, with enough memory to hold 3 pages, each useful page of Version 3 needs to be read only once through the whole retrieval process.

The above discussion is applicable to retrieving any version. That is, the I/O cost of reconstructing version V_i , with i pages in memory, is that of

1. reading edit scripts $E_i \cdots E_1$, plus
2. reading useful pages of version V_i.

Let S_i be the size of version V_i (in number of objects) and let B denote the capacity of a page. Clearly, the snapshot of V_i needs S_i/B pages. The number of useful pages created for version V_i is bounded by S_i/BU, where U is the required usefulness.

Let us consider the size of the database; this is determined by two parts: new objects and copied objects. New objects include first-time inserted new objects and updated objects. Since deleted objects are not removed from storage, deletions do not affect the size of database. Let S_{chg} denote the *total number of changes* in the document evolution (i.e., insertions, updates and deletions). Clearly, the new object part is bounded by $O(S_{chg})$. For the copied object part, the number of objects that got copied once is bounded by $U*S_{chg}$. Objects which got copied twice must be copied from those objects that have already been copied once. Therefore, the total number of objects copied twice is bounded by U^2*S_{chg}. Similarly, the number of objects that got copied i times is bounded by U^i*S_{chg}. Collectively, the total number of copied objects is bounded by :

$$\sum_{i=1}^{\infty} U^i * S_{chg} = S_{chg}/(1-U)$$

Hence the total number of copied objects is $O(S_{chg})$. Combining these two parts, the whole size of the database is linear $(O(S_{chg}))$.

4   Performance Evaluation

We evaluate the performance of UBCC scheme by examining its version retrieval cost and total database size. We compare its performance against the RCS scheme which uses no copies and thus has the least space requirements. We also compare UBCC against a *Snapshot* scheme that simply stores the whole document snapshot for each version. Obviously, the Snapshot scheme has the minimal version retrieval cost since each version is directly retrieved from the disk. In all experiments, the page size is set to 4K bytes.

We first examine the behavior of UBCC under various usefulness parameters, for a document whose size remains approximately the same between versions. More specifically, in the first set of experiments the size of each document version is about 100 pages while each version changes as much as 20% from the previous version (half of the changes are insertions and the other half are deletions). Changes are uniformly and randomly distributed among the document's data pages. The document evolution consists of 100 versions.

Figures 5 present the results. We examine the UBCC scheme under different usefulness requirement, namely, 25% useful, 50% useful and 75% useful. As expected, the Snapshot scheme has the lowest version retrieval cost (around 100 pages, since this is the document size per version). For the UBCC scheme, the retrieval cost is also proportional to the version size, but the actual cost depends on the usefulness parameter. Lower usefulness implies that a page can contain more invalid objects for a given version, or equivalently, a version's objects will be scattered among more data pages, thus increasing retrieval time. This is observed in Figure 5 where the UBCC with 25% usefulness has the largest retrieval overhead, followed by the 50% and 75%. The graph also shows that the RCS strategy needs to read the whole database prior to the target version. Therefore,

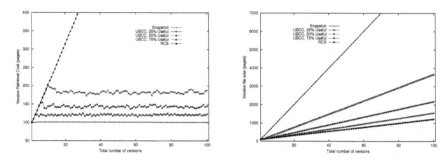

Fig. 5. Version retrieval and storage cost for various usefulness requirement (constant document size).

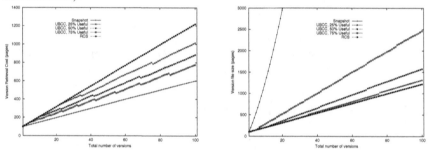

Fig. 6. Version retrieval and storage cost for an increasing document size evolution.

retrieving later versions gets more expensive than earlier versions. For example, the I/O cost of retrieving the 20th version is 320% of that version's size.

While the Snapshot scheme provides the minimal version retrieval cost, its storage cost is prohibitively expensive (at worst, it is quadratic to the total number of changes). RCS has the minimal storage cost since it stores only the changes. The space of all UBCC cases grows linearly with the number of changes, however, at a different rate. The storage overhead of the UBCC scheme is due to copied objects. With higher usefulness requirement, a page becomes useless faster and thus more copies are made.

The next experiments were designed to explore evolutions where the document's size expands or shrinks. In the expanding evolution experiment, a version increases the document's size by approximately 5% (at each version there are 10% insertions and 5% deletions). The performance results appear in Figure 6. Again, the version retrieval cost of the UBCC scheme is proportional to the document size (which now increases linearly). The actual overhead depends on the usefulness parameter. Similarly, the UBCC storage cost is linear in the size of total changes. Note that the UBCC with 25% or 50% usefulness has space cost very close to the minimal storage of RCS. That is because the small deletion percentage rarely causes UBCC to copy useless pages.

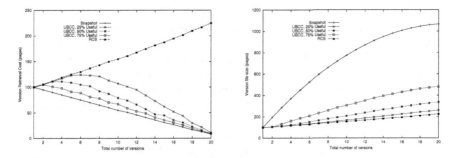

Fig. 7. Version retrieval and storage cost for a decreasing document size evolution.

Figure 7 illustrates the UBCC performance when the document size shrinks at a rate of 5%. Here, the version changes consist of 10% deletions and 5% insertions. The UBCC version retrieval cost decreases as the document shrinks. However, the RCS scheme retrieval cost grows linearly with the number of changes.

From the above experimental results we observe that the performance of the UBCC scheme can be tuned accordingly using the usefulness parameter. While using space that is close to the RCS scheme, its retrieval time approaches the optimal of the Snapshot scheme. The actual choice of the usefulness parameter can be set based on the application characteristics (document evolution, available space, required retrieval time).

5 Generalizing UBCC

5.1 Multiple Concurrent Versions

The paper so far has concentrated on linear sequences of versions where there is exactly one document version valid at a given time.

In this context, a notation such as *mydocument*[6] will be used to denote the sixth version of this document. Alternatively, this version number might be replaced by the time interval during which version 6 is valid.

In the software engineering world, it is instead common to use a tree-structured model for versions [2], [5], [11], [8], where a new version stems out as a new branch, which is normally called a 'minor' branch, while the original branch is called the 'major' branch. From that point on the two branches evolve independently.

For instance *mydocument*[4].*firstauthor*[3] would denote the third revision of the minor branch (named 'firstauthor') stemming out from version 4 of the major branch. Naturally, several minor branches can stem out from the same version, as in the case where several authors start revising the paper in parallel. Also, any branch can later subdivide into more branches.

In cooperative work, it is often the case that several branches are merged back, as in the case of multiple authors who revised different parts of a document in parallel, and their changes are now merged into the final paper. In this case, the overall document process can be represented as an directed acyclic graph (DAG).

This new version model is significantly more powerful than the original model which captured a document at different stages of its evolution. The new model provides for the verification of progress in authoring, guarantees fail-safe base-lines for exploratory changes; also it supports verification and comparison of the individual efforts in a multi-authoring situation.

Yet, this richer model adds very little complexity to our original UBCC scheme. Basically, the scheme needs to be revised as follows:

- A separate edit script must be kept for each minor branch. Strictly speaking, this script could share some part with the major script. However, to simplify the management, we assume that each new branch is started with a fresh edit script snapshot.
- When a minor branch is started, the usefulness of the current page is computed assuming that only the objects of the minor branch are alive. The rest of the page, including the part that is still empty, is considered expired. If this usefulness is below the threshold, the alive objects for the minor branch are copied into a new page (otherwise they are not), where all objects of the minor branch will then be written. New objects of the major branch are written in the current page (until this is full). From that point on, separate branches are managed independently, and objects from different branches are assigned to different pages. The usefulness of these pages is computed by viewing the empty part of a current page as useful.

Therefore, the only minor complication in our revised UBCC script involves the management of the current page at the time in which one or more minor branches are generated. If we allow both the minor and major branches to write (small revisions) onto our current page, this might fill with a mixture that fails the usefulness test for both branches. Then, a copy of the current page will have to be made for the major branch and another for the minor branch. We can avoid the unnecessary copying of the major branch, by letting it to be the only writer to the current branch from that point on. For the minor branch, we will first decide whether the current page is useful assuming that empty spaces are used by the major branch; then new pages are used for copied objects (if any) and other new objects of this branch.

The merging of two branches is even simpler; it can be accomplished by simply letting one the branches continue with objects taken from the other. The edit script of the continuing branch will simply refer to the objects from the other branch. If the percentage of objects copied from a page of this other branch falls below the usefulness level, a standard copying operation is performed.

5.2   Structuring and Indexing Document Versions

In the previous sections we have focused on the problem of retrieving *complete* versions of documents. In reality, users are frequently interested in retrieving particular parts or sections of a versioned document. For instance, after consulting the table of contents for a certain document version, the user could request, say, Chapter 6, or Sections 8.2 through 8.5 of that version. To support this partial retrieval, the edit script can be augmented with markers that facilitate the identification of the major logical structure of the document. The objective is to allow the retrieval of the desired sections of the desired versions by only retrieving the pertinent portions of the edit script, and the pages containing the desired segments identified by the script.

A similar problem occurs in the common situation where an index is used on a versioned document. The entries in such an index normally point to particular objects in the document that contain a keyword of interest, in the case of manual indexing, or any non-stop word, in the case of full-text inversion. A direct indexing into the database might succeed in retrieving the actual text, but we will then find it difficult to decide which version and section it belongs to. Therefore, we propose that, rather than pointing directly to the database, the index should point to the structured edit script, through which both the actual objects and the information about version number and section can be easily obtained.

The proposed solutions are made possible by the edit script with snapshots used in our UBCC scheme. Using the RCS scheme instead, the only general solution that would be possible for the Table-Of-Content and indexing problem is to reconstruct the appropriate version (up to the sections or chapters of interest) from the database. Thus, for RCS, the cost of reconstructing a single sections pointed by a table of contents or an index is not much less than that of reconstructing the whole document.

The *nested list* model is used to add logical structure. The following three markers are used in edit scripts: '[' , ']' , and ',', where '[' and ']' denote the start and end of a new level, and ',' is the separator between list elements. Much as any other entry in the edit script, each instance of these three markers is given with a position value that denotes its linear location in the edit script. For example, the version 1 in Figure 2 is structured as :

$$root, [ch\ A, [sec\ D, sec\ E], ch\ B, [sec\ F, sec\ G, sec\ H], ch\ C, [sec\ I, sec\ J]]$$

and its edit script E1 is :

$$ins(root), ins(','), ins('['), ins(ch\ A), ins('['), ins(sec\ D) \cdots$$
$$ins(sec\ J), ins(']'), ins(']')$$

Objects can also be uniquely identified via their logical position in the tree; For example, sec H is referred to as 1.2.3. To retrieve sec H, we can then use a depth-first search to traverse the structured edit script. With the structured edit scripts, queries, such as "Retrieve the document from the second chapter through the first section of the third chapter," can be easily answered by issuing a request of retrieving the document segment from position 1.2 to position 1.3.1.

The edit script is augmented for each new version to denote the changes. To maintain the structure of edit scripts, each inserted (or copied) object record is placed in the appropriate position in the structured script. The markers '[', ']', and ',' are inserted into or deleted from the edit script as needed to update the structure of the document.

To retrieve a part of a version, say, the segment from the second chapter through the first section of the third chapter, the structured edit script snapshot of the Version 2 is first built by the standard version object order reconstructing algorithm, as shown in Figure 4. We obtain the following edit script snapshot:

$$root, [chA, [sec\ E], chB, [sec\ F, sec\ G'], chK, [sec\ L], chC, [sec\ I, sec\ J, sec\ M]]$$

During the reconstruction process, the position of each object is checked to see if it is within the range of 1.2 to 1.3.1. If it is, the data page containing that object is read and the object is output, otherwise no data page is read. The reconstruction process stops as soon as it reaches the end of the required range. For our example, the reconstruction is completed when sec E is read.

Other index structures can be built on top of the structured edit script, for example, an *inverted index*. Assume that an entry for the keyword "Prozac" needs to be added to the index built on a versioned medical document. For each object which contains the key word "Prozac", one entry is recorded in the index. For example, the following index entries

$$(Version\ 2, Version\ 5, 1.1.9, (1.2.2, 1.2.7))$$
$$(Version\ 6, Version\ 8, (1.2.3, 1.3))$$

denote that our keyword appears in object 1.1.9, and in the segment from 1.2.2 through 1.2.7, for versions 2 through 5; also our keyword appears in versions 6 through 8 of the document segment from 1.2.3 to 1.3. Queries such as, "For versions 4 through 7, retrieve all chapters mentioning Prozac," can be answered by first checking the inverted index and locating the target document ranges and, then, locate these ranges for each version through structured edit scripts. No unnecessary versions or unwanted document segments are read.

An alternate approach could have the index entries to point to the actual objects; but then it would not be easy to reconstruct the logical structure of versions. Our generalized UBCC scheme provides a simple and flexible approach for implementing structure-oriented indexes for versioned documents. For each document type, the structure of the document could also have been represented using its specific XML tags. But the use of a generic tree structure yields better portability for generic applications, such as table of contents and keyword indexing.

6   Conclusion

In this paper, we have proposed a new strategy – usefulness-based copy control (*UBCC*) – to manage evolving structured documents. *UBCC* is I/O efficient and requires only minimal extra space. Compared with traditional strategies like RCS, the new strategy improves the efficiency of version retrieval at the cost of some controlled copying. In fact, in [4] we investigated the performance of UBCC against alternative techniques for storing versions, including extensions of a persistent paginated list method [6], and of the multiversioned B+ tree method used in temporal databases [1]. This comparison shows that the *UBCC* method performs better than these other approaches in terms of storage and retrieval efficiency [4].

Furthermore we have shown here that the UBCC method provides a flexible platform for supporting various kinds of document queries and computations, including, concurrent versioning and index on document structure. Other approaches, such as RCS [11], and the page list or the multiversion B+ methods discussed in [4] do not provide this flexibility.

We are currently investigating related issues, including querying and restructuring of versioned documents, and efficient generation for browser output and/or transport over the internet of versioned documents. These include the automatic generation of DTDs for versioned documents from the DTD of the unversioned document.

References

1. B. Becker, S. Gschwind, T. Ohler, B. Seeger, P. Widmayer, *"On Optimal Multiversion Access Structures"*, Proceedings of Symposium on Large Spatial Databases, Vol 692, 1993, pp. 123-141.
2. B. Berliner, *"CVS II: Parallelizing Software Development"*, http://www.cyclic.com/dev/source.html.
3. S-Y. Chien, V.J. Tsotras, and C. Zaniolo, *"Version Management of XML Documents"*, WebDB 2000 Workshop, Dallas, TX, 2000.
4. S-Y. Chien, V.J. Tsotras, and C. Zaniolo, *"A Comparative Study of Version Management Schemes for XML Documents"*, Submitted to ICDE 2001.
5. E. S. Cohen, D. A. Soni, R. Gluecker, W. M. Hasling, R. W. Schwanke and M. E. Wagner. *"Version Management in Gypsy"*, ACM SIGSOFT/SIGPLAN Software Engineering Symposium on Practical Software Development Environments. 1988.
6. A. Kumar, V. J. Tsotras, C. Faloutsos, *Access Methods for Bi-Temporal Databases*, IEEE Transactions on Knowledge and Data Engineering, Vol. 10, No. 1, 1998, pp 1-20.
7. D. Lomet and B. Salzberg, *Access Methods for Multiversion Data*, ACM SIGMOD Conference, pp: 315-324, 1989.
8. Marc J. Rochkind, *The Source Code Control System*, IEEE Transactions on Software Engineering, SE-1, 4, Dec. 1975, pp. 364-370.
9. D. Shasha, K. Zhang, *Fast algorithms for the unit cost editing distance between trees* Journal of Algorithms, 1990, 11:581-621.
10. B. Salzberg and V.J. Tsotras, *A Comparison of Access Methods for Time-Evolving Data*, ACM Computing Surveys, Vol. 31, No. 2, pp: 158-221, 1999.
11. Walter F. Tichy, *RCS–A System for Version Control*, Software–Practice & Experience 15, 7, July 1985, pp. 637-654.

Modeling Data Entry and Operations in WebML

Aldo Bongio[1], Stefano Ceri[2], Piero Fraternali[2], and Andrea Maurino[2]

[1] Politecnico di Milano, via Ponzio 34/5
20133 Milano Italy
bongio@fusberta.elet.polimi.it
[2] Politecnico di Milano, via Ponzio 34/5
20133 Milano Italy
{ceri,fraterna,maurino}@elet.polimi.it

Abstract. Web Modeling Language (WebML http://www.webml.org) is a notation for visually specifying complex Web sites at the conceptual level. All the concepts of WebML are specified both graphically and in XML; in particular, navigation and composition abstractions are based on a restricted number of hypertext components (units) which are assembled into pages and interconnected by links.

During implementation, pages and units are automatically translated into server-side scripting templates, which enable the display of data dynamically retrieved from heterogeneous data sources. This paper extends WebML with data entry and operation units, for gathering information from clients and invoking arbitrary operations.

Predefined operations are also proposed as built-in primitives for supporting standard updates on the content of the underlying data sources (represented as entities and relationships).

This natural extension of WebML permits the visual modeling of Web pages integrating read and write access, an essential aspect of many E-commerce applications (including user profiling and shopping cart management).

1   Introduction

Recently, important research efforts have addressed the conceptual modeling of data-intensive Web sites, under the assumption that the data content can be dynamically extracted from external data sources. Problems such as declarative Web specification [1,2,4,8], Web design patterns [9], or the semantic integration of data deriving from multiple sources [7,10] were extensively studied. In particular, [6] describes WebML, the conceptual model used within the W3I3 Project [5] for designing data-intensive Web sites. So far, most efforts have been focused on data retrieval, the most important aspect of Web site design. However, many applications require also the support of user-driven content generation and update; examples of such applications in E-commerce include the user profiles maintenance and shopping carts. Most conceptual Web design methods proposed so far do not include primitives for content production and update.

D. Suciu and G. Vossen (Eds.): WebDB 2000, LNCS 1997, pp. 201–214, 2001.

Another important problem concerns the seamless integration of automatically generated Web sites with external applications or with pre-existing Web pages, which are not described at the conceptual level. These legacy Web applications, which do not use the generative approach proposed by new-generation, model-based Web authoring tools, constitute the majority of current Web applications, and are a commodity that cannot be neglected by pragmatic Web design environments. This paper presents a solution for both the above problems, which smoothly extends WebML by adding two simple hypertext construction primitives for supporting data entry and operations. These abstractions are general and can be easily integrated in other conceptual Web design models. The novelty of the WebML approach to operation specification, e.g., with respect to object-oriented modeling languages, is the tight integration of the functional specifications into the composition and navigation model of the site, which is necessary to express the interplay between the design of the hypertext pages and of the operations applicable in the site.

WebML operations are simply added to a hypertext structure as side effects of navigating links, as indeed their effect is not only the execution of some computation, but also the navigation of one or more links between units and the production or transport of context information from one part of the hypertext to another one. This joint approach to hypertext and function specification is well suited to conceptual Web design also by non-technical people, because it does not require the expression of the functional aspects of a site in a separate notation, and can be easily integrated in the same automated code-generation process that transforms the read-only part of the site specifications into a concrete implementation.

The paper is organized as follows. Section 2 provides a short introduction of WebML. Section 3 describes the new concepts of Data Entry and operation units, by showing their syntax and some examples. Section 4 describes predefined operation units introduced to enable the change of database content. Then, Section 5 provides an example of use of Data Entry and operation units by modeling the CdNow's trolley. Finally, Section 6 draws the conclusions.

2   Preliminaries on WebML

The specification of a site in WebML consists of five orthogonal perspectives:

1. The **Structural Model** expresses the data content of the site, in terms of the relevant entities and relationships expressed by means of the E/R model [3].
2. The **Composition Model** specifies which pages compose the hypertext, and which content units make up a page.
3. The **Navigation Model** expresses links, which are drawn between pages and content units to form the hypertext.
4. The **Presentation Model** expresses the layout and graphic appearance of pages, independently of the output device and of the rendering language.

5. The **Personalization Model** expresses personalization requirements.

Figure 1 shows a graphic representation of a structural model, describing a simplified data source underlying a site for supporting the sale of records (freely inspired to the popular site http://www.cdnow.com). Artists are associated to

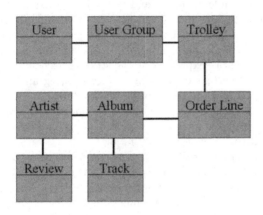

Fig. 1. Example of structural schema

their Reviews and Albums and each Album is associated to its Tracks. User and User Group are also modeled as application entities, and users can instantiate a trolley and fill it with orders, each one described by an Order Line.

The composition model of WebML supports six types of units, used to compose a hypertext:

- **Data units** show information about a single object, e.g., an instance of an entity or of a component. The definition of a data unit requires the indication of the concept (entity or component) to which the unit refers and the selection of the attributes to include in the unit content.
- **Multi-data** units show information about a set of objects, e.g., all the instances of an entity or all the components of a composite object. The definition of a multi-data unit requires the specification of the instances to be displayed (e.g., all entities related to a given one by a relationship) and of the data unit used to present such instances.
- **Index** units show a list of objects, where each entry is denoted by a descriptive key, i.e., a subset of the object's attributes. A selection from the index causes the access to another unit, which typically displays more information about the selected object.
- **Scroller** units show commands for accessing the elements of an ordered set of objects (the first, last, previous, next, i-th).
- **Filter** units show edit fields for inputting values used for searching within a set of object(s) those ones that meet a condition.

– **Direct** units denote the connection to a single object that is semantically related to another object by means of a one-to-one or many-to-one relationship.

Units are assembled into **pages**, which represent the abstraction of a self-contained region of the screen treated as an independent interface block (e.g., delivered to the user independently and in one shot). Examples of concrete implementations of the abstract concept of page in specific languages may be a frame in HTML or a deck in WML. Units and pages are connected to form a hypertext structure, by means of WebML **links**, which connect units in a way coherent to the semantics expressed by the structure schema of the application. Figure 2 shows a hypertext comprising a page showing an album, the (single) artist who issued it, and the index of its tracks. From the ArtistInfo unit it is possible to access other pages hosting the artist's biography and a list of reviews. More information about the semantics of units, links, and hypertexts in WebML can be found at http://webml.org and in [6].

WebML specifications are collected by means of user-friendly case tools and stored into an XML design repository. The XML representation is used for the automatic implementation and maintenance of Web sites: XSL-based technology is used for transforming WebML specifications into page templates in the rendering language of choice, (currently, we support HTML and WML). XSL translators assume that the application content is stored in a repository wrapped by an object-oriented API, and therefore map each unit into suitable calls to such an API. The WebML runtime API can retrieve data from multiple heterogeneous sources (presently, we support relational DBMSs and LDAP directories). This paper extends the "read only" approach (supported by the first version of WebML), to include generic data entry units and operations for enabling the interaction with external users and programs.

3   WebML Support for Data Entry and Operations

Data entry and operation units constitute the fundamental ingredients for adding to a Web modeling language the capability of expressing the collection of input from the user and the interaction with software functions of arbitrary complexity. Introducing data entry and operations affects composition and navigation modeling. The composition model is extended with two new units, called data entry and operation units, the navigation model is extended by adding to links the property of being operation-activating and by distinguishing a special class of links, called KO-links, associated with execution failure.

3.1   Data Entry Units

Data entry units are used for collecting input values into fields, which are then fed as parameters to operations for performing the required processing (e.g., content updates, searches, external operations). The value of each field

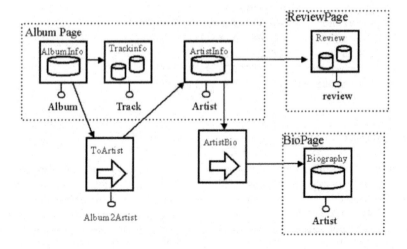

Fig. 2. Example of hypertext built with WebML composition and navigation primitives.

is either a constant expression, or extracted from the database, or provided by the user. If a field has mode "in" it is initialized by means of a default expression and then remains immutable; "out" fields are not initialized and specified interactively by the user; "inout" fields are initialized by means of a default expression and then modifiable interactively by the user. Default values are specified as expressions referencing context parameters of incoming links. Additional WebML properties of data entry units, not covered in this paper, describe integrity constraints on input fields, such as type information and Boolean expressions defining admissible values. Data entry units have one or more outgoing links, each of which corresponds to the acceptance of the user input and its submission to a given destination unit. These links have an associated context including all the parameter values of the data entry unit and are implemented in HTML and WML as the SUBMIT commands of a FORM.

The specification of data entry units (as of any other unit in WebML) is given in XML, according to the following syntax:

```
<!ELEMENT ENTRYUNIT (FIELD*, LINK*)>
<!ATTLIST ENTRYUNIT
        id      ID      #REQUIRED
        name    CDATA   #IMPLIED>

<!ELEMENT FIELD EMPTY >
<!ATTLIST FIELD
        id      ID      #REQUIRED
        name    CDATA   #IMPLIED
```

```
mode    (in|out|inout)   'out'
value       CDATA   #IMPLIED
link        IDREF   #IMPLIED
entity      IDREF   #IMPLIED
component       IDREF   #IMPLIED
relationship    IDREF   #IMPLIED
>
```

3.2   Operation Units

Operation units are used to invoke generic external operations implemented by externally defined Web pages. They take in input information received by means of one or more links; one of them is declared as **operation-activating** (optionally denoted by a circled A on the link's arc) and its navigation causes operation execution. Non-activating links may provide additional input information. After operation execution, which may entail an arbitrarily long interaction with external applications, context information can be brought (back) to WebML-modeled units, by one link dynamically selected among the operation's output links. All the required input parameters should be present when the operation is fired; controlling the correctness of the operation invocation, including the availability and suitability of input parameters, is part of the operation semantics.

WebML does not impose any specific requirement on the ACID properties of state changes, for instance there is no guarantee concerning the transaction's atomicity. In the future releases of WebML we exepect to provide model support for introducing the notion of atomic transactions. However, if the underlying data content is managed by a suitably interconnected data management system, then explicit built-in operations can be used to control the ACID properties of computations. In particular, a Commit-Work primitive atomically commits the entire collection of state changes occurred since the last invocation of the primitive (or since the first operation); similarly, a Rollback-Work primitive atomically rolls back all the state changes. Such built-in operations are translated in a straightforward way by invoking suitable services of the underlying data management software. The specification of operation units is given in XML, according to the following syntax:

```
<!ELEMENT OPERATIONUNIT (PARAMETER*, LINK*)>
<!ATTLIST OPERATIONUNIT
            id          ID      #REQUIRED
            name        CDATA   #IMPLIED
            operation   CDATA   #REQUIRED
        >
```

3.3   Example

Figure 3 describes an example of usage of a data entry unit coupled with an operation unit. The first unit collects user input and forwards it to a subscription operation, by means of an operation-activating link. The XML specification of the example is shown below.

```
<ENTRYUNIT id="MailEntryUnit">
    <FIELD id="userNameField"/>
    <FIELD id="emailAddressField"/>
    <LINK id="link1" to="SubscrUnit" type="activating"/>
</ENTRYUNIT>

<OPERATIONUNIT id="SubscrUnit"
    operation="subscribe">
    <PARAMETER id="uname"
  value="link1.userNameField">
    <PARAMETER id="email"
  value="link1.emailAddressField">
    <PARAMETER id="listName" value="'BestOffers'">
</OPERATIONUNIT>
```

The operation unit receives input from a single operation-activating link named link1, coming from a data entry unit, where the user can insert his username and email address. After the navigation of link1, rendered as a submit button, the "subscribe" operation is performed; this takes two parameters from the context of the incoming link (link1.userNameField and link1.emailAddressField), and a third constant parameter, which denotes the name of the mailing list to which the user is subscribing.

4   Predefined Operation Units

Several **predefined operation units** offer the standard operations for updating (at an abstract level) the content of the Web application; they support the creation, update, and deletion of entities and the creation and deletion of relationships. Operation units have a fixed number of input parameters, carried along one or two input links. They have an arbitrary number of output links, but exactly one of them is associated with the **failure of the operation**.

4.1   Entity Creation

The first built-in operation enables the creation of an entity or component. A *create* unit has as attributes the name of the entity or component being created, and receives from the input links the parameters which correspond to the entity's attributes. Omitted parameters are treated as null values. The *create* unit has two output links: a normal link is followed in case of success of the operation and a KO-link is followed in case of failure. The OID of the entity being created is one of the parameters implicitly associated with the OK output link. Figure 4 shows the creation of an artist object.

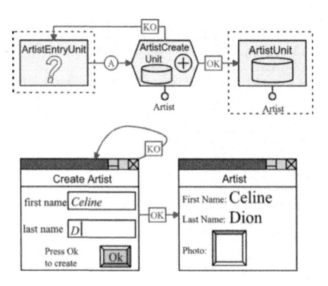

Fig. 3. Example of entity creation unit, coupled with a data entry unit; the OK link brings to the artist unit showing the newly created instance, the KO link brings back to the data entry unit.

4.2   Entity Deletion

A deletion unit is used to delete a given entity instance. The unit receives from its input link a single parameter, giving the object's OID. The example of Figure 5 shows a hypertext where an index unit is used to display the descriptive keys of several albums, among which the user may select the one to delete.

4.3   Entity Modification

A modification unit is used to change the content of a given entity or component instance. The operation receives from its input link a parameter, giving the object or component's OID; in addition, it requires a link from a data entry unit in order to receive the new attribute values from the user. The modification unit XML syntax explicitly lists the attributes to modify, and thus the update can be restricted to a subset of the object's attributes. Figure 6 shows how an artist's

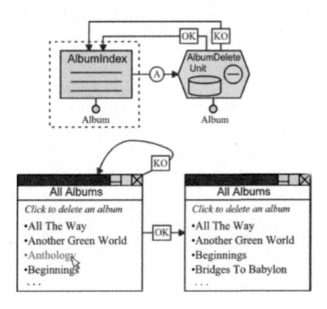

Fig. 4. Example of entity selection and deletion

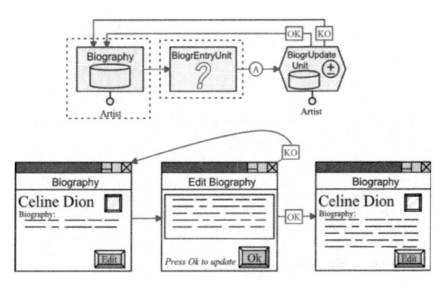

Fig. 5. Example of entity modification

biography can be updated, by first navigating the link to a data entry unit, and then activating the entity modification unit. Both the OK and KO links bring back to the Biography data unit.

4.4   Relationship Creation

A connection unit is used to create instances of relationships between pairs of entities, whose OIDs are the parameters required in input by the unit. Figure 7

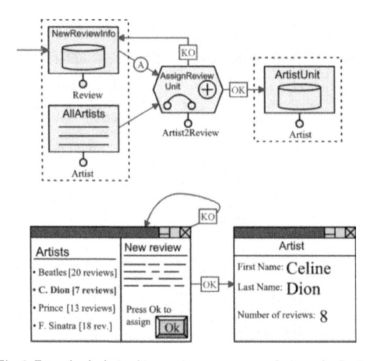

Fig. 6. Example of relationship creation to connect an Artist and a Review

shows an example of the connection unit. The user selects the artist to whom the review refers, and then activates the operation by navigating the activating link, whose effect is to connect the selected artist to the review. On success (OK link), a new page describing the selected artist is displayed; on failure (KO link), the initial page is presented again.

4.5   Relationship Deletion

A disconnection unit is used to drop instances of relationships between pairs of entities, whose OIDs are the parameters required in input by the unit. Figure 8 shows a page containing information about Artists and their albums, whose titles are displayed by an index. Once a title entry is selected, the information about the Album is displayed in the same page. With the selected album displayed, the relationship is deleted as an effect of an explicit navigation of the operation-activating link (as in Figure 3, such an explicit activation may be rendered by a button with an indication of the operation's side effect). Note that in this example the OIDs of both the instances that must be disconnected flow along a single activating link, as parameters of its context information. The activating link passes to the operation unit also the OID of the artist, taken from the input link coming from AlbumIndexUnit, which by default carries the OID of the object "owning" the relationship instances shown in the index.

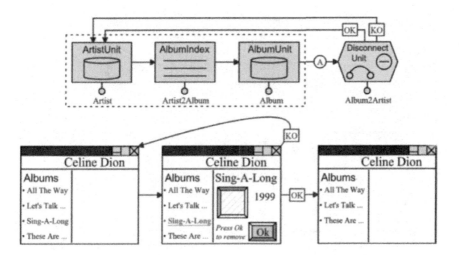

Fig. 7. Example of relationship deletion unit to disconnect an Album from an Artist

5   CDnow's Trolley

We show data entry and predefined units at work in the modeling of the CDnow. In the CDnow application, users can select one or more album to buy by clicking the *add to chart* link. The application·adds, in a transparent way, items into the trolley and displays the user's trolley page (see Figure 9). If the user wants to remove an item from his trolley he will select the *Remove* link, while if the user wants to change the quantity of an item he will select the *change quantity* link. If so the modify page will be displayed in order to change the quantity of selected item.

The hypertextual model of the CDnow trolley is shown in Figure 10. The user is implicitly asociated with a trolley instance when he is first connects to the CDnow site (anonymous trolley) but then, at any point, the user can identify

Fig. 8. The CDnow's trolley page

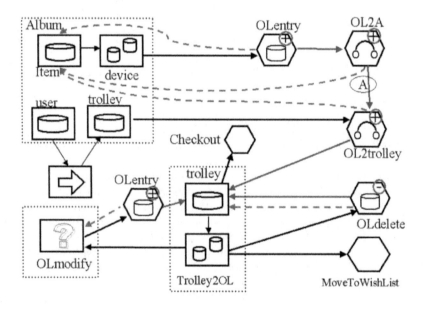

Fig. 9. The hypertextual model of CDnow's trolley. The dashed line are the KO links

himself; identification is required before any purchase. Thus, the trolley can be associated with the "anonymous" user while selections are being made. When the user pushes the "buy" button in the Album page, a chain of operations is activated, consisting in adding an order line with the selected album and quantity set to 1, then connecting the new order line with the user's trolley and with the selected album. If the chain of three operations is successfull, the trolley is shown on a page enclosing the trolley data unit (with current subtotal) and a multidata unit listing the selected CDs (see Fig. 9). For each of them it is possible removing the order line, changing the quantity (e.g. setting it to 2, buying two copies of the same record, or to 0, thus eliminating the order line), or calling an operation for moving the CD to a personalized wish list. Similarly, from the trolley unit it is possible to invoke an operation for the secure checkout and one for the standard checkout. Operations require the users to identify themselves if they are still anonymous; they are left unmodeled in our example.

6   Conclusion

This paper has shown two new Web modeling abstractions, which integrate data entry and operation invocation into WebML, an existing modeling notation for specifying read-only Web sites. These extensions can be orthogonally combined with primitives for composing hypertexts and defining their navigation, thus building on user skills matured in the conceptual specification of read-only Web sites. WebML is currently applied in the re-engineering of a large e-commerce site, where the write access primitives described in this paper are used to specify and implement a shopping cart connected to a legacy application for order confirmation and delivery. WebML read-only primitives are fully implemented in a Web design tool suite called ToriiSoft (http://www.toriisoft.com). The write extensions described in the paper are under implementation. Following the present implementation of WebML, the novel WebML primitives will be automatically translated into multiple rendering languages (including HTML, WML, XML+XSL, and special-purpose languages for TeleText applications) and server side scripting languages (including MicroSoft's Active Server Pages and JavaSoft's Java Server Pages).

References

1. C.R. Anderson, A. Levy, D.S. Weld, Declarative Web-Site Management with Tiramis, WebDb99 (Informal Proceedings), 1999.
2. P.Atzeni, G. Mecca, P. Merialdo, Design and maintenance of data-intensive web sites. In Proc. Int. Conf. Extending Database Technology EDBT), Valencia, Spain, 1998.
3. P. P. Chen, The Entity-Relationship Model, Towards a Unified View of Data, ACM Transactions on Database Systems, 1:1, 1976, pp. 9-36.
4. S. Ceri, P. Fraternali, S. Paraboschi: Design Principles for Data-Intensive Web Sites, ACM Sigmod Record, 27(4), Dec. 1998, pp.74-80.

5. S.Ceri, P.Fraternali, S.Paraboschi: Data-Driven, One-To-One Web Site Generation for Data-Intensive Applications. VLDB 1999, Edinburgh, Sept. 1999, 615-626.
6. S. Ceri, P. Fraternali, A. Bongio, Web Modeling Language (WebML): a Modeling Language for Designing Web Sites, in Proc. WWW9 Conference, Computer Networks 33 (2000) 137-157.
7. Mary F. Fernandez, Daniela Florescu, Jaewoo Kang, Alon Y. Levy, Dan Suciu: Catching the Boat with Strudel: Experiences with a Web-Site Management System. SIGMOD Conference 1998: 414-425
8. P. Fraternali, P.Paolini, A Conceptual model and a tool environment for developing more scalable, dynamic, and customizable Web applications. In Proc. Int. Conf. Extending Database Technology (EDBT), Valencia, Spain, 1998.
9. F. Garzotto, P. Paolini, D. Bolchini, and S. Valenti: "Modeling by patterns" of Web Applications, in Proc. Int. Workshop on the World Wide Web and Conceptual Modeling (Paris, Oct. 1999), Springer-Verlag, LNCS 1727., pp. 293-306
10. Hector Garcia-Molina, Yannis Papakonstantinou Dallan Quass, Anand Rajaraman, Yehoshua Sagiv, Jeffrey D. Ullman, Vasilis Vassalos, Jennifer Widom: The TSIMMIS Approach to Mediation: Data Models and Languages. JIIS 8(2): 117-132 (1997)
11. S. Ceri, P. Fraternali, A. Bongio: Specification of WebML, Deliverable W3I3.POLI.D21, March 2000.

An Optimization Technique for Answering Regular Path Queries

Gösta Grahne and Alex Thomo

Concordia University
{grahne,thomo}@cs.concordia.ca

Abstract. Rewriting queries using views is a powerful technique that has applications in data integration, data warehousing and query optimization. Query rewriting in relational databases is by now rather well investigated. However, in the framework of semistructured data the problem of rewriting has received much less attention. In this paper we identify some difficulties with currently known methods for using rewritings in semistructured databases. We study the problem in a realistic setting, proposed in information integration systems such as the Information Manifold, in which the data sources are modelled as sound views over a global schema. We give a new rewriting, which we call the *possibility rewriting*, that can be used in pruning the search space when answering queries using views. The possibility rewriting can be computed in time polynomial in the size of the original query and the view definitions. Finally, we show by means of a realistic example that our method can reduce the search space by an order of magnitude.

1 Introduction

Semistructured data is a self-describing collection, whose structure can naturally model irregularities that cannot be captured by relational or object-oriented data models [2]. Semi-structured data is usually best formalized in terms of labelled graphs, where the graphs represent data found in many useful applications such as web information systems, XML data repositories, digital libraries, communication networks, and so on. Semi-structured data is queried through regular path queries, which are queries represented by regular expressions. The design of the regular path queries is based on the observation that many of the recursive queries that arise in practice amount to graph traversals. These queries are in essence graph patterns and the answers to the query are subgraphs of the database that match the given pattern [21,16,9,10]. For example, the regular path query $(\_^* \cdot article) \cdot (\_^* \cdot ref \cdot \_^* \cdot (ullman + widom))$ specifies all the paths having at some point an edge labelled *article*, followed by any number of other edges then by an edge *ref* and finally by an edge labelled with *ullman* or *widom*.

In semistructured data, as well as in data integration, data warehousing and query optimization the problem of query rewriting using views is well known [20,25,9,19]. Simply stated, the problem is: Given a query Q and a set of views $\{v_1, \ldots, v_n\}$, find a representation of Q by means of the views and then answer

D. Suciu and G. Vossen (Eds.): WebDB 2000, LNCS 1997, pp. 215–225, 2001.

the query on the basis of this representation. Several papers investigate this problem for the case of conjunctive queries [20,25,11,24]. These methods are based on the query containment and the fact that the number of subgoals in the minimal rewriting is bounded from above by the number of subgoals in the query.

It is obvious that a method for rewriting of regular path queries requires a technique for the rewriting of regular expressions, i.e. given a regular expression E and a set of regular expressions $E_1, E_2, ..., E_n$ one wants to compute a function $f(E_1, E_2, ..., E_n)$ which approximates E. As far as the authors know, there are two methods for computing such a function f which best approximates E from below. The first one of Conway [12] is based on the derivatives of regular expressions introduced by Brzozowski [7], which provide the ground for the development of an algebraic theory of factorization in the regular algebra [8] which in turn gives the tools for computing the approximating function. The second method by Calvanese et al [9] is automata based. Both methods are equivalent in the sense that they compute the same rewriting, which is the largest subset of the query, that can be represented by the views. Posed in the framework of [17], we show that the rewriting produced by these methods is a (sometimes strict) subset of the *certain rewriting*. If we want to be able to produce the complete certain answer, the only alternative left is then to apply an intractable decision procedure of Calvanese et al [10] for *all* pairs of objects (nodes) found in the views. The contribution of this paper is an algorithm for computing a regular rewriting that will produce a superset of the certain answer. The use of this rewriting in query optimization is that it restricts the space of possible pairs needed to be fed to the decision procedure of Calvanese et al. We show by means of a realistic example that our algorithm can reduce the number of candidate pairs by an order of magnitude.

The outline of paper is as follows. In Section 2 we formalize the problem of query rewriting using views in a commonly occurring setting, proposed in information integration systems, in which the data sources are modelled as sound views over a global schema. We give some results about the applicability of previous work in this setting, and discuss further possibilities of optimization. At the end of Section 2 we sketch an algorithm for utilizing simultaneously the "subset" and a "superset" rewriting in query answering using views. In Section 3 we present our main results and method. First we give an algebraic characterization of a rewriting that we call the *possibility rewriting* and then we prove that the answer computed using this rewriting is a superset of the certain answer of the query, even when algebraically the rewriting does not contain the query. The computation of the possibility rewriting amounts to finding the transduction of a regular language and we give the appropriate automata-theoretic constructions for these computations.

2 Background

Rewriting regular queries. Let Δ be a finite alphabet, called the *database alphabet*. Elements of Δ will be denoted $R, S, T, R', S', \ldots, R_1, S_1, \ldots$, etc. Let $\mathbf{V} = \{V_1, \ldots, V_n\}$ be a set of *view definitions*, with each V_i being a finite or infinite regular language over Δ. Associated with each view definition V_i is a view name v_i. We call the set $\Omega = \{v_1, \ldots, v_n\}$ the *outer alphabet*, or *view alphabet*. For each $v_i \in \Omega$, we set $def(v_i) = V_i$. The substitution *def* associates with each view name v_i in Ω alphabet the language V_i. The substitution *def* is applied to words, languages, and regular expressions in the usual way (see e. g. [18]).

A *(user) query* Q is a finite or infinite regular language over Δ. A *lower-rewriting* (l-rewriting) of a user query Q using $\mathbf{V}$ is a language Q' over Ω, such that

$$def(Q') \subseteq Q.$$

If for any l-rewriting Q'' of Q using $\mathbf{V}$, it holds that $def(Q'') \subseteq def(Q')$ we say that Q' is *maximal*. If $def(Q') = Q$ we say that the rewriting Q' is *exact*.

Calvanese et al [9] have given a method for constructing an l-rewriting Q' from Q and $\mathbf{V}$. Their method is guaranteed to always find the maximal l-rewriting, and it turns out that the maximal l-rewriting always is regular. An exact rewriting might not exist, while a maximal rewriting always exists, although there is no guarantee on the lower bound. For an extreme example, if $\mathbf{V} = \emptyset$, then the maximal rewriting of any query is $\emptyset$.

Semistructured databases. We consider a database to be an edge labelled graph. This graph model is typical in semistructured data, where the nodes of the database graph represent the objects and the edges represent the attributes of the objects, or relationships between the objects.

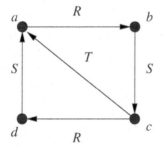

Fig. 1. An example of a graph database

Formally, we assume that we have a universe of objects D. Objects will be denoted $a, b, c, a', b', \ldots, a_1, b_2, \ldots$, and so on. A *database DB* over (D, Δ) is a pair (N, E), where $N \subseteq D$ is a set of nodes and $E \subseteq N \times \Delta \times N$ is a set of directed edges labelled with symbols from Δ. Figure 1 contains an example of a graph database.

If there is a path labelled $R_1, R_2, \ldots, R_k$ from a node a to a node b we write $a \xrightarrow{R_1 \cdot R_2 \ldots R_k} b$. Let Q be a query and $DB = (N, E)$ a database. Then the *answer* to Q on DB is defined as

$$ans(Q, DB) = \{(a, b) : \{a, b\} \subseteq N \text{ and } a \xrightarrow{W} b \text{ for some } W \in Q\}.$$

For instance, if DB is the graph in Figure 1, and $Q = \{SR, T\}$, then $ans(Q, DB) = \{(b, d), (d, b), (c, a)\}$

Views and answering queries using views. Let $\Omega = \{v_1, \ldots v_n\}$ be the view alphabet and let $\mathbf{V} = \{V_1, \ldots, V_n\}$ be a set of view definitions as before. Then a *source collection* $\mathcal{S}$ over $(\mathbf{V}, \Omega)$ is a a database over (D, Ω). A source collection $\mathcal{S}$ defines a set $poss(\mathcal{S})$ of databases over (N, Δ) as follows (cf. [17]):

$$poss(\mathcal{S}) = \{DB \; : \; \mathcal{S} \subseteq \bigcup_{i \in \{1, \ldots, n\}} \{(a, v_i, b) : (a, b) \in ans(V_i, DB)\}\}.$$

Suppose now the user gives a query Q in the database alphabet Δ, but we only have a source collection $\mathcal{S}$ available. This situation is the basic scenario in information integration (see e.g. [25,20,17]). The best we can do is to approximate Q by

$$\bigcap_{DB \in poss(\mathcal{S})} ans(Q, DB).$$

This approximation is called the *certain answer for Q using $\mathcal{S}$*. Calvanese et al [10], in a follow-up paper to [9] describe an algorithm $\mathcal{A}_{Q,\mathcal{S}}(a, b)$ that returns "yes" or "no" depending on whether given pair (a, b) is in the certain answer for Q or not. This problem is coNP-complete in the number of objects in $\mathcal{S}$ (data complexity), and if we are to compute the certain answer, we need to run the algorithm for *every* pair of objects in the source collection. A brute force implementation of the algorithm runs in time exponential in the number of objects in $\mathcal{S}$. From a practical point of view it is thus important to invoke algorithm $\mathcal{A}_{Q,\mathcal{S}}$ for as few pairs as possible.

Restricting the number of input pairs is not considered by Calvanese et al. Instead they briefly discuss the possibility of using rewritings of regular queries in answering queries using views. Since rewritings have proved to be highly successful in attacking the corresponding problem for relational databases [19], one might hope that the same technique could be used for semistructured databases. Indeed, when the exact rewriting of a query Q using $\mathbf{V}$ exists, Calvanese et al show that, under the "exact view assumption" the rewriting can be used to answer Q using $\mathcal{S}$. Unfortunately, under the more realistic "sound view assumption[1] " adopted in this paper we are only guaranteed to get a subset of the certain answer. The following propositions hold:

Theorem 1. *Let Q' be an l-rewriting of Q using **V**. Then for any source collection S over **V**,*

$$ans(Q', S) \subseteq \bigcap_{DB \in poss(S)} ans(Q, DB).$$

Proof. Let $(a, b) \in Q'(S)$ and let DB be an arbitrary database in $poss(S)$. Since $(a, b) \in Q'(S)$ there exists objects $c_{i_1} \ldots c_{i_k}$ and a path $a\, v_{i_1} c_{i_1} \ldots c_{i_k} v_{i_{k+1}} b$ in S such that $v_{i_1} \ldots v_{i_{k+1}} \in Q'$. Since $DB \in poss(S)$, there must be a path $a\, W_{i_1} c_{i_1} \ldots c_{i_k} W_{i_{k+1}} b$ in DB, where $W_{i_j} \in def(v_{i_j})$, for $j \in \{1, \ldots, k+1\}$. Furthermore we have that $W_{i_1} \ldots W_{i_k} \in def(Q') \subseteq Q$. In other words, $(a, b) \in ans(Q, DB)$. $\square$

Theorem 2. *There is a query Q and a set of view definitions **V**, such that there is an exact rewriting Q' of Q using **V**, but for some source collections S, the set $ans(Q', S)$ is a proper subset of $\bigcap_{DB \in poss(S)} ans(Q, DB)$.* $\square$

The data-complexity for using the rewriting is NLOGSPACE, which is a considerable improvement from coNP. There is an EXSPACE price to pay though. At the compilation time finding the rewriting requires exponential amount of space measured in the size of the regular expressions used to represent the query and the view definitions (expression complexity). Nevertheless, it usually pays to sacrifice expression complexity for data complexity. The problem is however that the l-rewriting is guaranteed only to produce a subset of the certain answer. We would like to avoid running the testing algorithm $\mathcal{A}_{Q,S}$ for all other pairs of objects in S.

In the next section we describe a "possibility" rewriting (p-rewriting) Q'' of Q using **V**, such that for all source collections S:

$$ans(Q'', S) \supseteq \bigcap_{DB \in poss(S)} ans(Q, DB).$$

The p-rewriting Q'' can be used in optimizing the computation of the certain answer as follows:

1. Compute Q' and Q'' from Q using **V**.
2. Compute $ans(Q', S)$ and $ans(Q'', S)$. Output $ans(Q', S)$
3. Compute $\mathcal{A}_{Q,S}(a, b)$, for each $(a, b) \in ans(Q'', S) \setminus ans(Q', S)$. Output those pairs (a, b) for which $\mathcal{A}_{Q,S}(a, b)$ answers "yes."

---

[1] If all views are relational projections, the exact view assumption corresponds to the pure universal relation assumption, and the sound view assumption corresponds to the weak instance assumption. For an explanation of the relational assumptions, see [26].

3   Computing the p-Rewriting

As discussed in the previous section, the rewriting Q' of a query Q is only guaranteed to be a contained rewriting. From Propositions 1 and 2 it follows that if we use Q' to evaluate the query, we are only guaranteed to get a subset of the certain answer (recall that the certain answer itself already is an approximation from below). In this section we will give an algorithm for computing a rewriting Q'' that satisfies the relation $ans(Q'', \mathcal{S}) \supseteq \bigcap_{DB \in poss(\mathcal{S})} ans(Q, DB)$. Our rewriting is related to the inverse substitution of regular languages and as consequence it will be a regular language.

Definition 1 Let L be a language over Ω^*. Then L is a *p-rewriting* of a query Q, using $\mathbf{V}$, if for all $v_{i_1} \ldots v_{i_m} \in L$, there exists $W_{i_1} \ldots W_{i_m} \in Q$ such that $W_{i_j} \in def(v_{i_j})$, for $j \in \{1, \ldots, m\}$, and there are no other words in Ω^* with this property.

The intuition behind this definition is that we include in the p-rewriting all the words in the view alphabet Ω, such that their substitution by *def* contains a word in Q. The p-rewriting has the following desirable property:

Theorem 3. *Let Q'' be a p-rewriting of Q using $\mathbf{V}$. Then*

$$ans(Q'', \mathcal{S}) \supseteq \bigcap_{DB \in poss(\mathcal{S})} ans(Q, DB),$$

for any source collection $\mathcal{S}$.

Proof. Assume that there exists a source collection $\mathcal{S}$ and a pair $(a, b) \in \bigcap_{DB \in poss(\mathcal{S})} ans(Q, DB)$, such that $(a, b) \notin ans(Q'', \mathcal{S})$. Since the pair (a, b) is in the certain answer of the query Q, it follows that for each database $DB \in poss(\mathcal{S})$ there is a path $a \xrightarrow{W} b$, where $W \in Q$. Now, we will construct from $\mathcal{S}$ a database $DB_{\mathcal{S}}$ such that $ans(Q, DB_{\mathcal{S}}) \not\ni (a, b)$. For each edge labelled v_i from one object x to another object y in $\mathcal{S}$ we chose an arbitrary word $W_i \in def(v_i)$ and put in $DB_{\mathcal{S}}$ the "new" objects $c_1, \ldots, c_{k-1}$, where k is the length of W_i, and a path $x, c_1, \ldots, c_{k-1}, y$ labelled with the word W_i. Each time we introduce "new" objects, so all the constructed paths are disjoint. Obviously, $DB_{\mathcal{S}} \in poss(\mathcal{S})$. It is easy to see that $ans(Q, DB_{\mathcal{S}}) \not\ni (a, b)$ because otherwise there would be a path $v_{i_1} \ldots v_{i_m}$ in $\mathcal{S}$ from a to b such that $def(v_{i_1} \ldots v_{i_m}) \cap Q \neq \emptyset$, that is $v_{i_1} \ldots v_{i_m} \in Q''$ and $(a, b) \in ans(Q'', \mathcal{S})$, From the fact that $ans(Q, DB_{\mathcal{S}}) \not\ni (a, b)$ it then follows that $\bigcap_{DB \in poss(\mathcal{S})} ans(Q, DB) \not\ni (a, b)$; a contradiction.   □

It is worth noting here that the Theorem 3 shows that $ans(Q'', \mathcal{S})$ contains the certain answer to the query Q even when algebraically $def(Q'') \not\supseteq Q$.

Recall that the definition of a view name $v_i \in \Omega$ is a regular language $def(V_i)$ over Δ. Thus *def* is in effect a *substitution* from Ω to 2^{Δ^*}. The *inverse* of this substitution is defined by, for each $W \in \Delta^*$,

$$def^{-1}(W) = \{U \in \Omega^* : W \in def(U)\}.$$

It is now easy to see that a p-rewriting Q'' of Q using $\mathbf{V}$ equals $def^{-1}(Q)$. This suggests that Q'' can be computed using finite transducers.

A *finite transducer* (see e.g. [27]) $T = (S, I, O, \delta, s, F)$ consists of a finite set of states S, an input alphabet I, and output alphabet O, a starting state s, a set of final states F, and a transition-output function δ from finite subsets of $S \times I^*$ to finite subsets of $S \times O^*$. An example of a finite transducer $(\{q_0, q_1, q_2\}, \{v_1, v_2\}, \{R, S\}, \delta, \{q_2\})$ is shown in Figure 2.

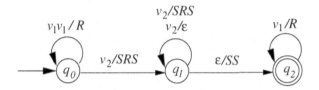

Fig. 2. A finite transducer T

Intuitively, for instance $(q_1, SRS) \in \delta(q_0, v_2)$ means that if the transducer is in state q_0 and reads word v_2, it can go to state q_1 and emit the word SRS. For a given word $U \in I^*$, we say that a word $W \in O^*$ is an *output of T for U* if there exists a sequence $(q_1, W_1) \in \delta(s, U_1)$, $(q_2, W_2) \in \delta(q_1, U_2)$, ..., $(q_n, W_n) \in \delta(q_{n-1}, U_n)$ of state transitions of T, such that $q_n \in F$, $U = U_1 \ldots U_n \in I^*$, and $W = W_1 \ldots W_n \in O^*$. We write $W \in T(U)$, where $T(U)$ denotes the set of all outputs of T for the input word U. For a language $L \subseteq I^*$, we define $T(L) = \bigcup_{U \in L} T(U)$.

A finite transducer $T = (S, I, O, \delta, s, F)$ is said to be in the *standard form* if δ is a function from $S \times (I \cup \{\epsilon\})$ to $2^{S \times (O \cup \{\epsilon\})}$. Intuitively. the standard form restricts the input and output of each transition to be only a single letter or ϵ. It is known that any finite transducer is equivalent to a finite transducer in standard form (see [27]).

From the above definitions, it is easy to see that a substitution can be characterized by a finite transducer. Start with one node representing both the starting state and the final state. Then build a "macro-transducer" by putting a self-loop corresponding to each $v_i \in \Omega$ on the sole state. In each such self-loop we first have the view symbol v_i as input and a regular expression representing the substitution of v_i as output. After that, we transform the "macro-transducer" into an ordinary one in standard form. The transformation is done by applying recursively the following three steps. First, replace each edge $v/(E_1 + \ldots + E_n)$, $n \geq 1$, by the n edges v/E_1, ..., v/E_n. Second, for each edge of the form $v/E_1 \ldots E_k$ from a node p to a node q (Figure 3, left), we introduce $k - 1$ new nodes r_1, $\ldots r_{k-1}$ and replace the edge $v/E_1 \ldots E_k$ by the edges v/E_1 from p to r_1, ϵ/E_2 from r_1 to r_2, ..., ϵ/E_k from r_{k-1} to q (Figure 3, right). Third, we get rid of "macro-transitions" of the form v/E^*. Suppose we have an edge labelled v/E^* from p to q in the "macro-transducer." (See Figure 4, left). We introduce a new

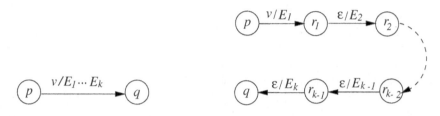

Fig. 3.

node r and replace the edge v/E^* by the edges v/ϵ from p to r, ϵ/E from r to r, and ϵ/ϵ from r to q, as shown in Figure 4, right.

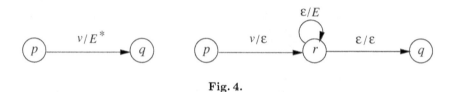

Fig. 4.

By interchanging the input and output of the finite transducer, we see that the inverse of a substitution can also be characterized by a finite transducer.

We now describe an algorithm that given a regular language L and finite transducer T constructs a finite state automaton that accepts the language $T(L)$. Let $A_L = (S_L, I, \delta_L, s_A, F_L)$ be an ϵ-free NFA that accepts L, and let $T = (S_T, I, O, \delta_T, s_T, F_T)$ be the finite transducer in standard form. We construct an NFA $A_{T_L} = (S_{T_L}, O, \delta_{T_L}, s_{T_L}, F_{T_L})$, where $S_{T_L} = S_L \times S_T$, $s_{T_L} = (s_L, s_{T_L})$, $F_{T_L} = F_L \times F_T$, and δ_{T_L} is defined by, for $(p, q) \in S_{T_L}$ and $v \in O \cup \{\epsilon\}$,

$$\delta_{T_L}((p, q), v) = \{(p', q') : \text{there exists } R \in I \text{ such that}$$
$$\delta_L(p, R) = p' \text{ and } (q', v) \in \delta_T(q, R),$$
$$\text{or } (q', v) \in \delta_{T_L}(q, \epsilon) \text{ and } p = p'\}$$

Theorem 4. *The automaton A_{T_L} accepts exactly the language $T(L)$.*   □

Collecting the results together, we now have the following methodology.

Corollary 1. *Let $\mathbf{V} = \{V_1, \ldots, V_n\}$ be a set of view definitions, such the $def(v_i) = V_i$, for all $v_i \in \Omega$, and let Q be a query over Δ. Then there is an effectively characterizable regular language Q'' over Ω that is the p-rewriting of Q using $\mathbf{V}$.*   □

Example 1. Let the query be $Q = \{(RS)^n : n \geq 0\}$ and the views be $v_1, v_2, v_3,$ and v_4, where $def(v_1) = \{R, SS\}$, $def(v_2) = \{S\}$, $def(v_3) = \{SR\}$, and $def(v_4) = \{RSRS\}$. The DFA[2] A accepting the query Q is given in Figure

---
[2] An ϵ-free NFA would do as well.

5, left, and the transducer characterizing the substitution *def* is given in Figure 5, right. We transform the transducer into standard form (Figure 6, left), and then interchange the input with output to get the transducer characterizing the inverse substitution (Figure 6, right). The constructed automaton A_{T_Q} is shown in Figure 7, where $r_0 = (p_0, q_0)$, $r_1 = (p_1, q_0)$, $r_2 = (p_0, q_2)$ and the inaccessible and garbage states have been removed.

Our algorithm computes the p-rewriting Q'' represented by $(v_4 + v_1 v_3^* v_2)^*$, and the algorithm of Calvanese et al [9] computes the l-rewriting Q' represented by v_4^*. Suppose that the the source collection $\mathcal{S}_n$ is induced by the following set of labelled edges: $\{(i, v_1, a_i) : 1 \le i \le n - 1\} \cup \{(a_i, v_2, i + 1) : 1 \le i \le n - 1\}$ $\cup \{(a_i, v_3, a_{i+1}) : 1 \le i \le n - 1\} \cup \{(i, v_4, i + 2) : 1 \le i \le n - 2\}$. We can now compute $ans(Q'', \mathcal{S}_n) = \{(i, j) : 1 \le i \le n - 1, i \le j \le n\}$, and $ans(Q', \mathcal{S}_n) = \{(i, 2k) : 1 \le i \le n - 1, 0 \le k \le n/2\}$. Then we have that the cardinality of $ans(Q'', \mathcal{S}_n)$ is $n + \ldots + 2 = \sum_{i=1}^{n-1}(i+1) = \frac{n(n-1)}{2} - 1 \approx \frac{n^2}{2}$ and the cardinality of $ans(Q', \mathcal{S}_n)$ is $\sum_{i=1}^{n-1}(\lfloor \frac{n-i}{2} \rfloor + 1) \approx \frac{n(n-1)-n}{4} + n \approx \frac{n^2}{4}$. Thus the cardinality of $ans(Q'', \mathcal{S}_n) \setminus ans(Q', \mathcal{S}_n)$ is approximately $n^2/2 - n^2/4 = n^2/4$, that is 16 times better that $(2n)^2$ which the number of all the possible pairs. □

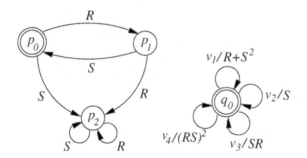

Fig. 5.

Now let us calculate the cost of our algorithm for computing the "possibility" regular rewriting.

Theorem 5. *The automaton characterizing Q'' can be built in time polynomial in the size of the regular expression representing Q and the size of the regular expressions representing* **V**. □

We note that the above analysis is wrt expression and not data complexity. Since the decision procedure of [10] is coNP-complete wrt data complexity, reducing the set of candidate pairs is very desirable.

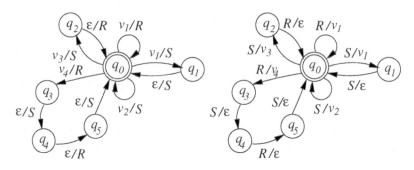

Fig. 6.

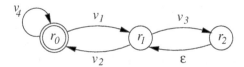

Fig. 7.

References

1. S. Abiteboul. Querying Semistructured Data. *Proc. of Intl. Conference on Database Theory (ICDT)* 1997, pp. 1–18.

2. S. Abiteboul, P. Buneman and D. Suciu. *Data on the Web : From Relations to Semistructured Data and Xml.* Morgan Kaufmann, San Francisco, 1999.

3. S. Abiteboul, R. Hull and V. Vianu. *Foundations of Databases.* Addison-Wesley, Reading, Mass. 1995.

4. S. Abiteboul, D. Quass, J. McHugh, J. Widom and J. L. Wiener. The Lorel Query Language for Semistructured Data. *Int. J. on Digital Libraries 1(1)* 1997, pp. 68–88.

5. P. Buneman. Semistructured Data. *Proc. of the 16th ACM Symposium on Principles of Database Systems (PODS)* 1997, pp. 117–121.

6. P. Buneman, S. B. Davidson, M. F. Fernandez and D. Suciu. Adding Structure to Unstructured Data. *Proc. of Intl. Conference on Database Theory (ICDT)* 1997, pp. 336–350.

7. J. A. Brzozowski. Derivatives of Regular Expressions. *J. of ACM 11(4)* 1964, pp. 481–494

8. J. A. Brzozowski and E. L. Leiss. On Equations for Regular Languages, Finite Automata, and Sequential Networks. *Theoretical Computer Science 10,* 1980, pp. 19–35

9. D. Calvanese, G. Giacomo, M. Lenzerini and M. Y. Vardi. Rewriting of Regular Expressions and Regular Path Queries. *Proc. of the 18th ACM Symposium on Principles of Database Systems (PODS)* 1999, pp. 194–204.

10. D. Calvanese, G. Giacomo, M. Lenzerini and M. Y. Vardi. Answering Regular Path Queries Using Views. *Proc. of Intl. Conference on Data Engineering (ICDE)* 2000, pp. 389–398

11. S. Cohen, W. Nutt, A. Serebrenik. Rewriting Aggregate Queries Using Views. *Proc. of the 18th ACM Symposium on Principles of Database Systems (PODS)* 1999, pp. 155–166

12. J. H. Conway. *Regular Algebra and Finite Machines*. Chapman and Hall, London, 1971.

13. A. Deutsch, M. F. Fernandez, D. Florescu, A. Y. Levy, D. Suciu. A Query Language for XML. *WWW8 / Computer Networks 31(11-16)* 1999, pp. 1155–116.

14. O. Duschka and M. R. Genesereth. Answering Recursive Queries Using Views. *Proc. of the 16th ACM Symposium on Principles of Database Systems (PODS)* 1997, pp. 109–116.

15. M. F. Fernandez and D. Suciu. Optimizing Regular path Expressions Using Graph Schemas *Proc. of Intl. Conference on Data Engineering (ICDE)* 1998, pp. 14–23.

16. D. Florescu, A. Y. Levy, D. Suciu Query Containment for Conjunctive Queries with Regular Expressions *Proc. of the 17th ACM Symposium on Principles of Database Systems (PODS)* 1998, pp. 139–148.

17. G. Grahne and A. O. Mendelzon. Tableau Techniques for Querying Information Sources through Global Schemas. *Proc. of Intl. Conference on Database Theory (ICDT)* 1999, pp. 332–347.

18. J. E. Hopcroft and J. D. Ullman *Introduction to Automata Theory, Languages, and Computation*. Addison-Wesley 1979.

19. A. Y. Levy. *Answering queries using views: a survey*. Submitted for publication 1999.

20. A. Y. Levy, A. O. Mendelzon, Y. Sagiv, D. Srivastava. Answering Queries Using Views. *Proc. of the 14th ACM Symposium on Principles of Database Systems (PODS)* 1995, pp. 95–104.

21. A. O. Mendelzon and P. T. Wood, Finding Regular Simple Paths in Graph Databases. *SIAM J. Comp. 24(6)*, 1995, pp. 1235–1258.

22. A. O. Mendelzon, G. A. Mihaila and T. Milo. Querying the World Wide Web. *Int. J. on Digital Libraries 1(1)*, 1997, pp. 54–67.

23. T. Milo and D. Suciu. Index Structures for Path Expressions. *Proc. of Intl. Conference on Database Theory (ICDT)*, 1999, pp. 277–295.

24. Y. Papakonstantinou, V. Vassalos. Query Rewriting for Semistructured Data. *Proc. of SIGMOD* 1999, pp. 455–466.

25. J. D. Ullman. Information Integration Using Logical Views. *Proc. of Intl. Conference on Database Theory (ICDT)* 1997, pp. 19–40.

26. M. Y. Vardi. The universal-relation model for logical independence. *IEEE Software 5(2)*, 1988, pp. 80–85.

27. S. Yu. Regular Languages. In: *Handbook of Formal Languages*. G. Rozenberg and A. Salomaa (Eds.) Springer Verlag, Berlin 1997, pp. 41–110

XDuce: A Typed XML Processing Language
(Preliminary Report)

Haruo Hosoya[1] and Benjamin C. Pierce[2]

[1] Department of CIS
University of Pennsylvania
hahosoya@cis.upenn.edu
[2] Department of CIS
University of Pennsylvania
bcpierce@cis.upenn.edu

1   Introduction

Among the reasons for the popularity of XML is the hope that the static typing provided by DTDs [XML] (or more sophisticated mechanisms such as XML-Schema [XS00]) will improve the safety of data exchange and processing. But, in order to make the best use of such typing mechanisms, we need to go beyond types for *documents* and exploit type information in static checking of *programs* for XML processing.

In this paper, we present a preliminary design for a statically typed programming language, *XDuce* (pronounced "transduce"). XDuce is a tree transformation language, similar in spirit to mainstream functional languages but specialized to the domain of XML processing. Its novel features are *regular expression types* and a corresponding mechanism for *regular expression pattern matching*. Regular expression types are a natural generalization of DTDs, describing, as DTDs do, structures in XML documents using regular expression operators (i.e., *, ?, |, etc.). Moreover, regular expression types support a simple but powerful notion of *subtyping*, yielding a substantial degree of flexibility in programming. Regular expression pattern matching is similar to ML pattern matching except that regular expression types can be embedded in patterns, which allows even more flexible matching.

In this preliminary report, we show by example the role of these features in writing robust and flexible programs for XML processing. After discussing the relationship of our work to other work, we briefly sketch some larger applications that we have written in XDuce, and close with remarks on future work. Appendices give a formal definition of the core language.

2   Programming in XDuce

We develop a series of examples of programming in XDuce, using regular expression types and regular expression pattern matching.

D. Suciu and G. Vossen (Eds.): WebDB 2000, LNCS 1997, pp. 226–244, 2001.

2.1   Regular Expression Types

Values and Types. XDuce's values are XML documents. A XDuce program may read in an XML document as a value and write out a value as an XML document. Even values for intermediate results during the execution of the program have a one-to-one correspondance to XML documents (besides some trivial differences).

As concrete syntax, the user has two choices: XML syntax or XDuce's native syntax. We can either write the following XDuce value (we assign it to the variable mybook for later explanation)

```
val mybook = addrbook[
                name["Haruo Hosoya"],
                addr["Tokyo"],
                name["ABC"],
                addr["Def"],
                tel["123-456-789"],
                name["Benjamin Pierce"],
                addr["Philadelphia"]]
```

in the native syntax, or the following corresponding document in standard XML syntax:

```
<addrbook>
  <name>Haruo Hosoya</name>
  <addr>Tokyo</addr>
  <name>ABC</name>
  <addr>Def</addr>
  <tel>123-456-789</tel>
  <name>Benjamin Pierce</name>
  <addr>Philadelphia</addr>
</addrbook>
```

XDuce provides term constructors of the form label[...], where ... is a sequence of other values. This corresponds to <label>...</label> in XML notation. We enclose strings in double-quotes, unlike XML.

Observe the sequence contained in addrbook. It is natural to impose a structure on the seven children so that they can be regarded as three "entries," each of which consists of fields tagged name, addr and optional tel. We can capture this structure by defining the following regular expression types.

```
type Addrbook = addrbook[(Name,Addr,Tel?)*]
type Name = name[String]
type Addr = addr[String]
type Tel = tel[String]
```

These XDuce definitions roughly correspond to the following DTD:

```
<!ELEMENT addrbook (name,addr,tel?)*>
<!ELEMENT name #PCDATA>
<!ELEMENT addr #PCDATA>
<!ELEMENT tel #PCDATA>
```

(Just as XDuce can read standard XML documents, we also provide a construct to import DTDs as regular expression types.) Type constructors `label[...]` have the same form as the term constructors that they classify. In addition, types may be formed using the regular expression operators * for repetition, | for alternation, and ? for optional elements. (We will show examples of alternations later.) For instance, the type `(Name,Addr,Tel?)*` stands for zero or more repetitions of the sequence of a `Name`, an `Addr`, and an optional `Tel`.

The notion of *subtyping* will play a crucial role in the calculation that justifies assigning the type `Addrbook` to the value `mybook`.

Subtyping. Before showing the subtyping relation, we need to clearly state this: the elements of every type in XDuce are *sequences*. For example, the type `Tel*` contains the following sequences.

`()`	the empty sequence
`tel["123"]`	sequence with one `Tel`
`tel["123"],tel["234"]`	sequence with two `Tel`'s
`...`	

In the type language, comma is the type constructor for concatenation of sequences. For example, the type `(Name,Tel*, Addr)` contains

```
name["abc"],addr["ABC"]
name["abc"],tel["123"],addr["ABC"]
name["abc"],tel["123"],tel["234"],addr["ABC"]
...
```

i.e., sequences with one `Name` value, followed by zero or more `Tel` values, then followed by one `Addr` value. The comma operator on types is associative: the types `((Name,Tel*),Addr)` and `(Name,(Tel*,Addr))` have exactly the same set of elements.

The *subtype* relation between two types is simply inclusion of the sets denoted by types(see Appendix A for the formal definition).

We now show the sequence of steps involved in verifying that `mybook` has type `Addrbook`. First, from the intuition that ? means "optional," we would expect the following relations:

$$\texttt{Name,Addr} \quad <: \texttt{Name,Addr,Tel?}$$
$$\texttt{Name,Addr,Tel} <: \texttt{Name,Addr,Tel?}$$

Notice that each right hand side has more possibilities than the left hand side. Similarly, * means "zero or more" intuitively, so in particular it could be three:

$$\texttt{T,T,T} <: \texttt{T*}$$

Combining these relations, we obtain

$$\texttt{(Name,Addr),(Name,Addr,Tel),(Name,Addr)} <: \texttt{(Name,Addr,Tel?)*}.$$

Since comma is associative, we can get rid of parentheses:

$$\text{Name,Addr,Name,Addr,Tel,Name,Addr}$$
$$= \text{(Name,Addr),(Name,Addr,Tel),(Name,Addr)}$$

(Here, we mean by T = U that both T <: U and U <: T.) Finally, combining these two relations and enclosing both sides by addrbook constructor, we obtain

$$\text{addrbook[Name,Addr,Name,Addr,Tel,Name,Addr]}$$
$$\text{<: addrbook[(Name,Addr,Tel?)*]}$$
$$\overset{\text{def}}{=} \text{Addrbook.}$$

Since the mybook value trivially has the type on the left hand side, it has also the type on the right hand side.

Union Types. XDuce also provides a union (or alternation) type constructor |. For example, we write (Name|Tel) to mean "either Name or Tel"; the basic subtyping relations for union types are the following.

$$\text{Name <: Name | Tel}$$
$$\text{Tel <: Name | Tel}$$

Notice that each right hand side offers more possibilities, and so describes a larger set of sequences.

Union types substantially increase our flexibility in programming. In particular, union types yield two interesting relations: "forget ordering" subtyping and "distributivity." These are the distinguishing points in union types, as opposed to conventional tagged sum types (as found, say, in ML). To illustrate these, let us consider the following scenario of a "database evolution."

Suppose we begin with a trivial database consisting of just a list of names, with type Name*. At some point, this database is copied to two different sites and maintained and evolved separately. At one site, address information is added to each name and the type of the database becomes (Name,Addr)*, while at the other telephone numbers are added and it becomes (Name,Tel)*.

Now, suppose we want to re-integrate these databases—that is, combine the copies src1, whose type is (Name,Addr)*, and src2 of type (Name,Tel)* by concatenating them: src1, src2. The type of this merged database is, of course, (Name, Addr)*, (Name,Tel)*.

Next, suppose we want to do something with our new database that involves extracting the common part (i.e., the name) from each record. Since we have two repetitions in the type, we might expect to need two loops in the program. (We do not show such a program explicitly, but it is easy to write.) However, we can do better by making the two loops into one, using the following "forget ordering" subtype relation:

$$\text{(Name,Addr)*, (Name,Tel)* <: ((Name,Addr) | (Name,Tel))*}$$

The intuition behind this relation is that the ordering information of the left hand side is forgotten on the right hand side. That is, on the left hand side, any (Name,Tel) pairs must occur after any (Name,Addr) pairs, while on the right hand side, these pairs can appear in any order.

Finally, since we have two alternatives joined by | in the new type, we might expect to need two branches in our inner loop, to extract the Name field from each of them. But we don't: we can use the following distributive subtyping law

$$(\texttt{Name,Addr}) \mid (\texttt{Name,Tel}) = \texttt{Name,(Addr} \mid \texttt{Tel})$$

to reorganize the type so that the Name field can be accessed directly.

2.2   Regular Expression Pattern Matching

Our term language is based on a powerful form of pattern matching. Our pattern matching is similar in spirit to ML's (or Haskell's, etc.), but somewhat more powerful, since it includes the use of regular expression types to dynamically match values of those types. Our patterns also require a different treatment of the usual checks for exhaustiveness and ambiguity of patterns.

The body of a XDuce program is a series of function definitions. As an example, the following function converts an address book into a telephone list.

```
fun mkTelList : (Name,Addr,Tel?)* → (Name,Tel)* =
    name[n:String], addr[a:String], tel[t:String],
                            rest:(Name,Addr,Tel?)*
      → name[n], tel[t], mkTelList(rest)
  | name[n:String], addr[a:String], rest:(Name,Addr,Tel?)*
      → mkTelList(rest)
  | ()
      → ()
```

This function takes a value of type (Name,Addr,Tel?)* and returns a value of type (Name,Tel)*. The body is a pattern match that breaks up the possibilities on the input values into three cases. The first case matches when the input value is a sequence beginning with name, addr, and tel labels, followed by some further sequence of type (Name,Addr,Tel?)*. In this case, we pick out the name and tel elements and prepend them to the result of calling mkTelList recursively on the remainder. The second case matches when we cannot find tel after addr, and simply calls mkTelList recursively. The third case matches the empty sequence, and returns the empty sequence.

As another example, consider the following function firstTriple, which takes out the first entry with a tel element.

```
fun firstTriple : (Name,Addr,Tel?)* → (Name,Addr,Tel)? =
    ps:(Name,Addr)*, t:(Name,Addr,Tel), rest:(Name,Addr,Tel?)*  → t
  | whole:(Name,Addr,Tel?)*  → ()
```

The function firstTriple has a pattern matching with two cases. In the first case, we skip all "pair" entries (i.e., (Name,Addr)) from the beginning and then pick out the first "triple" entry (i.e., (Name,Addr,Tel)) if such an entry exists. The second case matches otherwise and returns the empty.

The second example is more interesting in that the use of regular expression types is more critical there than in the first example. In the first case in the first example, the pattern matcher will walk over the first three elements of label name, addr, and tel, and then try to match the rest value against the pattern rest:(Name,Addr,Tel?)*. However, any value should already have this type. Therefore such a matching would not be meaningful. This is not true in the first case in the second example. When the pattern matcher looks at the first pattern ps:(Name,Addr)* in the first case, there is no hint about how many entries are "pairs." Therefore the matcher must walk through the input value to find where the chain of pairs ends. This matching for a *variable* length sequence is beyond ML pattern matching.

In these examples, pattern matchings are exhaustive. That is, all the values of type (Name,Addr,Tel?)* are covered by these patterns. In order to check exhaustiveness, we again use subtyping. For instance, in the first example, we check the following subtype relation

```
   (Name,Addr,Tel?)*
<: name[String], addr[String], tel[String], (Name,Addr,Tel?)*
 | name[String], addr[String], (Name,Addr,Tel?)*
 | ()
```

where the left hand side is the parameter type on the annotation and the right hand side is the type constructed from the patterns (i.e., the union of the patterns with all the term variables n, a, etc. removed). (Although in these examples subtyping of the other way around also holds, we do not check this since allowing this sometimes makes programming easier. Such a situation typically occurs when a pattern contains variables whose type information is useless in the body.)

Our pattern matchings can have two kinds of ambiguity. The first ambiguity occurs when multiple patterns match the same input value. For example, the patterns in firstTriple function above are ambiguous since any value that matches the first pattern also matches the second pattern. In such a case, we simply take the first matching pattern ("first matching policy"). The second ambiguity occurs when a single pattern can have multiple ways for variable bindings. This is intrinsic in regular expression pattern matching. For example, suppose we replace the first case in firstTriple with the following:

```
es:(Name,Addr,Tel?)*, t:(Name,Addr,Tel), rest:(Name,Addr,Tel?)*  → t
```

since we now skip both pair and triple entries at the beginning using the pattern es:(Name,Addr,Tel?)*, it is not clear which triple entry the variable t is bound to. We resolve this ambiguity by adopting a "longest match" policy where patterns appearing earlier have higher priority. In this example, the first (Name,Addr,Tel?)* matches as a long sequence as possible and therefore t is bound to the last triple entry. See Section Appendix C for a more formal treatment.

Another possible approach to resolving this ambiguity issue would be to simply disallow ambiguity. However, when we want to write a "default case" in a pattern matching, this restriction would force to write a somewhat cumbersome pattern that captures the "negation" of the other cases.

2.3   More Complex Example: Folder Manipulation

Up to now, the types that we have seen looked like regular expressions on strings. More interesting programs involve regular expressions on *trees*. Consider the following program.

```
type Folder = Record*
type Record = name[String], folder[Folder]
            | name[String], url[String], exists[Bool]

fun tidyFolder : Folder→Folder =
    record:Record, folder:Folder
       → tidyRecord(record), tidyFolder(folder)
  | () → ()

fun tidyRecord : Record→Record? =
    name[nm:String], folder[fl:Folder]
       → name[nm], folder[tidyFolder(fl)]
  | name[nm:String], url[s:String], exists[false[]]
       → ()
  | name[nm:String], url[s:String], exists[true[]]
       → name[nm], url[s], exists[true[]]
```

The mutually recursive types `Folder` and `Record` define a simple template for storing structured lists of bookmarks, as might be found in a web browser: a folder is a list of records, while a record is either a named folder or a named URL plus a boolean indicating whether the link is good or broken. The functions `tidyFolder` and `tidyRecord` traverse a bookmark list recursively, preserving leaves with good links and dropping ones with bad links.

3   Related Work

Mainstream XML-specific languages can be divided into query languages such as XML-QL [DFF+] and Lorel [AQM+97] and programming languages such as XSLT [XSL]. In general, when one is interested in rather simple information extraction from XML databases, programs in programming languages are less succinct than the same programs in a suitable query language. On the other hand, programming languages tend to be more suitable for writing complicated transformations like conversion to a display format. XDuce is categorized as a programming language.

Static typing of programs for XML processing has been approached from several different angles. One popular approach is to embed a type system for

XML in an existing typed language. The advantage is that we can enjoy not only the static safety and typechecking, but also all the other features provided by the host language. The cost is that XML values and their corresponding DTDs must be some how "injected" into the value and type space of the host language; this usually involves adding more layers of tagging than were present in the original XML documents, which inhibits subtyping. The lack of subtyping (or availability of only restricted forms of subtyping) is not a serious problem for simple traversal of tree structures; it becomes a stumbling block, though, in tasks like the "database evolution" that we discussed in Section 2, where forget-ordering subtyping and distributivity were critically needed.

A recent example of the embedding approach is Wallace and Runciman proposal to use Haskell as a host language [WR99] for XML processing. The only thing they add to Haskell is a mapping from DTDs into Haskell datatypes. This allows their programs to make use of other mechanisms standard in functional programming languages, such as higher-order functions, parametric polymorphism, and pattern matching. However, they do not have any notion of subtyping. Moreover, pattern matching in XDuce is more powerful than Haskell's in some cases. For instance, as shown in Section 2.2, we can concisely write patterns that skip a variable length sequence by using regular expression types. A difference in the other direction is that XDuce does not currently support higher-order functions or parametric polymorphism. (We are working on both of these extensions.)

Another piece of work along similar lines is the functional language XMλ for XML processing, proposed by Meijer and Shields [MS99]. Their type system is not described in detail in this paper, but seems to be close to Haskell's, except that they incorporate *Glushkov automata* in type checking, resulting in a more flexible type system.

A closer relative to XDuce is the query language YAT [CS98], which allows optional use of types similar to DTDs. The notion of subtyping between these types is somewhat weaker than ours (lacking, in particular, the distributivity laws used in the "database evolution" example in Section 2.1).

Milo, Suciu, and Vianu have studied a typechecking problem for their general framework called *k-pebble tree transducers*, which can capture a wide range of query languages for XML [MSV00]. The types there are based on tree automata and conceptually identical to those of XDuce. Papakonstantinou and Vianu present a typechecking algorithm for their query language *loto-ql* by using extensions to DTDs [PV00]. One of their extensions is equivalent to tree automata. The type checking algorithms presented in both papers are *semantically complete*, while XDuce's is not (since such typechecking would be undecidable in general for Turing-complete languages).

The type system of XDuce was originally motivated by the observation by Buneman and Pierce [BP99] that untagged union types corresponded naturally to forms of variation found in semistructured databases.

4   Conclusions and Future Work

We have presented several examples of XDuce programming and shown how we can write flexible and robust programs for processing XML by combining regular expression types and regular expression pattern matching.

We consider XDuce suitable for applications involving rather complicated tree transformation. Moreover, for such applications, our static typing mechanism would help in reducing development periods.

In this view, we have built a prototype implementation of XDuce and used it to develop some small but non-trivial applications:

Bookmarks can be viewed as a simple database query. It takes as input an Netscape bookmarks file of type `Bookmarks`, which is a subset of the (much larger) type HTML. It extracts a certain folder named "Public", formats it as a free-standing document, adds a table of contents at the front, and inserts links between the contents and the body. The result has type the full HTML type. (Total: 224 lines)

Html2Latex takes an HTML file (of type HTML) and converts it into LaTeX format (of type `String`). (264 lines)

Diff implements the "tree diff" algorithm proposed by Chawathe [Cha99]. It takes a pair of XML files of generic `Xml` type and returns a tree with annotations indicating whether each subtree has been retained, inserted, deleted, or changed between the two inputs. (300 lines)

The first two applications are written in the way that traverses the input tree by several simple recursive functions. The third one is more complex. The first phase is a dynamic programming algorithm, where regular expression types are used for representing the internal data structures; the second phase combines two input trees and inserts annotations at each node, where types ensure that the annotations and the actual trees are never confused. In the course of writing these applications, our type checker gave us tremendous help in finding silly mistakes.

The implementation of XDuce raises many algorithmic issues. The primary source of complication is that types and patterns in XDuce are essentially tree automata and therefore we need to use operations on tree automata [CDG+], which are in general expensive. For instance, decision for subtyping is inclusion of tree automata, which is known to be EXPTIME-complete [Sei90]. We have addressed this problem and obtained an algorithm that runs efficiently in practice [HVP00]. In particular, the HTML type[1] used in the above applications is generally considered to be one of the largest XML DTDs, yet type checking of our programs involving it takes a fraction of a second on stock hardware. As other implementation issues, we are working on a type inference algorithm to eliminate spurious type annotations in patterns, and a pattern compilation scheme to improve run-time efficiency [HP00].

---

[1] More precisely, we use XHTML, which is an XML implementation of HTML.

XDuce's language design is far from finished. We plan to add standard features from functional programming, such as higher-order functions and parametric polymorphism. We also consider a support for object-oriented features found in XML-Schema specifications [XS00]. The combination of these features with regular expression types raises some subtle issues, which we are now seeking to solve.

Our prototype implementation is written in O'Caml (6500 lines excluding libraries such as the XML parser). Interested readers are invited to visit our home page:

http://www.cis.upenn.edu/~hahosoya/xduce.html

Acknowledgments. Our main collaborators in the XDuce project are Peter Buneman, Jérôme Vouillon, and Phil Wadler. We have also learned a great deal from discussions with Nils Klarlund and Volker Renneberg, with the DB Group and the PL Club at Penn, and with members of Professor Yonezawa's group at Tokyo.

This work was supported by the University of Pennsylvania and by an NSF Career grant, CCR-9701826. Haruo Hosoya is supported by Japan Society for the Promotion of Science.

References

AQM+97. Serge Abiteboul, Dallan Quass, Jason McHugh, Jennifer Widom, and Janet L. Wiener. The Lorel query language for semistructured data. *International Journal on Digital Libraries*, 1(1):68–88, 1997.

BP99. Peter Buneman and Benjamin Pierce. Union types for semistructured data. In *Proceedings of the International Database Programming Languages Workshop*, September 1999. Also available as University of Pennsylvania Dept. of CIS technical report MS-CIS-99-09.

CDG+. Hubert Common, Max Dauchet, Rémy Gilleron, Florent Jacquemard, Denis Lugiez, Sophie Tison, and Marc Tommasi. Tree automata techniques and applications. Draft book; available electronically on http://www.grappa.univ-lille3.fr/tata.

Cha99. Sudarshan S. Chawathe. Comparing hierarchical data in external memory. In *Proceedings of the Twenty-fifth International Conference on Very Large Data Bases*, pages 90–101, Edinburgh, Scotland, U.K., September 1999.

CS98. Sophie Cluet and Jerome Simeon. Using YAT to build a web server. In *Intl. Workshop on the Web and Databases (WebDB)*, 1998.

DFF+. Alin Deutsch, Mary Fernandez, Daniela Florescu, Alon Levy, and Dan Suciu. XML-QL: A Query Language for XML. http://www.w3.org/TR/NOTE-xml-ql.

HP00. Haruo Hosoya and Benjamin Pierce. Tree automata and pattern matching. Available through http://www.cis.upenn.edu/~hahosoya/papers/tapat-full.ps, July 2000.

HU79. John E. Hopcroft and Jeffrey D. Ullman. *Introduction to Automata Theory, Languages, and Computation*. Addison-Wesley, 1979.

HVP00.   Haruo Hosoya, Jérôme Vouillon, and Benjamin C. Pierce. Regular expres-
          sion types for XML. In *Proceedings of the International Conference on
          Functional Programming (ICFP)*, 2000.
MS99.   Erik Meijer and Mark Shields. XMλ: A functional programming language
          for constructing and manipulating XML documents. Submitted to USENIX
          2000 Technical Conference, 1999.
MSV00.   Tova Milo, Dan Suciu, and Victor Vianu. Typechecking for XML transform-
          ers. In *Proceedings of the Nineteenth ACM SIGMOD-SIGACT-SIGART
          Symposium on Principles of Database Systems*, pages 11–22. ACM, May
          2000.
PV00.   Yannis Papakonstantinou and Victor Vianu. DTD Inference for Views of
          XML Data. In *Proceedings of the Nineteenth ACM SIGMOD-SIGACT-
          SIGART Symposium on Principles of Database Systems*, pages 35–46, Dal-
          las, Texas, May 2000.
Sei90.   Hermut Seidl. Deciding equivalence of finite tree automata. *SIAM Journal
          of Computing*, 19(3):424–437, June 1990.
WR99.   Malcolm Wallace and Colin Ranciman. Haskell and XML: Generic combina-
          tors or type-based translation? In *Proceedings of the Fourth ACM SIGPLAN
          International Conference on Functional Programming (ICFP'99)*, volume
          34-9 of *ACM Sigplan Notices*, pages 148–159, N.Y., September 27–29 1999.
          ACM Press.
XML.   Extensible markup language (XML™). http://www.w3.org/XML/.
XS00.   XML Schema Part 0: Primer, W3C Working Draft. http://www.w3.org/
          TR/xmlschema-0/, 2000.
XSL.   XSL Transformations (XSLT). http://www.w3.org/TR/xslt.

A Types

This section gives the formal definitions for types and subtyping.

A.1 Syntax

We assume a fixed set of base types, ranged over by B, and a countably infinite
set of labels, ranged over by l. Each base type B denotes a set V_B of base values,
ranged over by b_B. We assume that all V_B are disjoint.

Values are defined as follows.

$$v ::= M_1, \ldots, M_n \text{ sequence } (n \geq 0)$$

$$M ::= b_B \qquad \text{base element}$$
$$\quad\ l[v] \qquad \text{label element}$$

We write () for the empty value (i.e., the empty sequence). We write v,w for
the concatenation of values (i.e., sequences) v and w.

A XDuce program consists of a set of type definitions, a set of function
definitions, and an expression to be evaluated. Type definitions have the form

```
type X = T
```

where X ranges over variables and T ranges over type expressions. Type expressions are defined as follows.

$$
\begin{aligned}
\texttt{T} ::=\ &\texttt{X} &&\text{variable}\\
&\texttt{B} &&\text{base type}\\
&\texttt{()} &&\text{empty sequence}\\
&\texttt{l[T]} &&\text{label}\\
&\texttt{T,T} &&\text{concatenation}\\
&\texttt{T|T} &&\text{union}
\end{aligned}
$$

We sometimes write **type** $\overline{\texttt{X}}\texttt{=}\overline{\texttt{T}}$ to abbreviate a set of type definitions **type** $\texttt{X}_1\texttt{=}\texttt{T}_1,\dots,$**type** $\texttt{X}_n\texttt{=}\texttt{T}_n$. Since the set of type definitions is fixed for a given XDuce program, we lighten the notation below by assuming a fixed set of definitions $E = $ **type** $\overline{\texttt{X}}\texttt{=}\overline{\texttt{T}}$.

A.2 Semantics of Types

The denotation of each type is a set of values, defined as follows.

First, we define a function $[\![\cdot]\!]$, which takes a type and an environment mapping type variables to sets of values, and returns a set of values.

$$
\begin{aligned}
[\![\texttt{B}]\!]\rho &= V_{\texttt{B}}\\
[\![\texttt{()}]\!]\rho &= \{\,\texttt{()}\,\}\\
[\![\texttt{l[T]}]\!]\rho &= \{\,\texttt{l[f]} \mid \texttt{f} \in [\![\texttt{T}]\!]\rho\,\}\\
[\![\texttt{T}_1\texttt{,}\texttt{T}_2]\!]\rho &= \{\,\texttt{f,g} \mid \texttt{f} \in [\![\texttt{T}_1]\!]\rho \,\wedge\, \texttt{g} \in [\![\texttt{T}_2]\!]\rho\,\}\\
[\![\texttt{T}_1\texttt{|}\texttt{T}_2]\!]\rho &= [\![\texttt{T}_1]\!]\rho \cup [\![\texttt{T}_2]\!]\rho\\
[\![\texttt{X}]\!]\rho &= \rho(\texttt{X})
\end{aligned}
$$

Let μ be the smallest mapping satisfying $\mu(\texttt{X}_i) = [\![\texttt{T}_i]\!]\mu$ for all the definitions **type** $\texttt{X}_i\texttt{=}\texttt{T}_i$ in E. Finally, write $[\![\texttt{T}]\!]$ for $[\![\texttt{T}]\!]\mu$.

A.3 Derived Forms

The regular expression type constructors are derivable as combinations of the above constructs. We represent the Kleene closure T* by a variable X that is recursively defined as follows (cf. lists as a datatype in ML).

```
type X = T,X | ()
```

The other regular expression constructors are defined as follows.

$$
\begin{aligned}
\texttt{T+} &\equiv \texttt{T , T*}\\
\texttt{T?} &\equiv \texttt{T | ()}
\end{aligned}
$$

A.4   Regularity

As we have defined them so far, types correspond to arbitrary context-free grammars—for example, we can write definitions like:

```
type X = Int,X,String | ()
```

Since the decision problem for inclusion between context free languages is un-decidable [HU79], we need to impose an additional restriction to reduce the power of the system so that types correspond to regular tree languages. Decid-ing whether an arbitrary context-free grammar is regular is also undecidable [HU79], so we adopt a simple syntactic condition, called *well-formedness*, that ensures regularity. Intuitively, well-formedness allows recursive uses of variables to occur only in tail positions. For example, we allow the following type defini-tions:

```
type X = Int,Y
type Y = String,X | ()
```

More precisely, we define well-formedness in terms of a "right-linearity" judg-ment of the form $\sigma \vdash T : rl(X)$, where σ is a set of variables. It should be read "T is right-linear in X, assuming that all bodies of variables in σ are right-linear in X." This judgment uses an auxiliary "disconnectedness" judgment of the form $\sigma \vdash T : dc(X)$, read "T is disconnected from X (i.e., X does not occur in the top level of T), assuming that all bodies of variables in σ are disconnected from X." These two judgments are defined by the following rules (where $X \neq Y$):

$$\sigma \vdash T : rl(X) \quad \text{for } T = \text{() or } 1\text{[T] or } X$$
$$\sigma \vdash Y : rl(X) \quad \text{if } Y \in \sigma$$
$$\sigma \vdash Y : rl(X) \quad \text{if } Y \notin \sigma \text{ and } \sigma \cup \{Y\} \vdash E(Y) : rl(X)$$
$$\sigma \vdash T|U : rl(X) \text{ if } \sigma \vdash T : rl(X) \text{ and } \sigma \vdash U : rl(X)$$
$$\sigma \vdash T,U : rl(X) \text{ if } \emptyset \vdash T : dc(X) \text{ and } \sigma \vdash U : rl(X)$$

$$\sigma \vdash T : dc(X) \quad \text{for } T = \text{() or } 1\text{[T]}$$
$$\sigma \vdash Y : dc(X) \quad \text{if } Y \in \sigma$$
$$\sigma \vdash Y : dc(X) \quad \text{if } Y \notin \sigma \text{ and } \sigma \cup \{Y\} \vdash E(Y) : dc(X)$$
$$\sigma \vdash T|U : dc(X) \text{ if } \sigma \vdash T : dc(X) \text{ and } \sigma \vdash U : dc(X)$$
$$\sigma \vdash T,U : dc(X) \text{ if } \sigma \vdash T : dc(X) \text{ and } \sigma \vdash U : dc(X)$$

The empty sequence, a label, and the variable X are right-linear in X. For variables Y other than X, we recursively check the right-linearity of the body of Y. To ensure termination, we keep track in σ of variables that have already been checked. For (T|U), both T and U should be right-linear in X. For (T,U), we check if U is right-linear in X, while T is disconnected from X. The disconnectedness judgment is defined similarly, except for the first rule, in which X is *not* disconnected from X. Now, the set of type definitions E is said to be *well-formed* if

$$\emptyset \vdash E(X) : rl(X) \text{ for all } X \in dom(E)$$

A.5   Subtyping

We define the subtyping relation in the simplest possible way:

$$S <: T \quad \text{iff} \quad [\![S]\!] \subseteq [\![T]\!].$$

A.1 Theorem: There is an algorithm to decide the subtyping relation.

The concrete algorithm and its soundness, completeness, and termination theorems are given in our another paper [HVP00].

B   Terms

B.1   Syntax

At the top level, we have a set of declarations of mutually recursive functions, each of the following form.

```
fun f : S→T =
    p1 → e1
  | p2 → e2
  | ...
  | pn → en
```

Each function has type annotations for both the parameter and the result. The body consists of one or more pattern matching clauses. Each clause has a pattern and a term for the body. (We write `fun f:S→T = ` $\overline{p} \rightarrow \overline{e}$ to abbreviate the above form.) In addition to the fixed set E of type definitions, we fix a set F of function definitions for the remainder of the document.

The syntax of terms and patterns is:

$$
\begin{array}{llll}
e ::= & x & \text{variable} \\
& b_B & \text{base value} \\
& () & \text{empty sequence} \\
& l[e] & \text{label} \\
& e,e & \text{concatenation} \\
& f(e) & \text{application} \\
\\
p ::= & x:T & \text{variable} \\
& () & \text{empty sequence} \\
& l[p] & \text{label} \\
& p,p & \text{concatenation}
\end{array}
$$

B.2   Typing Rules

A context Γ is a mapping from variables to types, written $x_1 : T_1, \ldots, x_n : T_n$. We have three judgments:

$\Gamma \vdash e \in T$ $\qquad\qquad$ e has type T

$\vdash p \in T \Rightarrow \Gamma'$ $\qquad\quad$ p accepts type T and yields context Γ'

$\vdash \texttt{fun } \texttt{f} : \texttt{S} \rightarrow \texttt{T} = \overline{\texttt{p}} \rightarrow \overline{\texttt{e}}$ $\quad$ f is well-typed

The typing relation for terms is:

$$\frac{\Gamma(x) = T}{\Gamma \vdash x \in T} \qquad\qquad (\text{TE-Var})$$

$$\Gamma \vdash b_B \in B \qquad\qquad (\text{TE-Base})$$

$$\Gamma \vdash () \in () \qquad\qquad (\text{TE-Emp})$$

$$\frac{\Gamma \vdash e \in T}{\Gamma \vdash 1[e] \in 1[T]} \qquad\qquad (\text{TE-Lab})$$

$$\frac{\Gamma \vdash e_1 \in T_1 \qquad \Gamma \vdash e_2 \in T_2}{\Gamma \vdash e_1, e_2 \in T_1, T_2} \qquad\qquad (\text{TE-Cat})$$

$$\frac{\begin{array}{c} \texttt{fun } f : S \rightarrow T = \ldots \in F \\ \Gamma \vdash e \in S' \end{array}}{\Gamma \vdash f(e) \in T} \qquad\qquad (\text{TE-App})$$

$$\frac{\Gamma \vdash e \in S \qquad S <: T}{\Gamma \vdash e \in T} \qquad\qquad (\text{TE-Sub})$$

For patterns:

$$\vdash x : T \in T \Rightarrow x : T \qquad\qquad (\text{TP-Var})$$

$$\vdash () \in () \Rightarrow \cdot \qquad\qquad (\text{TP-Emp})$$

$$\frac{\vdash p \in T \Rightarrow \Gamma}{\vdash 1[p] \in 1[T] \Rightarrow \Gamma} \qquad\qquad (\text{TP-Lab})$$

$$\frac{\vdash p_1 \in T_1 \Rightarrow \Gamma_1 \qquad \vdash p_2 \in T_2 \Rightarrow \Gamma_2}{\vdash p_1, p_2 \in T_1, T_2 \Rightarrow \Gamma_1, \Gamma_2} \qquad\qquad (\text{TP-Cat})$$

For functions:

$$\frac{\vdash p_i \in S_i \Rightarrow \Gamma_i \qquad \Gamma_i \vdash e_i \in T_i}{S <: S_1 | .. | S_n} \tag{TF}$$
$$\overline{\vdash \texttt{fun } f:S{\rightarrow}T = \overline{p}{\rightarrow}\overline{e}}$$

The rule TF needs a little explanation: each pattern p_i accepts type S_i and yields the context Γ_i, under which the body e_i can be given the result type T (as annotated). Also, the parameter type S is required to be a subtype of the union of all S_i's. This subtype checks exhaustiveness of patterns.

C   Operational Semantics

The operational semantics consists of evaluation relations for terms and pattern matching. The former is fairly standard, the latter a little unusual due to "ambiguity" in patterns.

There are two kinds of ambiguity. One appears when there are multiple clauses whose patterns match the input value. For example, in the function

```
fun is_single : Int*→Bool =
    x:Int   →   true
  | x:Int*  →   false
```

we have two possibilities when the input is a single integer.

The other source of ambiguity is when there are multiple ways in which a single clause can match a given value. For example, in the function

```
fun f : Int*→Int* =
    x:Int*, y:Int*  →   x
```

it is unclear how many integers x takes from the beginning of the input. We address the first source of ambiguity by adopting a "first match" policy, as in ML. For the second one, we adopt a "longest match" policy as in Emacs.

In fact, the longest-match policy turns out to be just a special case of the first-match policy. Recall that Int* is a derived form meaning a variable X defined as follows:

```
type X = Int,X | ()
```

The ordering of the branches in the definition is significant: Int,X comes before (). Now, in the above example, we first process the pattern x:Int*, traversing the input value and the definition of X in parallel and taking the first clause (Int,X) as often as possible. When the input value is exhausted and the second clause (()) is taken, we move on to the pattern y:Int*, where we can now only take the second clause because the remaining of the input value is the empty sequence.

To describe the first-match policy, we use a notion of *choice sequence*. During pattern matching, we remember the index of the branch we take at each choice point. A choice sequence is a sequence of such indices, listed according to the order of traversal—from left to right and from outer to inner. Finally, we take the *smallest* choice sequence in the dictionary order (written $\prec$).

The evaluation relations are defined with respect to an environments V—a mapping from variables to values. There are three judgments.

$$V \vdash \mathsf{e} \Downarrow \mathsf{v} \qquad \text{e evaluates to v}$$
$$\vdash \mathsf{p} \triangleright \mathsf{v} \Rightarrow V \,/\, \alpha \quad \text{p matches v and yields } V \text{ and choice sequence } \alpha$$
$$\vdash \mathsf{T} \triangleright \mathsf{v} \Rightarrow \alpha \qquad \text{T matches v and yields choice sequence } \alpha$$

Evaluation of terms is defined as follows:

$$V \vdash \mathsf{x} \Downarrow V(\mathsf{x}) \tag{EE-Var}$$

$$V \vdash \mathsf{b_B} \Downarrow \mathsf{b_B} \tag{EE-Base}$$

$$V \vdash \mathsf{()} \Downarrow \mathsf{()} \tag{EE-Emp}$$

$$\frac{V \vdash \mathsf{e} \Downarrow \mathsf{v}}{V \vdash \mathsf{l[e]} \Downarrow \mathsf{l[v]}} \tag{EE-Lab}$$

$$\frac{V \vdash \mathsf{e_1} \Downarrow \mathsf{v} \qquad V \vdash \mathsf{e_2} \Downarrow \mathsf{w}}{V \vdash \mathsf{e_1,e_2} \Downarrow \mathsf{v,w}} \tag{EE-Cat}$$

$$\frac{\begin{array}{c} V \vdash \mathsf{e} \Downarrow \mathsf{v} \\ \mathtt{fun}\ \mathsf{f}\!:\!\mathsf{S}{\to}\mathsf{T} = \overline{\mathsf{p}}{\to}\overline{\mathsf{e}} \in F \\ \vdash \mathsf{p_i} \triangleright \mathsf{v} \Rightarrow W \,/\, \alpha \\ \forall j, \beta.(\vdash \mathsf{p_j} \triangleright \mathsf{v} \Rightarrow U \,/\, \beta \implies (i,\alpha) \prec (j,\beta)) \\ W \vdash \mathsf{e_i} \Downarrow \mathsf{w} \end{array}}{V \vdash \mathsf{f(e)} \Downarrow \mathsf{w}} \tag{EE-App}$$

Pattern matching:

$$\frac{\vdash \mathsf{T} \triangleright \mathsf{v} \Rightarrow \alpha}{\vdash \mathsf{x}\!:\!\mathsf{T} \triangleright \mathsf{v} \Rightarrow \mathsf{x} \mapsto \mathsf{v} \,/\, \alpha} \tag{EP-Var}$$

$$\vdash \mathsf{()} \triangleright \mathsf{()} \Rightarrow \cdot \,/\, \cdot \tag{EP-Emp}$$

$$\frac{\vdash \mathsf{p} \triangleright \mathsf{v} \Rightarrow V \,/\, \alpha}{\vdash \mathsf{l[p]} \triangleright \mathsf{l[v]} \Rightarrow V \,/\, \alpha} \tag{EP-Lab}$$

$$\frac{\begin{array}{c} \vdash \mathsf{p} \triangleright \mathsf{v} \Rightarrow V \,/\, \alpha \\ \vdash \mathsf{q} \triangleright \mathsf{w} \Rightarrow W \,/\, \beta \end{array}}{\vdash \mathsf{p,q} \triangleright \mathsf{v,w} \Rightarrow V, W \,/\, \alpha, \beta} \tag{EP-Cat}$$

Type matching:

$$\frac{\text{type } X\text{=}T \in E \qquad \vdash T \triangleright v \Rightarrow \alpha}{\vdash X \triangleright v \Rightarrow \alpha} \qquad \text{(ET-VAR)}$$

$$\vdash B \triangleright b_B \Rightarrow \cdot \qquad \text{(ET-BASE)}$$

$$\vdash () \triangleright () \Rightarrow \cdot \qquad \text{(ET-EMP)}$$

$$\frac{\vdash T \triangleright v \Rightarrow \alpha}{\vdash 1[T] \triangleright 1[v] \Rightarrow \alpha} \qquad \text{(ET-LAB)}$$

$$\frac{\vdash T \triangleright v \Rightarrow \alpha \qquad \vdash U \triangleright w \Rightarrow \beta}{\vdash T,U \triangleright v,w \Rightarrow \alpha, \beta} \qquad \text{(ET-CAT)}$$

$$\frac{\vdash T \triangleright v \Rightarrow \alpha}{\vdash T|U \triangleright v \Rightarrow 1, \alpha} \qquad \text{(ET-OR1)}$$

$$\frac{\vdash U \triangleright v \Rightarrow \alpha}{\vdash T|U \triangleright v \Rightarrow 2, \alpha} \qquad \text{(ET-OR2)}$$

The third and fourth premises in EE-APP say that we choose the match that yields the smallest choice sequence in the dictionary order. Also, notice that in EP-CAT and ET-CAT we concatenate the choice sequences left to right, and that in ET-OR1 and ET-OR2 we adjoin the present choice number to the front. These reflect our policy that the priority of choice is from left to right and from outer to inner.

We can prove the following type soundness: a well-typed term evaluates to a value inhabiting the expected type.

C.1 Theorem [Type Soundness]: Suppose $\vdash$ fun $f:S{\to}T = \overline{p}{\to}\overline{e}$ for all functions in F. Then, $\emptyset \vdash e \Downarrow v$ and $\emptyset \vdash e \in T$ imply $v \in [\![T]\!]$.

Proof: We prove the result by showing the following stronger statements:

- If $\vdash T \triangleright v$, then $v \in T$.
- If $\vdash p \triangleright v \Rightarrow V \,/\, \alpha$ and $\vdash p \in T \Rightarrow \Gamma$, then $\Gamma \vdash V$.
- If $V \vdash e \Downarrow v$ and $\Gamma \vdash e \in T$ where $\Gamma \vdash V$, then $v \in [\![T]\!]$.

(Here, $\Gamma \vdash V$ means that $dom(\Gamma) = dom(V)$ and $V(x) \in [\![\Gamma(x)]\!]$ for each $x \in dom(\Gamma)$.) Each statement can be proved by induction on the derivation of the type matching, pattern matching, or term evaluation relation. For the last statement, we need the following inversion properties.

- $\Gamma \vdash \mathtt{x} \in \mathtt{T}$ implies $\Gamma(\mathtt{x}) <: \mathtt{T}$.
- $\Gamma \vdash \mathtt{b_B} \in \mathtt{T}$ implies $\mathtt{B} <: \mathtt{T}$.
- $\Gamma \vdash \mathtt{()} \in \mathtt{T}$ implies $\mathtt{()} <: \mathtt{T}$.
- $\Gamma \vdash \mathtt{1[e]} \in \mathtt{T}$ implies $\Gamma \vdash \mathtt{e} \in \mathtt{S}$ with $\mathtt{1[S]} <: \mathtt{T}$ for some S.
- $\Gamma \vdash \mathtt{e_1,e_2} \in \mathtt{T}$ implies $\Gamma \vdash \mathtt{e_1} \in \mathtt{S_1}$ and $\Gamma \vdash \mathtt{e_2} \in \mathtt{S_2}$ with $\mathtt{S_1,S_2} <: \mathtt{T}$ for some $\mathtt{S_1}$ and $\mathtt{S_2}$.
- $\Gamma \vdash \mathtt{f(e)} \in \mathtt{T}$ implies $\Gamma \vdash \mathtt{e} \in \mathtt{S}$ where $\mathbf{fun}\ \mathtt{f:S} \rightarrow \mathtt{T'} = \ldots \in F$ and $\mathtt{T'} <: \mathtt{T}$.

∎

Automatic Classification of Text Databases through Query Probing

Panagiotis G. Ipeirotis[1], Luis Gravano[1], and Mehran Sahami[2]

[1] Computer Science Department, Columbia University,
1214 Amsterdam Avenue, Mailcode: 0401,
New York, NY 10027-7003, USA
{pirot, gravano}@cs.columbia.edu
[2] E.piphany, Inc.
1900 South Norfolk Street, Suite 310,
San Mateo, CA 94403, USA
sahami@epiphany.com

Abstract. Many text databases on the web are "hidden" behind search interfaces, and their documents are only accessible through querying. Traditional search engines typically ignore the contents of such search-only databases. Recently, Yahoo-like directories have started to manually organize these databases into categories that users can browse to find these valuable resources. We propose a novel strategy to automate the classification of search-only text databases. Our technique starts by training a rule-based document classifier, and then uses the classifier's rules to generate probing queries. The queries are sent to the text databases, which are then classified based on the number of matches that they produce for each query. We report some initial exploratory experiments that show that our approach is promising to automatically characterize the contents of text databases accessible on the web.

1 Introduction

Text databases abound on the Internet. Sometimes users can browse through their documents by following hyperlinks. In many other cases, text databases are "hidden" behind search interfaces, and their documents are only available through querying. For those databases, web search engines cannot crawl inside, and they just index the "front pages", ignoring the contents of possibly rich sources of information. One example of such a search-only text database is the archive of a newspaper. Many newspapers do not offer a browsing interface for past issues, but they do offer search capabilities to retrieve old articles. This is the case, for example, for The New York Times newspaper.

One way of facilitating the access to this kind of searchable databases is to build metasearchers. A metasearcher sends user queries to many search engines, retrieves and merges the results and then returns the combined results back to the user (see [6,12,17,16,5,11]). Alternatively, users can browse Yahoo-like directories to locate databases of interest and then submit queries to these databases.

D. Suciu and G. Vossen (Eds.): WebDB 2000, LNCS 1997, pp. 245–255, 2001.

Some sites have started in the last few years to provide such services. For example, *Invisible Web*[1] and *SearchEngine Guide*[2] classify various search engines into a hierarchical classification scheme. A user can then locate relevant text databases and submit queries only to them to obtain more accurate and focused results than when searching a more general text database. Other services (e.g., *Copernic*[3]) combine the metasearching approach with "browsing." Users can select a specific category (e.g., Recipes, Newspapers, etc.) and the metasearcher then sends the user queries to the searchable databases previously classified in the given category.

Unfortunately, existing approaches for text database classification involve manual intervention of a human expert and do not scale. In this paper we will describe a way of automating this classification process by issuing *query probes* to the text databases. More specifically, in Section 2 we define what it means to classify a text database. Then, in Section 3 we focus on the design of our query probing classification strategy. Finally, in Section 4 we present some initial experiments over web databases.

Related Work: Query probing has been used in [15] for automatic extraction of information from web-based databases. Manually constructed query probes have been used in [4] for the classification of text databases. Query probes were used in [7] to rank databases by similarity to a given query. This algorithm assumes that the query interface can handle differently normal queries and query probes. Reference [1] probes text databases with queries to determine an approximation of their vocabulary and associated statistics. This technique requires retrieving the documents in the query results for further analysis. Finally, guided query probing has been used in [13] to determine sources of heterogeneity in the algorithms used to index and search locally at each text database.

2   Text-Database Classification

In this section we will describe two basic approaches for the classification of text databases. One approach classifies a database into one category when the database *contains a substantial number of documents* in this category. The other approach classifies a database into one category when *the majority of its documents* are in this category.

Example 1. Consider two databases D_1, D_2 with 1,000 and 10,000,000 documents, respectively, and a topic category *"Health."* Suppose that D_1 contains 900 documents about health while D_2 contains 200,000 such documents. Our decision whether to classify D_1 and D_2 in the *"Health"* category will ultimately depend on how users will take advantage of our classification and the databases. Some users might prefer a "focus-oriented" classification (i.e., might be looking

---

[1] http://www.invisibleweb.com/
[2] http://www.searchengineguide.com/
[3] http://www.copernic.com/

for text databases having mostly documents about health and little else). Such users might not want to process documents outside of their topic of interest, and might then prefer that database D_1 be classified in the *"Health"* category (90% of its documents are on health). In contrast, D_2 should not be classified in that category. Although D_2 has a large number of documents on health, these documents represent only a small fraction of the database (i.e., 2%). Hence, it is likely that our "focus-oriented" users would be exposed to non-health documents while exploring D_2. Alternatively, other users might be looking for text databases having a sufficiently large number of documents on health. It might be unimportant for such users what else is at each database. These users might then prefer D_2 to be classified in the *"Health"* category because of its large number of documents on health (i.e., 200,000). D_1 (with 900 documents on health) might or might not be classified in that category, depending on what we consider a "sufficiently large" number of documents.

Consider a set of categories $C_1, \ldots, C_k$ and a text database D that we want to classify in one or more of these categories. Each of D's documents has been classified in one of the categories $C_1, \ldots, C_k$ that we use to classify D. Given this classification of the documents in D we can compute a vector $C = (n_1, \ldots, n_k)$, which indicates the number of documents n_i in category C_i, for $i = 1, \ldots, k$. Vector C is a good summary of the contents of database D and we will use it to classify the database, as we describe next. As illustrated in Example 1 above, to categorize databases we need to capture how "focused" D is and how many documents it contains for a given category. For this we define the following two metrics.

Definition 1. *Consider a text database D and a category C_i. Then the* coverage *of D for C_i is the number of documents in D in category C_i. The* specificity *of D on C_i is the fraction of documents in D in category C_i:*

$$\text{Coverage}(D, C_i) = n_i$$
$$\text{Specificity}(D, C_i) = \frac{n_i}{|D|}$$

Specificity defines how "focused" a database is on a given category. One problem with the definition above is that we do not always know the number of documents in a database. We will discuss how we can approximate this value in Section 3. *Coverage* defines the "absolute" amount of information that a database contains about a specific category. An alternative definition for coverage could divide n_i by the total number of documents in all databases. This would capture what fraction of the existing documents in category C_i are present in a given database. Although this definition is interesting, it has the undesirable property of depending on a universe of known databases. On the Internet, databases come and go constantly so this definition would make the resulting classification scheme that we describe quite unstable. Moreover, since the *Coverage* value would have the same normalizing constant for all databases, excluding this factor will have no bearing on the relative ranking of databases by their coverage of a certain topic.

Using the definitions above, each database D has a specificity and a coverage value for each category. We can use these values to decide how to classify D into one or more of the categories. As described above, we could classify a database into one category when the majority of the documents it contains are of a specific category. Our classification could alternatively be based on the number of documents of a specific category that a database contains.

Definition 2. *Consider a database D and a category C_i and let $\tau_s, \tau_c \geq 0$ to be two pre-specified thresholds. Then D is in category C_i according to a "coverage-oriented" classification if* Coverage$(D, C_i) \geq \tau_c$. *Similarly, D is in category C_i according to a "specificity-oriented" classification if* Specificity$(D, C_i) \geq \tau_s$.

Example 1. **(cont.)** Consider the two databases D_1, D_2 described above, and the category *"Health."* Using Definition 2, *Coverage*$(D_1, \text{"Health"}) = 900$, since D_1 has 900 documents on health. Similarly, *Coverage*$(D_2, \text{"Health"}) = 200,000$. If threshold τ_c for our *"coverage-oriented" classification* is set to, say, 10,000, then D_2 will be classified in category "Health" while D_1 will not, since it does not have a sufficiently large number of documents in this category. Analogously, *Specificity*$(D_1, \text{"Health"}) = \frac{900}{1000} = 0.9$ while *Specificity*$(D_2, \text{"Health"}) = \frac{200,000}{10,000,000} = 0.02$. If threshold τ_s for our *"specificity-oriented" classification* is set to, say, 0.3 then D_1 will be classified in category "Health" while D_2 will not, since it is not sufficiently focused on health and holds too many documents in other categories.

The two alternative database classification schemes above assume that we somehow know the number of documents that each database has in each category, which is clearly unrealistic in most Internet settings. In effect, as discussed in the Introduction, many times we do not have access to a database's contents other than through a query interface. In the next section we introduce techniques for approximating the classification of text databases in this limited-access scenario.

3   Classifying Databases through Probing

The previous section described how to classify a database given the number of documents it contains in each of our categories. Unfortunately, text databases do not export such metadata. In this section we introduce a technique to classify text databases in the absence of any information about their contents. Our technique starts by training a rule-based *document* classifier over our categories (Section 3.1) and then uses the classifier's rules to design a set of probing queries (Section 3.2). The database will be classified based on the number of matches returned for each of these queries, without accessing the documents per se (Section 3.3).

3.1   Training a Document Classifier

Our technique for classifying databases over a set of categories $C_1, \ldots, C_k$ starts by training a rule-based *document* classifier over those categories. We use RIP-PER, an off-the-shelf tool developed at AT&T Research Laboratories[2,3]. Given a set of training, pre-classified documents, this tool returns a classifier that might consist of rules like the following:

```
Computers IF mac
Computers IF graphics windows
Religion  IF god christian
Hobbies   IF baseball
```

The first rule indicates that if a document contains the term `mac` it should be classified in the *"Computers"* category. A document should also be classified into that category if it has the words `graphics` and `windows`. Similarly, if a document has the words `god` and `christian`, it is a *"Religion"* document, whereas if it has the word `baseball`, it is a *"Hobbies"* document.

Once we have trained a document classifier using a tool like RIPPER, we could apply it to every document in a *database* D that we want to classify. This procedure would produce a close approximation to the $C = (n_1, \ldots, n_k)$ vector of category frequencies for D (Section 2), which we could use to classify D according to Definition 2. Unfortunately, we often do not have access to all the documents in a database, other than indirectly through a query interface, as discussed above. Next, we define a query probing strategy to deal with such databases.

3.2   Probing a Database

Our goal is to create a set of queries for each category that will retrieve exactly the documents for that category from the database we are classifying. We will construct these queries based on the document classifier discussed above. To create our queries, we turn each rule into a query. The number of matches for each query will be the number of documents in the database that satisfy the corresponding rule. These numbers will then be used to approximate the distribution of documents in categories within a text database, as the following example illustrates.

Example 2. Consider a database D with 500 documents, all about *"Computers,"* and suppose that our categories of interest are *"Computers," "Hobbies,"* and *"Religion."* Then D has associated with it a vector $C = (500, 0, 0)$ (Section 2), showing the distribution of documents over these three categories. Suppose also that we have trained a rule-based document classifier and obtained the four rules shown above for the three categories. If we do not have access to all the documents of D, we can still characterize its contents by issuing probing queries constructed from the document classifier as discussed above. Our first probe will be the query `mac`. The database will return a result of the form "92 documents found." We send a second query `graphics AND windows`. Again, we get a result like "288 documents found." Queries `god AND christian` and `baseball` return 0 and 2 matches respectively. From these results we conclude that D has $288+92=380$ "Computers" documents, 0 "Religion" documents, and 2 "Hobbies" documents. Thus we approximate the ideal vector C, with $C' = (380, 0, 2)$.

RIPPER can produce either an ordered set of rules or an unordered set of rules. When the rules are ordered, the first rule that is satisfied by a document fires and gives a classification for that document. No subsequent rules are matched against that document. We should formulate our queries properly in order to simulate the actions of the classifier as much as possible. For example, if the rules above were ordered rules, our second probing query would have been `graphics AND windows AND NOT mac`, to avoid retrieving any documents that would match the first, earlier rule.

If the query interface of a database does not support the kind of queries described above, we break these queries into smaller pieces that we can send separately. A detailed description of this technique is beyond the scope of this paper. For completeness, we mention that we submit the probing queries in such a way that we can use the inclusion-exclusion principle to calculate the number of results that would have been returned for the original queries.

A significant advantage of our probing approach is that we do not need to retrieve documents to analyze the contents of a database [1]. Instead, we count only the number of matches for these queries. Thus, in our approach we only require a database to report the number of matches for a given query. It is common for a database to return something like "X documents found" before returning the actual results.

3.3   Using Probing Results for Classification

After the probing phase, we have calculated an approximation of the coverage of a database for our categories. To calculate the specificity values, we would need the size of the database $|D|$, and we approximate it by $|D| \simeq \sum_{i=1}^{k} n_i$. This means that we will use only the documents that are classified into the given categories to calculate the size of the database. This approximation, especially for a small number of queries, is not close to the real size of the database, but it is sufficient for our purposes. Our estimates will be accurate as long as the fraction of matches for a category, as determined by the query probes, is representative of the actual fraction of documents in that category in the database. Unfortunately, this approach can give poor results when there are many documents that do not belong to any of the given categories. In such a case, it is also difficult to categorize this text database into the given classification scheme, since no category will accurately reflect the database contents.

An extra step that we applied to our method to improve the results is the following. For each of the rules, we know its accuracy from the training phase of the classifier. For example, the rule `Computers IF mac` may have correctly classified 90 documents and incorrectly classified 10 other documents during the training phase, resulting in an accuracy of 0.9. We adjust our results from the probing phase by multiplying the number of documents matched by each rule by the accuracy of that rule. Also, for the set of rules that classified documents into one category, we know their "recall," i.e., how many documents they recalled over all the documents in this category. For example if category Computers in the training phase had 150 documents and the rules retrieved 100, then recall is 0.67. This means that only this portion of all the documents of this category were retrieved. To adjust our results further, we divide each element of the C' approximation vector with the recall for this category. This regularization of the values n_i helps account for the fact that rules generally do not (and need not) have perfect recall on real document databases.

4   Initial Experiments

Using RIPPER, we created a classifier using a collection of 20,000 newsgroup articles from the UCI KDD archive[4]. This collection has been used in previous text categorization experiments [8,14], and is composed of 1,000 newsgroup articles from each of 20 newsgroups. We further grouped the articles into five large sets according to their originating newsgroups: *Computers* (comp.*), *Science* (sci.*), *Hobbies* (rec.*), *Society* (alt.atheism, talk.*, soc.*) and *Misc* (misc.sale). We have removed all the headers (except for the "Subject:" line), the e-mail addresses from the body of the articles and all punctuation. Subsequently, we eliminated all words that appeared in fewer than three documents in the collection and the 100 most frequent words. Such feature reduction is in accordance with Zipf's Law [18], which shows that there are many infrequently used words in document collections. For purposes of classification, however, such infrequent terms generally provide little discriminating power between classes (due to their rarity), and can thus be safely eliminated with little, if any, reduction in subsequent classification accuracy. Similarly, very frequent words, that often tend to appear in virtually all articles, will also provide little ability to make classification distinctions, and can likewise be eliminated. After this step we applied an information theoretic feature selection algorithm [9,10] to reduce the terms from about 40,000 to 5,000. This algorithm eliminates features that have the least impact on the class distribution of documents (as measured by the relative entropy of the distribution of the document class labels conditioned on the appearance of a given feature). Features that have little impact on the class distribution are likely to also have little discriminating power between classes, and can thus be eliminated without much adverse impact on the final classification accuracy. For the training set we used a random sample of 10,000 documents and the remaining 10,000 documents were used for testing.

The initial document classifier generated by RIPPER consisted of 534 ordered rules. Many of the rules were covering very few (one or two) examples from the training set. These rules did not contribute much to the overall accuracy of the

---

[4] http://kdd.ics.uci.edu/

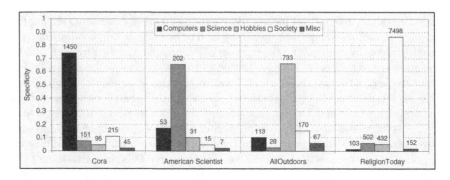

Fig. 1. Specificity and coverage values for four web-accessible databases.

document classifier, and would result in too many probing queries during the classification stage. Thus, we decided to restrict the classifier to produce only rules that covered at least 50 examples from the training set. This resulted in a classifier with 29 ordered rules that included a total of 32 words. We also tried to produce a rule set that would include rules with negations (NOT clauses). The resulting classifier had 31 rules with much better accuracy, but, in this case, a total of 92 words were used to form the rules. The queries for this classifier were much longer and we opted to use the simpler classifier (that had only 29 rules and 32 words) for the sake of query efficiency. The rules given in Section 3.1 are, in fact, examples of rules used by this classifier.

After constructing the classifier, we selected four sites from *Invisible Web*[5] to test our method. These four sites are topically cohesive, and should be classified in the same category by both the specificity- and the coverage- oriented classification alternatives of Definition 2:

- *Cora*[6]: A repository of technical papers about Computer Science. This repository should be classified under the category *"Computers."*
- *American Scientist*[7]: An on-line version of a magazine on science and technology. This database should be classified under the category *"Science."*
- *AllOutdoors*[8]: A site with articles about fishing, hunting, and other outdoor activities. This site should be classified under the category *"Hobbies."*
- *ReligionToday*[9]: A site with news and discussion about religion. This site should be classified under the category *"Society."*

We probed these sites using the techniques described in Section 3.2. One problem that arose during the probing phase was a limitation on the length of the queries that we could submit to the "American Scientist" site. We truncated

---

[5] http://www.invisibleweb.com/
[6] http://www.cora.jprc.com/
[7] http://www.amsci.org/
[8] http://www.alloutdoors.com/
[9] http://www.religiontoday.com/

the long queries by eliminating terms that did not cover any documents (e.g., instead of issuing a query `baseball AND NOT god`, if the query `god` returned 0 results, we issue only the query `baseball`).

The results of our probing phase can be seen in Figure 1. Consider, for example, the results for Cora. After submitting the queries for the class Computer, the database reported 1450 matches for all the queries. For classes Science, Hobbies, Society, and Misc, it reported 151, 95, 215, and 45 matches respectively. Using these coverage values we estimated specificity as in Section 2. The specificity values are depicted using the bars, and it can be clearly seen that the results indicate that Cora is a site that is "focused" on Computers. Similarly for the other sites, we probed them using the same rules. The results clearly indicate the focus of each site. For example, if we had a threshold value for specificity of $\tau_s = 0.6$, then each site would be classified correctly. Moreover, to measure the significance of our results, we performed a Chi-squared test comparing the distribution of the classes for each database given by the probes to the uniform distribution. This test gives us a measure for how likely the skew in the class distribution (toward the correct class) is likely to have been gotten by chance. The Chi-square test reveals that the skews in the class distributions for each database are significant at the 99.9% level. Thus, it appears that, in every case, the probes generated by the RIPPER rules have accurately captured the concept represented by each class of documents.

5   Conclusions and Future Work

In this paper, we have described a method that uses probing queries produced by a classifier to classify a text database. We have also shown some promising initial experiments. The method managed to identify the right category for each database, using only the number of matches for a small set of queries and without retrieving any documents. Our technique could also be used to characterize web sites that offer a browsable interface as well. The only requirement is the existence of a search interface for the local contents, which many sites offer. By using only a small set of probe queries, we can get a coarse idea about the contents of a web site.

Our future work includes the expansion of our strategy into a hierarchical classification scheme. We believe that hierarchical organization of the categories will allow our scheme to handle a large number of categories. A fundamental question that we will also study is how to find training sets that would be representative of the kinds of data sets available on the web. Our technique relies on good document classifiers, so having appropriate training sets is a crucial issue. We will explore the efficiency of our algorithm for various indexing environments and for search interfaces that support different sets of boolean operators. We also plan to compare our approach against an adaptation, for the database classification problem, of the technique in [1]. Finally, we will expand our adjustment technique (that currently uses only the precision of each rule and the recall for each category) to use the full set of statistics (i.e., confusion matrices) from the document classifier. This could produce better approximations of the contents of the search-only text databases.

Acknowledgments. This material is based upon work supported by the National Science Foundation under Grants No. IIS-97-33880 and IIS-98-17434. Any opinions, findings, and conclusions or recommendations expressed in this material are those of the authors and do not necessarily reflect the views of the National Science Foundation.

Panagiotis Ipeirotis is partially supported by Empeirikeio Foundation and he thanks the Trustees of Empeirikeio Foundation for their support.

We also thank Pedro Falcao Goncalves for his contributions during the initial stages of this project.

References

1. James P. Callan, Margaret Connell, and Aiqun Du. Automatic discovery of language models for text databases. In *SIGMOD 1999, Proceedings of the ACM SIGMOD International Conference on Management of Data, Philadelphia, Pennsylvania, USA*, pages 479–490. ACM Press, 1999.
2. William W. Cohen. Fast effective rule induction. In *Machine Learning, Proceedings of the Twelfth International Conference on Machine Learning (ICML'95), Tahoe City, California, USA*, pages 115–123. Morgan Kaufmann, 1995.
3. William W. Cohen. Learning trees and rules with set-valued features. In *Proceedings of the 13th National Conference on Artificial Intelligence and Eighth Innovative Applications of Artificial Intelligence Conference, AAAI 96, IAAI 96, Portland, Oregon*, volume 1, pages 709–716. American Association for Artificial Intelligence, AAAI Press / The MIT Press, 1996.
4. Susan Gauch, Guijun Wang, and Mario Gomez. Profusion*: Intelligent fusion from multiple, distributed search engines. *The Journal of Universal Computer Science*, 2(9):637–649, September 1996.
5. Luis Gravano, Chen-Chuan K. Chang, Héctor García-Molina, and Andreas Paepcke. *STARTS*: Stanford proposal for Internet meta-searching. In *SIGMOD 1997, Proceedings of the ACM SIGMOD International Conference on Management of Data, Tucson, Arizona, USA*, pages 207–218. ACM Press, 1997.
6. Luis Gravano, Héctor García-Molina, and Anthony Tomasic. *GlOSS*: Text-Source discovery over the Internet. *ACM Transactions on Database Systems*, 24(2):229–264, June 1999.
7. David Hawking and Paul B. Thistlewaite. Methods for information server selection. *ACM Transactions on Information Systems*, 17(1):40–76, January 1999.
8. Thorsten Joachims. A probabilistic analysis of the Rocchio algorithm with TFIDF for text categorization. Technical Report CMU-CS-96-118, School of Computer Science, Carnegie Mellon University, March 1996.
9. Daphne Koller and Mehran Sahami. Toward optimal feature selection. In *Machine Learning, Proceedings of the Thirteenth International Conference (ICML'96), Bari, Italy*, pages 284–292. Morgan Kaufmann, 1996.
10. Daphne Koller and Mehran Sahami. Hierarchically classifying documents using very few words. In *Machine Learning, Proceedings of the Fourteenth International Conference on Machine Learning (ICML'97), Nashville, Tennessee, USA*, pages 170–178. Morgan Kaufmann, 1997.

11. Steve Lawrence and C. Lee Giles. Inquirus, the NECI meta search engine. In *Proceedings of the Seventh International World Wide Web Conference, Brisbane, Australia*, pages 95–105, 1998.
12. Weiyi Meng, King-Lup Liu, Clement T. Yu, Xiaodong Wang, Yuhsi Chang, and Naphtali Rishe. Determining text databases to search in the Internet. In *VLDB'98, Proceedings of the 24th International Conference on Very Large Data Bases, New York City, New York, USA*, pages 14–25. Morgan Kaufmann, 1998.
13. Weiyi Meng, Clement T. Yu, and King-Lup Liu. Detection of heterogeneities in a multiple text database environment. In *Proceedings of the Fourth IFCIS International Conference on Cooperative Information Systems, Edinburgh, Scotland*, pages 22–33. IEEE Computer Society Press, 1999.
14. Tom Mitchell. *Machine Learning*. McGraw Hill, 1997.
15. Mike Perkowitz, Robert B. Doorenbos, Oren Etzioni, and Daniel S. Weld. Learning to understand information on the Internet: An example-based approach. *Journal of Intelligent Information Systems*, 8(2):133–153, March 1997.
16. Erik Selberg and Oren Etzioni. Multi-Service search and comparison using the MetaCrawler. In *Proceedings of the Fourth International World-Wide Web Conference*, 1995.
17. Jinxi Xu and James P. Callan. Effective retrieval with distributed collections. In *SIGIR'98, Proceedings of the 21st Annual International ACM SIGIR Conference on Research and Development in Information Retrieval, Melbourne, Australia*, pages 112–120. ACM Press, 1998.
18. George K. Zipf. *Human Behavior and the Principle of Least Effort*. Addison-Wesley, 1949.

Locating and Reconfiguring Records in Unstructured Multiple-Record Web Documents

David W. Embley and L. Xu

Department of Computer Science
Brigham Young University
Provo, Utah 84602, U.S.A.
{embley,lx,}@cs.byu.edu

Abstract. Record extraction from data-rich, unstructured, multiple-record Web documents works well [9], but only if the text for each record can be located and isolated. Although some multiple-record Web documents present records as contiguous, delineated chunks of text (which can thus be located and isolated [10]), many do not. When some values of textual records are factored out, are split unnaturally across boundaries, are joined unnaturally within boundaries, or are linked by off-page connectors, or when desired records are interspersed with records that are not of interest, it is difficult to automatically cull records and piece values together to form clean, delineated chunks of text that each represent a single record of interest. In this paper we address this problem and propose an algorithm to find and rearrange (if necessary) records in an HTML document. The essential idea is to attempt to maximize a record-recognition heuristic with respect to a given application ontology. Tests we conducted for two widely differing applications show that this technique properly locates and reconfigures records.

1   Introduction

The World Wide Web contains abundant repositories of information in Web documents. Many of these Web documents contain lists of unstructured text whose contents can be extracted to form database records. As an example, Figure 1 shows a list of car advertisements; each ad is an unstructured record that contains values such as the year of the car, its make and model, its features, and its selling price. We call these Web documents *multiple-record Web documents.*

Over the past two years, we have experimented successfully with extracting record data from data-rich, unstructured, multiple-record Web documents. Applications have included car ads, job ads, obituaries, real estate, precious gems, computer monitors, games, musical instruments, stocks, and personals [9,15]. As a measure of success, we have computed recall and precision ratios for each attribute for each application. We achieved recall ratios in the range of 90% and precision ratios near 98% for both car ads and job ads. For obituaries, a much more complex challenge, recall ratios ranged from 70% to 100%, and precision ratios ranged from 93% to 100% (except for names of relatives, which dropped

D. Suciu and G. Vossen (Eds.): WebDB 2000, LNCS 1997, pp. 256–274, 2001.

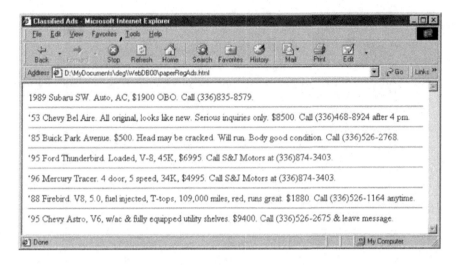

Fig. 1. Regular Car Ads

to 71%). Our results compare favorably with the results others have obtained (e.g. [1,2,4,5,6,8,12,16,17,18,13,21,22]). [1]

In our experiments, however, we have assumed that the input is a set of clean, plain-text record chunks. Initially, we obtained these unstructured records by hand, but we have since developed an algorithm to discover record boundaries automatically and to clean and present unstructured records to our downstream data-extraction system [9]. This record-boundary-discovery algorithm works well (near 100%) for Web documents such as the one in Figure 1 in which each unstructured record exists as an isolated text chunk. Because it only finds record delimiters, however, it fails for Web documents that have characteristics like the ones in Figure 2, where the car ads are: (1) *factored*—the year values 1999 and 1998 appear only once for each group of car ads in Figure 2(a); (2) *joined*—the next to last ad in Figure 2(a) mentions three cars jointly; (note also that the dealer and phone number are factored to the end of the ad); (3) *off-page*—the second ad in Figure 2(a) contains an off-page link to the page in Figure 2(b); (4) *split*—the natural white-space boundary splits the third ad in Figure 2(b); and (5) *interspersed*—the second 1998-ad in Figure 2(a) is an ad for a washer and dryer, which is interspersed among the car ads.

The contribution of this paper is that it shows how to resolve each of these problems. The technique for each is similar. The main idea is to define a record-recognition heuristic which we can use in an algorithm to locate and reconfigure unstructured records. We adapt the Vector Space Model (VSM) [20] from the field of information retrieval to define our record-recognition heuristic.

We use VSM measures to locate the information of interest in a Web document with respect to an application description by analyzing the Web doc-

---

[1] For a specific comparison between our work and the work cited here, see [9].

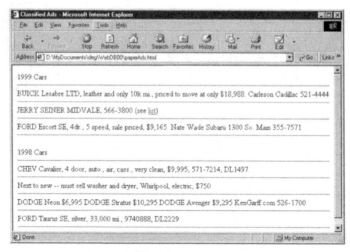

(a) Base Car Ads

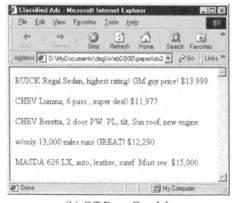

(b) Off-Page Car Ads

Fig. 2. Irregular Car Ads

ument's tree structure, i.e., the document's DOM tree. The basic idea is to compute VSM measures for each subtree and find the subtree whose VSM measures most closely match the application description. As part of traversing the DOM tree and computing VSM measures, we also gather in the text of all hyperlinked documents whose VSM measures exceed an application-dependent threshold. This included text becomes part of an augmented DOM tree for the document both for computing VSM measures to locate the records of interest and for further processing in which records are rearranged.

To reconfigure records, we use VSM measures to detect how well individual unstructured records match an application description. Record reconfiguration works only within the located (possibly augmented) subtree containing the information of interest with respect to the application description. We base our approach to reconfiguring records on the idea of hill climbing. VSM measures increase when we "defactor" a set of records (e.g. distribute the years in Figure 2(a) to each of the records); increase when we divide joined records that appear within a delimited record group and increase even more when we defactor end values in joined record groups; and increase when we group records split across apparent boundaries. As a result, when we rearrange a multiple-record Web document to "maximize" VSM measures, the result becomes a list of cleaned text chunks, one for each individual unstructured record.

Section 2 describes application ontologies, which are the application descriptions we use in our work. Section 3 explains how we adapt VSM for use in record location and record reconfiguration. Section 4 presents an algorithm that uses our adapted record-location and record-reconfiguration VSM measures to find the records in a multiple-record HTML document and to rearrange them (if necessary) to produce automatically the ontology-applicable, cleaned, unstructured records contained within the document. Section 5 discuss the results of applying our record location and reconfiguration algorithm to several Web documents for car-ads and obituaries. We chose these two applications because together they cover the patterns of interest: patterns (1), (2), and (5) in Figure 2 are common in car-ad Web documents, whereas patterns (3) and (4) are common in obituary Web documents. Further, applying the heuristic algorithm in two different applications helps justify our claim that the algorithm has general applicability independent of the application domain. We make concluding remarks in Section 6.

2 Application Ontology

For our work in data extraction, we define an *application ontology* to be a conceptual-model instance that describes a real-world application in a narrow, data-rich domain of interest (e.g. car advertisements, obituaries, job advertisements) [9]. Each of our application ontologies consists of two components: (1) an *object/relationship-model instance* that describes sets of objects, sets of relationships among objects, and constraints over object and relationship sets, and (2) for each object set, a *data frame* that defines the potential contents of the object set. A data frame for an object set defines the lexical appearance of constant objects (if any) for the object set and establishes appropriate keywords that are likely to appear in a document when objects in the object set are mentioned.

In this paper, we consider two application ontologies. One is for car-ads; the other is for obituaries. Figure 3 shows part of the car-ad application ontology, including object and relationship sets and cardinality constraints (lines 1-8) and a few lines of the data frames (lines 9-18). (The full ontology for car ads is about 600 lines in length.) Figure 4 shows the graphic version for the obituary ontology. A graphic ontology provides only the object and the relationship sets and the constraints among the object and relationship sets—the data frames must have separate specifications [14]. Observe that the obituary ontology, which has 18 object sets, is much more complex than the car-ad ontology, which has only 8.

1. Car [-> object];
2. Car [0:0.911:1] has Year [1:*];
3. Car [0:0.708:1] has Make [1:*];
4. Car [0:0.775:1] has Model [1:*];
5. Car [0:0.538:1] has Mileage [1:*];
6. Car [0:2.328:*] has Feature [1:*];
7. Car [0:0.866:1] has Price [1:*];
8. PhoneNr [1:*] is for [1:1.061:*];
9. Year matches [4]
10.   constant {extract "\d{2}";
11.   context "\b'[4-9]\d\b";
12.   substitute "^" -> "19"
13.   ...
14. Mileage matches [8]
15.   ...
16.   keyword "\bmiles\b", "\bmi\.", "\bmi\b",
17.   "\bmileage\b";
18. ...

Fig. 3. Car-Ads Application Ontology (Partial)

An object set in an application ontology represents a set of objects which may either be lexical or nonlexical. Data frames with declarations for constants that can potentially populate the object set represent lexical object sets, and data frames without constant declarations represent nonlexical object sets. *Year* (Line 9) and *Mileage* (Line 14) are lexical object sets whose character representations have a maximum of length 4 characters and 8 characters respectively. *Make*, *Model*, *Price*, *Feature* and *PhoneNr* are the remaining lexical object sets in our car-ads application, and *Car* is the only nonlexical object set.

We describe the constant lexical objects and the keywords for an object set by regular expressions using Perl syntax. When applied to a textual document, the **extract** clause in a data frame causes a string matching a regular expression to be extracted, but only if the **context** clause also matches the string and its surrounding characters. A **substitute** clause lets us alter the extracted string before we store it in an intermediate file, in which we also store the string's position in the document and its associated object-set name. One of the nonlexical object sets is designated as the *object set of interest*—*Car* for the car-ad ontology and *Deceased Person* for the obituary ontology. The notation "[-> object]" in Line 1 of Figure 3 and the notation "-> •" in the *Deceased Person* object set in Figure 4 designate the object sets of interest.

Textually, we denote a relationship set by a name that includes its object set names (e.g. *Car has Year* and *PhoneNr is for Car*). Graphically, we denote a

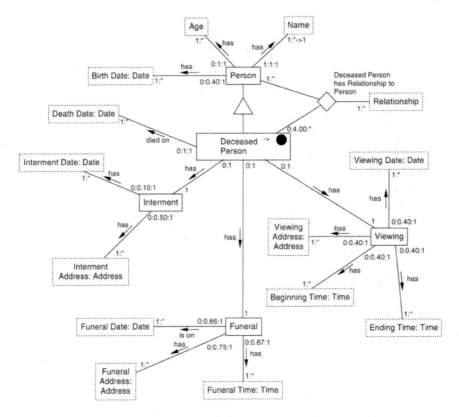

Fig. 4. Obituary Application Ontology(Graphic)

relationship set by a labeled edge connecting object sets (e.g. *Person has Age* and *Deceased Person has Relationship to Person*).

The *min:max* pairs and *min:ave:max* triples in the relationship-set name are *participation constraints*: *min* designates the minimum number of times an object in the object set can participate in the relationship set; *ave* designates the average number of times an object is expected to participate in the relationship set; and *max* designates the maximum number of times an object can participate, with * designating an unknown maximum number of times. The participation constraint on *Car* for *Car has Feature* in Figure 3, for example, specifies that a car need not have any listed features, that a car has 2.328 features on the average, and that there is no specified maximum for the number of features listed for a car.

We call a lexical object set with a 1 as the maximum participation constraint with respect to the object of interest a *1-max lexical object set*. Otherwise, if a lexical object set has a maximum participation constraint larger than 1, we call it a *n-max lexical object set*.

For our car-ad and obituary application ontologies, we obtained participation constraints as follows. We selected 10 different regions covering the United States and found one car-ad page and one obituary page from each of these regions. From each of these pages we selected 12 individual car-ads/obituaries by taking every $n/12$-th car-ad/obituary where n was the total number of car-ads or obituaries on the page. We then counted by hand and obtained minimum, average, and maximum values for each object set in each relationship set.

3   Record-Location and Record-Recognition Heuristics

We are interested in recognizing the existence of chunks of unstructured text that constitute record information both for individual records and for groups of records. We have adapted the Vector Space Model (VSM) [20], a common information-retrieval measure of document relevance, for this purpose. VSM measures the cosine between two vectors—in our case, between an ontology vector OV representing what we expect to find and a document (or subdocument) vector DV representing we actually find. VSM also measures the magnitudes of the two vectors.

We construct the ontology vector OV based on the static specification of the predefined application ontology. To construct the ontology vector OV, we (1) identify the lexical object-set names—these become the names of the coefficients of OV, and (2) determine the average participation for each lexical object set with respect to the object set of interest specified in O—these become the values of the coefficients of OV. For example, the ontology vector for the car-ads application in Figure 3 is < Year:0.911, Make:0.708, Model:0.775, Mileage:0.538, Price:0.866, Feature:2.328, PhoneNr:1.061 >.

The names of the coefficients of a document vector DV are the same as the names of the coefficients of OV. We obtain the value of each coefficient of DV by automatically counting the number of appearances in the document of constant values that belong to each lexical object set. By applying the car-ad application ontology in Figure 3 to the entire document in Figure 1 we find 7 $Year$ values, 6 $Make$ values, and so forth, and obtain the document vector < Year:7, Make:6, Model:6, Mileage:3, Price:6, Feature:7, PhoneNr:7 >. We can construct a document vector for an entire document or for any subpart part of a document.

We have discussed the creation of a document vector as if correctly detecting and classifying the lexical values in a document is easy—but it is not easy. We identify potential lexical values for an object set using regular expressions as explained in Section 2. This can be error-prone, but we can adjust the regular expressions to improve this initial identification and achieve good results [9]. After initial identification, we must decide which of these potential object-set/constant pairs to accept. In our downstream processes, we use sophisticated heuristic based on keyword proximity, application-ontology cardinalities, record boundaries, and missing-value defaults to best match object sets with potential constants. For upstream rearrangement of records we use techniques that are far less sophisticated. In our simple upstream procedures we consider only, two cases: (1) a recognized string has no overlap either partially or completely with any other recognized string, and (2) a recognized string does overlap in some way with at least one other recognized string. For Case 1, we accept the recognized string for an object set even if the sophisticated downstream processes would reject it. For Case 2, we resolve the overlap simplistically, as follows. There are three subcases: (1) exact match, (2) subsumption, and (3) partial overlap. (1) If a lexical value v is recognized as potentially belonging to more than one lexical object set, we use the closest keyword that appears before or after v to determine which object set to choose; if no applicable keyword is found, instead of choosing one of the object sets arbitrarily, we discard this lexical value v. (2) If a lexical value v is a proper substring of lexical value w, we retain w and discard v (3) If lexical value v and lexical value w appear in a Web document, such that a suffix of v is a prefix of w, we retain v and discard w.

The *VSM measure* defined in [20], calculates the acute angle between an ontology vector OV and a document (or subdocument) vector DV as $\cos \theta = P/N$, where P is the inner product of the two vectors and N is the product of the lengths of the two vectors. So, if n is the number of lexical object sets and $OV =< o_1, o_2, ..., o_n >$ and $DV =< d_1, d_2, ..., d_n >$, then

$$\cos \theta = \frac{\sum_{i=1}^{n}(o_i d_i)}{(\sqrt{\sum_{i=1}^{n} o_i^2})(\sqrt{\sum_{i=1}^{n} d_i^2})} \tag{1}$$

When OV is the ontology vector for the car-ads application ontology (given above) and DV is the document vector for the car-ads document in Figure 1 (given above), the cosine measure is 0.894. When the distribution of values among the object sets in DV closely matches the expected distribution specified in OV, the angle θ is close to zero degrees, and $\cos \theta$ is close to one.

The VSM measures used in this paper also includes one other measure—the magnitude. The magnitude measures the vector lengths $|OV|$ and $|DV|$, which can be calculated by the following formulas.

$$|OV| = \sqrt{\sum_{i=1}^{n} o_i^2} \tag{2}$$

$$|DV| = \sqrt{\sum_{i=1}^{n} d_i^2} \tag{3}$$

When applying the record-location and record-reconfiguration heuristics, both OV and DV are adjusted but the calculation of the VSM measures remain the same as given in formulas (1), (2), and (3). We adjust OV and DV differently and for different reasons when applying record-location and record-reconfiguration heuristics. We explain these adjustments next.

3.1 Record-Location Heuristic

When we construct the two vectors OV and DV for record location, we would like to apply the VSM measure to detect which subpart of the document contains the data related to our application ontology. We have found, however, as others have also [3], that it is difficult to use the ontology and document vectors directly. Our particular problem is that the n-max object sets tend to carry much more weight than they should. We therefore normalize our vectors by letting

$$OV =< \frac{o_1}{o_1}, \frac{o_2}{o_2}, ..., \frac{o_n}{o_n} >=< 1, 1, ..., 1 >$$

and

$$DV =< \frac{d_1}{o_1}, \frac{d_2}{o_2}, ..., \frac{d_n}{o_n} >$$

before we apply our VSM measures. Using these normalized vectors,

$$cos\ \theta = \frac{\sum_{i=1}^{n}(\frac{o_i}{o_i}\frac{d_i}{o_i})}{\sqrt{\sum_{i=1}^{n}(\frac{o_i}{o_i})^2}\sqrt{\sum_{i=1}^{n}(\frac{d_i}{o_i})^2}} = \frac{\sum_{i=1}^{n}\frac{d_i}{o_i}}{\sqrt{n}\sqrt{\sum_{i=1}^{n}(\frac{d_i}{o_i})^2}} \tag{4}$$

and the lengths of the adjusted vectors OV and DV are

$$|OV| = \sqrt{\sum_{i=1}^{n}(\frac{o_i}{o_i})^2} = \sqrt{n} \tag{5}$$

$$|DV| = \sqrt{\sum_{i=1}^{n}(\frac{d_i}{o_i})^2} \tag{6}$$

Since the vector coefficients for OV are the estimates for one record and the vector coefficients for DV are the values identified for one or more records, the length $|DV|$ divided by the length $|OV|$ is a rough estimate of the number of records in the document (or the part of the document) being measured. For our car-ads example for the document in Figure 1, using formulas (5) and (6), $|DV| \div |OV| = 7.365$.

3.2 Record-Reconfiguration Heuristic

For record reconfiguration we need to be able to determine how well the data extracted from a text component matches a single record. As will be explained when we present our algorithm in Section 4, we use the idea of hill climbing to determine whether to combine adjacent text components and candidate factored text components. The main idea is to rearrange the text in an attempt to maximize the VSM measures for one record, making the record as close to perfect as possible.

To implement the record-reconfiguration heuristic, we first normalize OV and DV as described in Section 3.1. Then, we use the VSM magnitude measure

$|DV|$, which can be calculated by formula (6), to decide if a text component contains multiple records based on an application dependent threshold value. If a text component contains multiple records, we split the text component into fine-grained components that can each be a single record or a subpart of a single record.

At this level of granularity, the cosine measure is sensitive to variations in the number of appearances of objects for each object set. To mitigate this problem, we reduced the document vector to essentially only note whether an object for an object set occurs in a text component by letting

$$
e_i = \begin{cases} 0 & \text{if } d_i = 0 \\ 1 & \text{if } d_i > 0 \text{ and the } i\text{th coefficient is for a 1-max object set} \\ \lceil \frac{d_i}{C_i} \rceil & \text{if } d_i > 0 \text{ and the } i\text{th coefficient is for an } n\text{-max object set} \end{cases} \tag{7}
$$

for $1 \leq i \leq n$ where C_i is the expected maximum number of occurrences for the ith n-max object set and is obtained by taking the maximum seen for object set i in the training set. Hence, $DV =< e_1, e_2, ..., e_n >$ where e_i is normally 0 or 1, with the rare exception of an integer larger than 1 if more than the the expected maximum number of objects appear in a text component for an n-max object set.

When considering whether to combine two text components TC_1 and TC_2 together into $TC_{1,2}$, we consider the respective document vectors DV_1 for TC_1, DV_2 for TC_2, and $DV_{1,2}$ for TC_1 and TC_2 combined together:

$$DV_1 =< f_{11}, f_{12}, ..., f_{1n} >$$

$$DV_2 =< f_{21}, f_{22}, ..., f_{2n} >$$

$$DV_{1,2} =< f_1, f_2, ..., f_n >$$

For DV_1, $f_{1i} = e_{1i}$ as defined in formula (7). DV_2, however, may represent previously combined components, numbered for notational convenience as components 2, 3, ..., p. Thus,

$$
f_{2i} = \begin{cases} \sum_{j=2}^{p} e_{ji} & \text{if the } i\text{th coefficient is for a 1-max object set} \\ \lceil \frac{\sum_{j=2}^{p} d_{ji}}{C_i} \rceil & \text{if the } i\text{th coefficient is for an } n\text{-max object set} \end{cases}
$$

where e_{ji} is the the e-value computed by formula (7) for the ith coefficient in the jth text component under consideration, and d_{ji} is the occurrence count for the ith coefficient in the jth text component under consideration. $DV_{1,2}$ represents the combination of DV_1 and DV_2 and is thus

$$
f_i = \begin{cases} e_{1i} + \sum_{j=2}^{p} e_{ji} & \text{if the } i\text{th coefficient is for a 1-max object set} \\ \lceil \frac{d_{1i} + \sum_{j=2}^{p} d_{ji}}{C_i} \rceil & \text{if the } i\text{th coefficient is for an } n\text{-max object set} \end{cases} \tag{8}
$$

Using these vectors for DV_1, DV_2, and $DV_{1,2}$, we obtain the following adjusted cosine measures.

$$
cos_1 = \frac{\sum_{i=1}^{n} f_{1i} \frac{o_i}{o_i}}{\sqrt{\sum_{i=1}^{n} (\frac{o_i}{o_i})^2} \sqrt{\sum_{i=1}^{n} f_{1i}^2}} = \frac{\sum_{i=1}^{n} f_{1i}}{\sqrt{n} \sqrt{\sum_{i=1}^{n} f_{1i}^2}} \tag{9}
$$

$$cos_2 = \frac{\sum_{i=1}^{n} f_{2i} \frac{o_i}{o_i}}{\sqrt{\sum_{i=1}^{n} (\frac{o_i}{o_i})^2} \sqrt{\sum_{i=1}^{n} f_{2i}^2}} = \frac{\sum_{i=1}^{n} f_{2i}}{\sqrt{n} \sqrt{\sum_{i=1}^{n} f_{2i}^2}} \qquad (10)$$

$$cos_{1,2} = \frac{\sum_{i=1}^{n} f_i \frac{o_i}{o_i}}{\sqrt{\sum_{i=1}^{n} (\frac{o_i}{o_i})^2} \sqrt{\sum_{i=1}^{n} f_i^2}} = \frac{\sum_{i=1}^{n} f_i}{\sqrt{n} \sqrt{\sum_{i=1}^{n} f_i^2}} \qquad (11)$$

Here n is the number of the lexical object sets. Observe that in formulas (9), (10), and (11), $\sqrt{n}$, which represents the $|OV|$, is static. We can therefore ignore this while computing cosine measures for hill climbing. Observe also that the adjusted vector lengths for $|DV_1|$, $|DV_2|$, and $|DV_{1,2}|$ are respectively the following.

$$|DV_1| = \sqrt{\sum_{i=1}^{n} f_{1i}^2} \qquad (12)$$

$$|DV_2| = \sqrt{\sum_{i=1}^{n} f_{2i}^2} \qquad (13)$$

$$|DV_{1,2}| = \sqrt{\sum_{i=1}^{n} f_i^2} \qquad (14)$$

Intuitively, what is happening here is that we combine text components so long as we do not get "too many" 1-max objects or "too many" n-max objects. In making this test, the VSM measures let us consider all the object sets together as a unit as we attempt to hill climb by concatenating text components together. We stop concatenating whenever we start going down hill.

4   Record Location and Reconfiguration Algorithm

Figure 5 shows our algorithm for locating and reconfiguring records within a given Web document D. We assume that D has been identified as a multiple-record Web document suitable for the application.[2] D may contain only a list of regular car ads or obituaries, in which case the algorithm simply outputs the list, or D may contain a mixture of any or all of the categorized problems: having records that are factored, joined inside boundaries, off-page or partially off-page, split across boundaries, or interspersed among inapplicable records. The algorithm locates the appropriate subpart of the document that contains the data of interest for the application ontology and brings in any hyperlinked pages with data of interest for the application ontology.. After a best-guess boundary tag is detected within the (possibly augmented) subpart of the document containing the data of interest, the algorithm uses hill climbing to improve the VSM

---

[2] In other work [11], we have shown how to identify both car-ad Web documents and obituary Web documents with over 90% accuracy.

input: Application ontology O and applicable Web document D.
output: Data file F containing reorganized individual records.
1. Parse O and compute the magnitude of the ontology vector OV;
2. Parse D into a DOM tree T, then:
    For each off-page link
        Compute the VSM measure for the linked page;
        Retain the page if the VSM measure exceeds a threshold;
    Compute the VSM measure for every subtree (including retained link pages);
3. Analyze T and the VSM measures of the tree elements and locate the subtree S
    that contains the data of interest for O;
4. Obtain the best-guess record boundary, $btag$, in S;
5. For each text component TC in S between successive $btags$:
    Let pTC be the previously text component, if any;
    Let fv be the current potential outside-boundary
        factored value, if any;
    5a. Use the VSM measure to reorganize and process
        joined and inside-boundary factored records in TC:
    Obtain any inside-boundary factored values;
    Divide the joined records into individual records;
    Distribute any inside-boundary factored values to the
        previously-joined but now individual records;
    5b. Use the VSM measure to recognize and combine
        adjacent record fragments and distribute
        outside-factored values to individual records:
    If $VSMmeasure(pTC + TC) > VSMmeasure(TC)$ and
       $VSMmeasure(pTC + TC) > VSMmeasure(pTC)$
       Combine pTC and TC as the next pTC;
    Else
       Add pTC to F;
       If $VSMmeasure(fv + TC) > VSMmeasure(TC)$ and
         $VSMmeasure(fv + TC) > VSMmeasure(fv)$
         Combine fc and TC as the next pTC
       Else
          If the VSM measure determines that TC
            is a new potential factored value;
          fv is set to TC;
       pTC is set to TC;
  After considering all text components, add the last pTC to F
6. Use the VSM measure to discard inapplicable interspersed records in F;

Fig. 5. Record Location and Rearrangement (RLR) Algorithm

measures for each record. When processing a text component within D, the algorithm checks for the possibility that the current record is factored, split, or joined and rearranges record components to maximize VSM measures. Comments on the steps of our Record Location and Rearrangement (RLR) Algorithm follow:

Step 1: We construct the ontology vector OV as a normalized vector as described in Section 3.1. The magnitude of the ontology vector OV, $|OV|$, is calculated by formula (5) in Section 3.1. Thus $|OV| = \sqrt{n}$, where n is the number of the lexical object sets for the application ontology.

Step 2: We use a standard algorithm [7] to parse D into a DOM tree T. We then follow each off-page link and check the data in the linked document as follows. We construct the normalized document vector for the linked page as described in Section 3.1. We then compute the VSM measures for the off-page document by formulas (4) and (6) and determine based on an application-dependent threshold value whether we should retain the linked document as part of D.

Then, for each leaf node or internal node in the DOM tree T, we collect the text corresponding to the node. For a leaf node, the collected text is the text of the leaf node. For an internal node, the text is recursively collected from each node within the subtree rooted at the internal node. While collecting text, if the node contains an off-page link and the corresponding off-page document is retained, the text of the off-page document is collected as part of the text. Finally, for each node we construct the normalized document vector as described in Section 3.1 and calculate the VSM measures by formulas (4) and (6).

Step 3: Given these VSM measures for each node in T, we analyze T to locate the subtree S in T that contains the data of interest. We find S according to how close the VSM measures are to the VSM measures of T and according to whether the VSM measures of the siblings of S show that they do or do not contain useful data for the application ontology. We use the subtree S rather than T for further processing.

Step 4: We use several heuristics to obtain the best-guess record boundary tag, $btag$, within S. We apply each of these heuristics and then use Stanford Certainty Theory to calculate a combined value for each possible boundary tag. The best-guess record boundary is the HTML tag that has the largest value. The details of this step are in [10].

Step 5: We split the text of subtree S between successive $btags$ into a list of text components TCs. Initially, we construct a document vector and calculate VSM measures for each text component by formulas (4) and (6).

Step 5a: We use threshold values for the VSM measures to check whether a text component TC contains multiple records. We also check the head and the tail of a text component to see if there are inside-boundary factored values that do not appear in the middle of the joined multiple records. When distributing the data into individual records, the algorithm uses a multiple-slot template and assumes that the layout pattern for these records is regular.

Steps 5b: We look (1) for adjacent components, which when joined together would improve the VSM measures, and (2) for outside-boundary factored values, which when distributed to the text components would improve the VSM measures. In this step we construct the document vectors for text components by formula (7), and we adjust the document vectors when we combine components by formula (8). In the presentation of our algorithm in Figure 5, we denote the VSM measures for a text component TC by $VSMmeasure(TC)$. We decide whether to combine a text component TC we are considering with a previous (possibly already combined) text component pTC by computing the VSM measures for TC by formulas (9) and (12), by computing the VSM measures for pTC by formulas (10) and (13), and by computing the VSM measures for TC and pTC together by formulas (11) and (14).

Thus, if we have a previous text component, we may have already joined it with even earlier text components, if appropriate, and we may have already distributed factored values into it, if appropriate. We compare this (possibly adjusted) prior text component with the current text component. If the VSM measure improves, we join the two together and proceed to the next text component. If not, we add the prior text component to the output file and continue our consideration of the current text component by checking whether the current factored value, if any, improves the VSM measure. If it does, we combine the current text component with the factored value and let it be the prior text component for the next iteration. Otherwise, we consider the possibility that the text component itself is the next factored value. We use VSM measures to make this determination. Either we assign the current text component to be the current outside-boundary factored value and also assign it as the prior text component for the next iteration, or we simply let the current text component be the prior text component for the next iteration.

Step 6 After the rearrangements in Step 5, we have a list of potential records. We use a C4.5 [19], machine-learned threshold [11] to check each one. To calculate the VSM measures, we construct document vector for each potential record as discussed in Section 3.1. We thus compute the VSM measure by formulas (4) and (6). If the record exceeds the threshold, we keep it; otherwise we discard the record.

5   Results

For both car ads and obituaries we provided two sets of documents, one to act as a training set and the other to act as a test set.

5.1   Car-Ads

To guide us in creating the Record Location and Rearrangement (RLR) Algorithm, we used twelve artificial car-ad Web documents. We designed these documents to span the various cases covered in the algorithm—the Web document in Figure 1 represented the extreme case with no irregularities and the combination document in Figure 2 represented the extreme case with all types of irregularities. We constructed these two documents and the other ten from actual car-ad documents, but we made them "short" (less than a dozen car ads) and "sweet" (stripped of superfluous information beyond the basic record information).

Once our RLR algorithm successfully processed these twelve "training" documents, we tested our RLR algorithm on 30 actual Web documents. We had selected these 30 Web documents, three from each of 10 different geographic regions in the U.S., before developing our RLR algorithm. Indeed, we selected these documents for an entirely different purpose. Table 1 shows the results.

An examination of these 30 documents revealed the following: ten contained only regular car ads; thirteen contained joined car ads inside of record boundaries, all with inside-boundary factored values; one contained outside-boundary factoring; thirteen contained non-car-ads interspersed with car ads; and none contained split or off-page car ads. Altogether in these documents we found 498 car ads that needed to be rearranged and 49 non-car-ads that needed to be discarded. Our RLR algorithm correctly rearranged 92% of the 498 and correctly discarded 80% of the 49. The combined output of our RLR algorithm over all ads in the 30 documents (including regular ads) correctly produced 1,562 (1,562 = 1,104+316+142) of the grand total of 1,616 car ads, for an accuracy of 97%.

Over all 30 car-ad documents, our RLR algorithm produced 54 false drops (54 = 1,616-1,562) and 10 false positives. Seven of the ten false positives were all ads for snowmobiles, which are a lot like car ads. The other three false positives were ads for car dealers without mention of specific cars. Of the 54 false drops, 14 were regular car ads and 40 were rearranged car ads. For all 14 of the regular car ads and 20 of the 40 rearranged car ads, the ontology failed to find enough values (mostly models) to bring the VSM measures above the threshold, and these 34 car ads were thus improperly discarded. We can fix this problem by improving our ontology. Twenty of the false drops all came from the same "strange" joined record groups of one source Web document—"strange" because it repeated an identical phone number five times, once for every five car ads. This is a in-boundary factored pattern we had not anticipated. Out RLR algorithm properly split the joined records, but it lost the factored information.

An interesting problem appeared in one source document—each record included a header and a body. Each record body contained the complete, detailed information for a car, while the header contained only the summary information for the car. The algorithm split the header and the body into two records. Indeed, a human would judge each isolated header and each isolated body as being a car ad. As a pair, however, it is clear that the information in the body subsumes the information in the header. We cannot use VSM measures to solve this problem, and we therefore do not resolve this problem as part of our work for this paper. To solve the problem, we intend to send both header records and body records downstream for data extraction. Then, once the downstream processes extract the data and place records in a database, we can check the records—if the information in one record subsumes the information in another, we can discard the subsumed record.

Table 1. Car ontology test results.

	Combined Total	Regular		Joined-Factored		Factored		Interspersed	
		Total	Correct	Total	Correct	Total	Correct	Total	Correct
1.	20	20	20						
2.	66	24	24	42	41				
3.	20	20	20					3	3
4.	8	8	8						
5.	315	132	132	183	166			10	10
6.	63	47	47	16	16			1	1
7.	9	4	4	5	5				
8.	66	66	66					1	1
9.	27	25	25	2	2			3	3
10.	12	12	12						
11.	30	30	30						
12.	57	47	45	10	10				
13.	116	94	94	22	22			10	10
14.	7	7	7					7	0
15.	35	22	22	13	13				
16.	143					143	142		
17.	47	24	23	23	23				
18.	15	13	13	2	1			1	1
19.	20	20	18						
20.	9	7	7	2	2			1	1
21.	20	20	20						
22.	57	47	46	10	10				
23.	18	18	18					5	3
24.	40	40	40						
25.	10	10	10					5	4
26.	42	42	42						
27.	153	153	150					1	1
28.	55	55	55						
29.	68	43	42	25	5			1	1
30.	68	68	63						
	1616	1118	1104	355	316	143	142	49	39

5.2   Obituaries

For the obituary application ontology, we used 30 Web document to guide us in tuning the RLR Algorithm for obituaries. Once we obtained obituary threshold values, we tested the RLR algorithm on 30 additional Web documents. As was the case for our car-ad documents, we had selected these 60 Web documents, six from each of ten different geographic regions in the U.S., before developing our RLR algorithm. The results are in Table 2.

The 30 test documents revealed the following: twenty two contained only regular obituaries; five contained off-page obituaries; and three contained split obituaries. Altogether in these documents we found 42 obituaries that needed to be rearranged. Our RLR algorithm correctly rearranged 100% of the 42. The combined output of our RLR algorithm over all ads in the 30 documents

Table 2. Obituary ontology test results.

	Combined Total	Regular		Hyperlinked		Split	
		Total	Correct	Total	Correct	Total	Correct
1.	9	9	9				
2.	10	10	10				
3.	4	4	4				
4.	10	10	10				
5.	5	5	5				
6.	2	2	2				
7.	8	8	8				
8.	10	10	10				
9.	3			3	3		
10.	10	10	10				
11.	7	7	7				
12.	14	14	14				
13.	10	10	8				
14.	8	8	8				
15.	7			7	7		
16.	9	9	9				
17.	4					4	4
18.	10	10	10				
19.	10	10	8				
20.	6	6	6				
21.	10	10	10				
22.	10	10	10				
23.	2					2	2
24.	7			7	7		
25.	6	6				6	6
26.	3			3	3		
27.	5	5	5				
28.	9			9	9		
29.	3	3	3				
30.	4	4	4				
	215	174	170	29	29	12	12

(including regular obituaries) correctly produced 211 of the grand total of 215 obituaries, for an accuracy of 98%.

For our obituary documents, our RLR algorithm produced four false drops and two false positives. All four false drops were for regular obituaries; two each appeared in two different documents. These false drops happened because the ontology failed to find some of the expected values in these obituaries. Thus, the algorithm dropped them because their VSM measures did not exceed threshold values as they should have. Further, these same problems also caused the two false-positive errors. It just so happened that in both documents the false drops were adjacent. Since the ontology recognized only some of the expected values, a combination of the two obituaries appeared to be a better obituary (according to the VSM measures) than the two separate obituaries. Thus, our algorithm combined the two pairs of false drops creating two false-positive obituaries.

6 Concluding Remarks

We presented an approach to locating, delineating, and rearranging records in unstructured multiple-record Web documents. The key idea to the success of this approach is to heuristically maximize a VSM measure of similarity between the expectations for value occurrences specified in an application ontology and the actual occurrences found in a document. We encoded two variations of these VSM measures—one to locate records and discard interspersed inapplicable records and the other to combine factored and split records. Our work here shows that we can recognize and properly deal with records that have been factored, "unnaturally" split across boundaries, "unnaturally" joined within boundaries, linked to additional off-page information, and interspersed with records not applicable to the application ontology. Results from tests we conducted showed that we correctly located, delineated, and rearranged 97% of the car-ad records we encountered and 98% of the obituary records we encountered.

References

1. B. Adelberg. NoDoSE—a tool for semi-automatically extracting structured and semistructured data from text documents. In *Proceedings of the 1998 ACM SIG-MOD International Conference on Management of Data*, pages 283–294, Seattle, Washington, June 1998.
2. N. Ashish and C. Knoblock. Semi-automatic wrapper generation for Internet information sources. In *Proceedings of the CoopIS'97*, 1997.
3. R. Baeza-Yates and B. Ribeiro-Neto *Modern information retrieval*. ACM Press and Addison Wesley, New York, 1999.
4. S. Brin. Extracting patterns and relations from the World Wide Web. In *Proceedings of the WebDB Workshop (at EDBT'98)*, 1998.
5. J. Cowie and W. Lehnert. Information extraction. *Communications of the ACM*, 39(1):80–91, January 1996.
6. M. Craven, D. DiPasquo, D. Freitag, A. McCallum, T. Mitchell, K. Nigam, and S. Slattery. Learning to extract symbolic knowledge from the World Wide Web. In *Proceedings of the 15th National Conference on Artificial Intelligence (AAAI-98)*, pages 509–516, Madison, Wisconsin, July 1998.
7. Docuverse DOM SDK, 2000. URL: http://www.docuverse.com/htmlsdk/.
8. R. Doorenbos, O. Etzioni, and D. Weld. A scalable comparison-shopping agent for the World-Wide Web. In *Proceedings of the First International Conference on Autonomous Agents*, pages 39–48, Marina Del Rey, California, February 1997.
9. D. Embley, D. Campbell, Y. Jiang, S. Liddle, D. Lonsdale, Y.-K. Ng, and R. Smith. Conceptual-model-based data extraction from multiple-record Web pages. *Data & Knowledge Engineering*, 31(3):227–251, November 1999.
10. D. Embley, Y. Jiang, and Y.-K. Ng. Record-boundary discovery in Web documents. In *Proceedings of the 1999 ACM SIGMOD International Conference on Management of Data (SIGMOD'99)*, pages 467–478, Philadelphia, Pennsylvania, 31 May - 3 June 1999.

11. D. Embley, Y.-K. Ng, and L. Xu. Filtering multiple-record Web documents based on application ontologies. 2000. (submitted for publication).
12. D. Freitag. Information extraction from HTML: Application of a general machine learning approach. In *Proceedings of AAAI/IAAI*, pages 517–523, 1998.
13. J. Hammer, H. Garcia-Molina, J. Cho, R. Aranha, and A. Crespo. Extracting semistructured information from the Web. In *Proceedings of the Workshop on Management of Semistructured Data*, Tucson, Arizona, May 1997.
14. K. Hewett *An integrated ontology development environment for data extraction.* Masters Thesis, Brigham Young University, April 2000.
15. Home Page for BYU Data Extraction Group, 2000. URL: http://www.deg.byu.edu.
16. N. Kushmerick, D. Weld, and R. Doorenbos. Wrapper induction for information extraction. In *Proceedings of the 1997 International Joint Conference on Artificial Intelligence*, pages 729–735, 1997.
17. W. Lehnert, C. Cardie, D. Fisher, J. McCarthy, E. Riloff, and S. Soderland. Evaluating an information extraction system. *Journal of Integrated Computer-Aided Engineering*, 1(6), 1994.
18. I. Muslea, S. Minton, and C. Knoblock. STALKER: Learning extraction rules for semistructured, Web-based information sources. In *Proceedings of AAAI'98: Workshop on AI and Information Integration*, Madison, Wisconsin, July 1998.
19. J. Quinlan. *C4.5: Programs for Machine Learning.* Morgan Kaufmann, San Mateo, California, 1993.
20. G. Salton and M. McGill. *Introduction to Modern Information Retrieval.* McGraw-Hill, New York, 1983.
21. D. Smith and M. Lopez. Information extraction for semi-structured documents. In *Proceedings of the Workshop on Management of Semistructured Data*, Tucson, Arizona, May 1997.
22. S. Soderland. Learning to extract text-based information from the World Wide Web. In *Proceedings of the Third International Conference on Knowledge Discovery and Data Mining*, pages 251–254, Newport Beach, California, August 1997.

Author Index

Lecture Notes in Computer Science

For information about Vols. 1–1931
please contact your bookseller or Springer-Verlag